THE COOLER KING

Also by Patrick Bishop

NON-FICTION

The Reckoning

Wings

Target Tirpitz

Ground Truth

Battle of Britain

3 Para

Bomber Boys

Fighter Boys

The Irish Empire

The Provisional IRA

The Winter War

FICTION

Follow Me Home

A Good War

THE
COOLER
KING

The True Story of
William Ash:
Spitfire Pilot, POW and
WWII's Greatest Escaper

Patrick Bishop

THE OVERLOOK PRESS

NEW YORK, NY

First published in the United States in hardcover in 2016 by
The Overlook Press, Peter Mayer Publishers, Inc.

141 Wooster Street
New York, NY 10012
www.overlookpress.com
For bulk and special sales please contact sales@overlookny.com,
or to write us at the above address.

Library of Congress Cataloging-in-Publication Data
Names: Bishop, Patrick (Patrick Joseph) author.
Title: The Cooler King : the true story of William Ash, the greatest
escaper
of World War II / Patrick Bishop.
Other titles: True story of William Ash, the greatest escaper of World
War II
Description: New York, NY : The Overlook Press, [2016]
Identifiers: LCCN 2015039894 | ISBN 9781468312737
Subjects: LCSH: World War, 1939-1945--Prisoners and prisons, German. |
Ash,
William, 1917-2014. | Prisoners of war--Germany--Biography. |
Prisoners of
war--Canada--Biography. | Canada. Royal Canadian Air
Force--Officers--Biography. | Escapes. | Prisoner of war
escapes--Germany.
| World War, 1939-1945--Germany.
Classification: LCC D805.G3 B5525 2016 | DDC 940.54/7243092--dc23
LC record available at http://lccn.loc.gov/2015039894

Manufactured in the United States of America

ISBN: 978-1-4683-1273-7
1 3 5 7 9 10 8 6 4 2

To Nina

ACKNOWLEDGEMENTS

I would like to thank Bill Ash's widow Ranjana Sidhanta and his friend and collaborator Brendan Foley for generously allowing me to quote from his publications and reproduce photographs from his early years. I am also grateful to Juliet Ash for sharing memories of her father and to Betty Barthropp for talking to me about her late husband Paddy's friendship with Bill. The staffs of the National Archives, the Imperial War Museum, the London Library and the Bishopsgate Institute were helpful and efficient.

The work has been made easier and more pleasurable by the professionalism of the Atlantic team, in particular my editor James Nightingale and copyeditor Will Atkins who saved me from many errors.

I would also indebted to my friend Annabel Merullo for shepherding the project through, from inception to realization.

ILLUSTRATIONS

SECTION ONE

The formal portrait Bill sent home in 1941. (*Courtesy of Brendan Foley*)

Bill with his sister Adele at home in Dallas in 1925. (*Courtesy of Brendan Foley*)

Bill during training. (*Courtesy of Brendan Foley*)

At the controls of his Spitfire in late 1941. (*Courtesy of Brendan Foley*)

Canadian Prime Minister Mackenzie King greets Bill during a visit to 411 Squadron. (*Courtesy of Brendan Foley*)

The squadron at Digby.

At dispersal, waiting for action, Digby, late summer 1941. (*Courtesy of Brendan Foley*)

411 pilots just before or after an operation.

Squadron Leader Stan Turner.

Bill is entertained by Buck McNair. (*Courtesy of Brendan Foley*)

The church at Vieille Église today. (*Patrick Bishop*)

The house where the Boulanger family once had their *estaminet*.
  (*Patrick Bishop*)
The cover of Bill's prisoner-of-war file at Stalag Luft III.
  (*Courtesy of Brendan Foley*)
Paddy Barthropp.
Sketch map of Stalag Luft III. (*The National Archives*)

SECTION TWO
Stalag Luft III, *c.* 1944. (*Keystone / Hulton Archive / Getty Images*)
Watchtower at Stalag Luft III, *c.* 1942. (*Hulton Archive / Getty
  Images*)
Robert Kee, 1951. (*John Chillingworth / Picture Post / Getty Images*)
Wing Commander Harry Day briefs Kenneth Moore for his
  role as Douglas Bader in *Reach for the Sky* (1955). (*Kurt Hutton /
  Picture Post / Getty Images*)
Prisoners laying the foundations for a hut in Stalag Luft III.
  (*Hulton Archive / Getty Images*)
Prisoners in a hut in Stalag Luft III, 1943. (*Keystone / Getty
  Images*)
Prisoners and camp staff in the Red Cross parcel store, Stalag
  Luft III. (© *IWM, HU 20926*)
Prisoners prepare a news sheet, Stalag Luft III. (© *IWM, HU
  20928*)
Prisoners tend their garden at Stalag Luft III. (© *IWM, HU
  20930*)
A church service for POWs at Stalag Luft III, *c.* 1944. (*Hulton
  Archive / Getty Images*)
An American military funeral at Stalag Luft III, February 1945.
  (*Topfoto / The Granger Collection, New York*)

The avenue leading away from Stalag Luft III. (© *James Finlay,*
   www.jamesfinlay.com)

Halbau today. (© *James Finlay, www.jamesfinlay.com*)

Liberated POWs at Marlag und Milag Nord at Westertimke,
   29 April 1945. (© *IWM, BU 4835*)

Release of prisoners in Westertimke Camp, 5 May 1945.
   (*Keystone-France / Gamma-Keystone via Getty Images*)

Steve McQueen in *The Great Escape* (1963). (© *John Springer*
   Collection / Corbis)

'The real escaper is more than a man equipped with compass, maps, papers, disguise and a plan. He has an inner confidence, a serenity of spirit which make him a Pilgrim.'

Airey Neave, Colditz escaper

PROLOGUE

The Spitfire slithered to a halt. For a few seconds he savoured the wonderful silence. He opened his eyes. Framed in the windshield in front of his face was the outline of a church tower. The church seemed to be upside down. He realized that he was hanging, inverted by the straps of his safety harness. He felt for the triangular release catch, pressed, and slumped onto the soft earth. He had jettisoned the perspex canopy just before the landing. It made getting out a lot easier. He could smell petrol and hear the tick of hot aluminium. He knew what was likely to come next: a sickening *whoompf* and an explosion of flame. He wriggled through the gap between the humped fuselage and the ground, rolled clear and staggered upright. He raised his arms and cautiously clenched and unclenched his hands. Amazingly, he felt OK.

He looked back at the wreckage of the Spitfire, which lay there like a spent comet, trailing a long tail of churned dirt. A thought floated through his head, something they drummed into him during training: *In the case of a crash landing in hostile territory it is vital to ensure that your aircraft does not fall intact into enemy hands.* There was no danger of that. The airframe was bent, the wings were torn from their roots and the propeller blades twisted like wrought iron.

The sound of an aeroplane engine made him look up. One of the German fighters was circling, checking whether he had survived the crash. He felt the pilot's eyes locking onto him and looked around frantically for somewhere to hide. Across the field lay the church and a line of houses. The pilot would be radioing back to his base at Saint-Omer, reporting the Spitfire's last resting place. He set off, jogging across the furrows towards the cover of the village. The heavy clay stuck to his boots, turning his limbs to lead, as if he was running in a nightmare.

The village had just a single street. The houses either side were low and built of dull red brick with thick wooden shutters framing the windows. It was two o'clock in the afternoon yet nobody was about. The place was as deserted as a ghost town in his native Texas. The German plane had cleared off, its engine note fading to a distant pulse. The silence that followed felt sinister. It was broken by a rusty creaking. The front door of one of the cottages opened. In the doorway stood a little girl, about nine or ten years old, he guessed. She stepped forward, beckoning to him.

He took a few paces back. It seemed wrong to involve her in his drama. Yet she kept walking towards him, holding out her hand. Instinctively he reached out and took it. She turned round and led him towards the house.

The door shut behind him. He was in a small, dim room.

In the gloom he made out the shape of a woman, youngish and attractive, with a sad, kind face. She smiled and beckoned him to follow her as she climbed the stairs.

He tried to remember some of the little French he had learned at school and could only come up with 'bonjour'. He felt a need to talk, to explain who he was, although it must have been obvious, speaking urgently in English, even though it was clear she didn't understand a word. She pressed a finger to her lips and he got the message and shut up. Then she tugged at his tunic, opened a wardrobe and pulled out a man's jacket and some trousers – her husband's? Her brother's? He stifled the impulse to ask.

He took off his flying jacket and boots. As he went to pull down his trousers, he saw mother and daughter watching him, and a foolish spurt of modesty made him hesitate. The woman jabbed a finger at the window, motioning for him to hurry before the Germans arrived. He dropped his trousers and pulled on the new pair. They were a bit short but otherwise OK. The little girl clapped. The black jacket was a tight fit but it would have to do. The woman reached again into the wardrobe and bought out a pair of boots and some wooden clogs. He chose the clogs, thinking they would look more authentic. A few seconds later he was regretting it as he clopped unsteadily back down the stairs.

After the horrors of the last half-hour he felt tears pricking his eyes at such unconditional kindness. He had neither the words nor the time to pour out his thanks. Impulsively he gave the woman a quick, heartfelt hug, and kissed the little girl. They led him to the back door. Behind a small garden lay flat fields. He hurried away with no idea where he was heading. He looked back. The door was already closed, as if his saviours had never existed.

It was the end of March. The land looked drab and dead. It was flat and watery, criss-crossed by drainage ditches. Between the ridged planes of the fields stood lines of bare poplars, stabbing like rows of spears into the vaulting grey sky.

To the left of the house was a hedge and behind it a lane ran south of the village. He walked purposefully, not too fast, not too slow, a man with things to do and a home to go to. Over the fields drifted the sound of clashing gears. He looked back. A lorry was driving into the village and behind it a motorcycle with a grey-helmeted rider. The black peasant jacket and the clogs no longer felt like any protection. He had to get out of sight. There was a channel running along the side of the road, a drainage ditch or a narrow canal. He remembered from trips to the movies in Dallas how escapees from chain gangs waded down rivers to throw the bloodhounds off the scent.

He slithered down the bank. The water was cold and slimy. It stank dreadfully. He was standing waist-deep in the village sewer. He waded southwards, crouching down below the bank until he was out of sight of the houses. When he could stand the stench no more he climbed out and trudged across fields and ditches, avoiding anywhere where he might encounter humans.

At six o'clock it was getting dark. He was exhausted, hungry, cold and soaking wet. An isolated copse, etched black against the sinking sun, offered a possible sanctuary for the night. He ducked under the bare branches, stretched out on the mulch of dead leaves and closed his eyes. It was Tuesday, 24 March 1942. In the space of a few hours Flying Officer William Ash's war had changed utterly.

ONE

The men's boots crunched softly on the sandy track. It was a midsummer day in June, 1942 but here, deep in the forest, the air was cool and the sun barely penetrated the pine woods that stretched out into infinity on either side of the path. They rounded a bend and there, rising out of a vast clearing, stood the camp. It was a forlorn sight. Rows of grey-green wooden huts lay in neat lines surrounded by tall barbed-wire fences. Watchtowers had been erected at regular intervals around the perimeter from which guards leaned over their machine guns and looked down impassively at the new arrivals.

The men halted at the entrance while their escort consulted with the sentries. Then the gates swung open. The men marched through, shoulders back, arms swinging, in an effort to show they were not beaten yet. A depressing rattle of chains and padlocks confirmed the new reality. They had reached the end of their journey into captivity. From now on the boundaries of their lives would extend no further than the wire walls of Stalag Luft III.

It had taken William Ash more than two months to get there. After crash-landing his Spitfire in a field close to the church in the village of Vieille-Église in the flat lands of the Pas-de-Calais he spent several days wandering the countryside avoiding German patrols before being rescued by a French family who passed him on to a resistance network. He had been taken to Paris where he spent a dreamlike few weeks hiding in the apartment of a young couple. Then one morning he was woken by the sound of the door being kicked in. He was dragged off for interrogation by the Gestapo who, after getting nothing from him, announced their intention to shoot him as a spy. He had resigned himself to death when good luck – a frequent visitor in his short life – intervened. The Luftwaffe somehow learned he was in the hands of the Gestapo. Air force pride demanded the prisoner be handed over to them. The Gestapo reluctantly disgorged him. He spent a brief spell at the Dulag Luft reception centre outside Frankfurt, where all Allied airmen who survived being shot down over German territory were interrogated and processed. And now he was at the end of the line, with every prospect of remaining here until the war was over.

Inside the gates of Stalag Luft III the new prisoners were counted off before being taken into the administration area for processing. They were watched by a gaggle of prisoners who had come over to the compound fence to look over the latest arrivals. They themselves had only been there a few months at most but already they seemed like old lags. Bill stood chatting with the others while he waited his turn, smelling the clean scent of pine resin mixed with the tobacco smoke. First came registration, which meant being fingerprinted, photographed and issued with an identity disc inscribed with the name of the camp and an identifying number. Then they were all marched into the compound and the Germans melted away. Inside the compound, it looked as if organizational matters were in the hands of the prisoners themselves. An efficient man in RAF uniform told Ash he would be billeted in Block 64 on the northern side of the compound. He was pleased to hear that a friend he had made in Dulag Luft would be sharing the same barrack. He and Patrick Barthropp had first met a few weeks before. Ash's first impression had not been favourable. Barthropp seemed to be a 'fighter boy' from central casting, a 'young, hard-nosed Spitfire pilot with a devil-may-care attitude to life and death and a passion for anything fast, including aeroplanes, horses and women', he wrote years later in a memoir. There was some truth in the caricature, but he had already come to see that the studied carelessness hid something more complicated and more interesting, and in time would judge him to be 'one of the kindest, most generous men I have ever met'.[1]

On the face of it they were chalk and cheese. Their backgrounds could scarcely have been more different. Bill Ash was twenty-two and had already had enough adventures for several lifetimes. He had grown up in Texas during the Depression, the son of a travelling salesman who, through no fault of his own, never seemed to hang on to a job. Money was always tight, sometimes non-existent. He been forced to work almost as soon as he could walk. He had paid his own way through university only to find it impossible to get a foot on the ladder to a proper career. In the end Hitler had chosen his future for him. Unlike most of his fellow Texans he had followed closely events in Europe and was determined to fight against Fascism as soon as he could. Long before the United States entered the war he headed north to join the Royal Canadian Air Force, renouncing his American citizenship in the process. He was posted to Britain and had been flying Spitfires with 411 Squadron when his career had come to an end, bounced by a swarm of Focke-Wulf 190 fighters when returning from a raid on the town of Comines, on the Franco-Belgian border.

Paddy Barthropp was twenty-one but his blond hair, slight build and pink cheeks made him look younger. He sprang from the Anglo-Irish gentry, and moved in a world of country houses, shooting parties and horses. He had nonetheless suffered some of life's knocks. His father had gambled away the family fortune, forcing Paddy to leave his Catholic private school early. The setback had been the making of him. After a brief period as an engineering apprentice he joined the RAF as an officer cadet in 1938 and fought in the Battle of Britain. He had been shot down six weeks after Bill, in the same area of the Pas-de-Calais.

They approached life from opposite directions. Bill liked classical music and serious literature. Paddy hardly read anything but the racing pages of the papers, and was happy to listen to whatever was playing on the anteroom gramophone. Bill was a committed left-winger. Paddy had no interest in politics. These differences, though, were insignificant compared with the attitudes that bound them together. Among them were a broad streak of irresponsibility, an addiction to romance and a feeling of personal affront at the injustices with which the world abounded. Above all they shared an appreciation of the absurd and a great capacity for fun and laughter. As they stowed away their few possessions in the lockers next to their bunk beds and went out to explore their new domain, it was clear they were going to need their sense of humour to deal with what lay ahead.

Stalag Luft III was only a few months old. Its name was an abbreviation of *Stammlager Luft* – aircrew camp – and it had been built to accommodate the increasing number of fliers being shot down as the Royal Air Force stepped up its campaigns. The air war had moved on. While fighter squadrons still mounted aggressive operations across the Channel to harass the Germans wherever they could reach them, much of the effort was now in the hands of Bomber Command, which launched raids almost nightly on targets inside Germany. From now on American bomber fleets would become increasingly involved in the campaign.

The first airmen prisoners had been housed in Stalag Luft I at Barth, on a lagoon on the Baltic Sea in north-eastern Germany. When that became too small the inmates were dispersed around other sites. Now all aircrew were to be concentrated in a single camp again – one that was designed to be as difficult to escape from as possible.

The Germans knew from their experience of captured British aviators in the First World War that air force prisoners were troublesome. A number had refused to opt for a quiet life and set about planning escapes, some ingenious, some foolhardy. The prisoners at Barth had continued the tradition. Stalag Luft III was therefore sited as far from a friendly frontier as geography allowed. It lay near the town of Sagan, on the old frontier with Poland, about ninety miles south-east of Berlin. The Baltic Sea, from where an escaper stood a chance of finding a ship to take him to neutral Sweden, was two hundred miles to the north and Switzerland was more than five hundred miles to the south-west. In between stretched vast areas of territory, controlled and surveilled with all the efficiency that the Nazi state could muster.

From the outset, the Germans emphasized the futility of trying to break out. 'The camp staff... hammered into us that Sagan was so remotely sited that even if we did escape there was nowhere to go,' remembered Wing Commander Henry Lamond, who arrived there from Barth in March 1942.[2] 'Therefore there was no point in escaping and we might as well think of something else to do with our time.' Lamond was inclined to agree. 'After we were moved into it and had studied the general layout the general opinion was that they had got it right and this place would be very hard to escape from.'

Nonetheless the very look of the place was enough to make you want to try. 'If any spur had been needed to induce prisoners to escape from the compounds at Sagan, the bleakness of the surroundings would have provided it,' wrote Aidan Crawley, another early arrival. 'The areas inside the barbed wire were covered with tree stumps and were without a blade of grass. And the soil, which was mainly pine needles on top and sand underneath, crumbled into dust in summer and in winter became mud. Outside the wire a monotonous and unbroken vista of fir trees was all that the prisoners could see.'[3]

In June 1942, the camp had two compounds, though more would be added in the coming years as the influx of prisoners forced repeated expansions. Central Compound was reserved for non-commissioned ranks – the sergeants who flew as pilots, navigators, bomb-aimers, wireless-operators and aerial gunners, but who, according to the class-conscious criteria of the RAF, did not qualify as officer material. In the mid summer of 1942, only a handful of NCOs had arrived and Central Compound was practically empty.

East Compound, though, was filling up rapidly and by the end of the year would house seven hundred prisoners.[4] At this early stage it comprised eight single-storey barrack huts, a cook-house, a bathhouse and two latrine blocks, laid out in rows. The huts were built out of pine boards planed from trees felled in the surrounding forest, stained grey-green or pale brown by wood preservative, with pitched, tar-paper-covered roofs. They were mounted on blocks about a foot off the ground. In the middle of the compound was a concrete-lined pool from which water could be pumped in the not unlikely event of a fire. An open space in the south-east corner was set aside for sports.

Each hut had twelve large rooms holding eight to ten prisoners, who slept in bunk beds. Three small rooms served as kitchen, bathroom and night urinal. A large window in each room let in some light. For heating there was a single pot-bellied stove which, though adequate for much of the year, made little impression on the cold of a Central German winter, and there were never enough of the coal briquettes which served as fuel.

Prisoners bathed, shaved, and did their laundry in the compound washroom, fitted with cold-water taps, wooden benches and tin basins. The two latrine blocks consisted of twenty holes cut in planks suspended over a cesspit that was emptied according to a haphazard schedule. In high summer the stench was almost unbearable. To make matters worse the cesspit was home to millions of flies which would take off from time to time to patrol the camp in search of other sustenance. An American officer arriving in August 1942 reported that when the prisoners sat down to eat they first had to conduct a 'fly purge' by opening the window, closing the doors, then standing shoulder to shoulder and flailing bath towels to drive the flies out of the window before slamming it shut again.[5] Unsurprisingly, the camp was plagued with dysentery.

East Compound was bounded on its northern side by a long oblong enclosure, the *Vorlager* or camp annexe. In the top left-hand corner stood a cement blockhouse housing both the shower area and the punishment cells. Next to it was the sick quarters and next to that the coal store. Standing at right angles were four more buildings. The first was a barrack for the Russian prisoners, who were used as slave labour. To the right was the Red Cross parcel store, adjoined by the office where books and mail were censored. Last in line was a dental surgery and more accommodation for the Russians. Running down the west side of both enclosures was the *Kommandantur*, containing the German administrative headquarters and the staff living quarters.

The camp was surrounded by two concentric perimeter fences, seven feet apart. Each fence was nine feet high, constructed from strands of barbed wire stretched across concrete stanchions which curved in at the top. The ground in between was littered with drifts of coiled barbed wire. Every hundred yards or so the barbed wire was surmounted by wooden towers, mounted on stilts and equipped with machine guns. They were manned by guards – 'goons', in camp slang – who worked brief two-hour shifts to ensure maximum alertness. The towers were known to the prisoners as 'goon boxes'.

The most daunting barrier was the least impressive. A warning fence, consisting of a wooden rail two feet high, was situated fifteen yards inside the perimeter fence, in full view of the goon boxes. Almost the first thing newcomers learned were the rules concerning the warning fence. 'The area between this and the perimeter fence was "no man's land",' according to the official camp history, based on the inmates' testimony recorded after the war.[6] 'Prisoners of war were forbidden to cross the fence or even to touch it and were shot at if they did so.' If a ball from the games field landed behind the fence, a prisoner had to get permission from a goon to fetch it, or prevail on one of the camp security staff to do so. From September 1942, sentries patrolled inside the perimeter fence during the day and outside at night. When darkness fell, *Hundeführers*, with Alsatian sniffer dogs, roamed the compound, which was bathed in light from powerful lamps mounted along the fence. Even the ground below the prisoners' feet was under surveillance. A ring of microphones was sunk nine feet into the soil around the perimeter at ten-yard intervals, connected to a listening post in the *Kommandantur* where monitors listened for sounds of tunnelling.

At first it took 500 to 600 Germans to run and guard the camp. They were all drawn from the Luftwaffe, as the authorities had decided that each service should be responsible for its prisoner-of-war counterparts. Many of the guards were flak-gunners who had been allowed a break from their duties on the Eastern Front and were grateful for a temporary respite from the carnage. Above them were the camp security staff, the *Abwehr*, who operated separately from both the camp administration and the companies of guards. They were under the control of the camp security officer, a Major Peschel. He had a small staff of three or four junior officers who controlled specialist teams of five or six men which were under the command of a sergeant. They wore dark blue overalls and Luftwaffe field caps but carried no weapons. The prisoners called them 'ferrets'. Their job was to counter escape activity. To begin with they were as amateur in detecting escapes as the prisoners were in planning them. But like their charges they were quick learners. Soon a battle of wits began that would never reach a conclusion. The ferrets seemed to relish the contest. They were conscientious and cunning. 'They crouched under huts looking for tunnels, dug spikes into the ground... peered through windows, eavesdropped and entered rooms,' the camp history reported.[7]

The ferrets and the prisoners had a complicated relationship. They soon recognized each other as worthy adversaries. Experience of each others' wiles brought a wary mutual respect that sometimes shaded into affection. The chief ferret was Ober-feldwebel (Warrant Officer) Hermann Glemnitz. The prisoners called him 'Dimwits', but he was far from stupid and his sharp ears and keen eyes would detect many a tunnel in the early stages of construction. He and his charges got on surprisingly well. As a young man he had worked abroad – in Britain or America, according to different accounts – and he could speak good

English. Aidan Crawley, a pre-war journalist and man about town, and a prominent figure on successive escape committees, remembered his 'friendly and bluff manner. Prisoners liked him because as far as was known he was one of the few incorruptible Germans and yet he had a sense of humour.' Glemnitz never seemed depressed and enjoyed cracking jokes. 'Well, why are you not digging today?' he would ask. 'It's bad weather to be above ground.' There was method, though, in his bonhomie. 'Glemnitz was talkative and observant, going frequently into prisoners' rooms and haranguing them about politics or any other subject: yet all the time he was on the lookout for signs of escape activity.'[8]

Corporal Karl Pilz, known as 'Charlie', was another cunning adversary, 'a curious mixture of humanity and subversiveness. He had a genuine understanding of what a prisoner's life was like and frequently overlooked small irregularities which it was his duty to report.' He treated his struggle with the prisoners in a sporting manner, as a game with recognized rules. 'Tunnels in particular he regarded with the eye of an expert. If they were the efforts of new recruits he would pour scorn on them and ask why they were wasting their time. On the other hand a good tunnel aroused his admiration and he would take endless photographs for his escape museum.' Not that he ever neglected his duties. He 'could smell a tunnel from a hundred yards away and had a nasty criminal mind which worked on exactly the same wavelength as any escaper's,' wrote Tommy Calnan, a serial escaper. 'Charlie was a menace.'[9]

The Luftwaffe were always keen to establish common ground with their captives. Those who had flying experience encouraged

the idea that, whatever differences might divide their govern-
ments, aviators shared a common code. On the train taking Bill
Ash from Paris to Dulag Luft were some Luftwaffe fighter pilots
from Saint-Omer, returning home on leave. It was the home
base of the aircraft that had shot him down. 'When they learned
that an RAF pilot was on board, they came to our compartment
to meet me and, since several of them spoke reasonable English,
to have a professional chat,' he wrote.[10] He was not in the mood.
'Ideas of the camaraderie of the air and the whole conflict being
something the higher-ups arranged among themselves and
nothing to do with us little fellows who simply laid our lives on
the line… belonged as far as I was concerned to another war
and another film.' He had nothing to say to them and if they
left thinking his reticence was due to the fact that he had been
bested by them in an air battle, 'that was all right with me'.

The captors' desire to show a human face to their prisoners
was not insincere. As the prisoners soon learned, the Germans
were able to operate with equal ease at either extreme of the
spectrum of human behaviour. To those such as the British
who they regarded as blood kin, they showed consideration and
respect. For those languishing at what the Nazis believed to be
the foot of the racial totem pole there was only unbounded cruelty. At the same time as Stalag Luft III was being built, other
camps were under construction all over the German empire,
to imprison the Reich's enemies. Those inside them, the Jews,
Gipsies and homosexuals, the political and religious undesir-
ables, could expect only starvation, brutalization and, sooner
or later, death. Occasionally, the British and Allied prisoners
of war would catch a glimpse of this parallel world from which

pity had been banished. The temptation was to shudder and count your blessings. But the knowledge of the depravity that lay beneath the authorities' civilized veneer hovered at the back of every prisoner's mind.

The camp's commandant seemed the antithesis of Nazi inhumanity. Colonel Friedrich-Wilhelm von Lindeiner-Wildau was an efficient and civilized man who spoke English well. In the summer of 1942 he was sixty-one years old, a First World War veteran who had been wounded three times and won the Iron Cross twice. He came out of retirement in 1937 to join the staff of the Luftwaffe chief, Hermann Göring. Acting as chief jailer to Allied aviators was not much to his taste. The prisoners, even those who caused him the most trouble, nonetheless found him 'an erect, elderly soldier of the old school, very fair and correct'.[11] Bill Ash, who would cause him endless trouble, shared this opinion. 'He generally had our respect,' he wrote, 'if rarely our obedience.'[12]

Lindeiner-Wildau followed, as closely as circumstances allowed, the policy for the treatment of prisoners of war laid down in the Geneva Convention of 27 July 1929, to which the Germany of the Weimar Republic had been a signatory. Given the Nazis' innate contempt for international law and their record of tearing up inherited agreements which placed any restraints on their actions, it seems at first sight strange that they continued to stick to this one. The explanation for this uncharacteristic behaviour is probably that by honouring it they ensured good treatment for their own prisoners in British hands. In any event, this document would, to an important degree, shape the lives of Allied prisoners for much of the war.

The ninety-seven articles, drawn up by the International Committee of the Red Cross, prescribed a regime based on the highest civilized principles. It decreed that prisoners of war 'shall at all times be humanely treated and protected, particularly against acts of violence'.[13] Under its provisions, captives were to be held well away from battle zones, enjoying the same shelter, food and medical care as German troops in barracks. In addition to official rations they were entitled to receive comforts from outside – most significantly the famous food parcels supplied by the Red Cross itself. Officers were not required to work. Other ranks might be, but under the same conditions as German workers. The authorities were expected to 'encourage as much as possible the organization of intellectual and sporting pursuits'. They took this seriously. The camp was awash with books and the inmates put on regular theatrical productions, sometimes with costumes brought in from Berlin. The safeguards and provisions went on and on. If implemented they provided an environment in which prisoners would be kept reasonably healthy and well-nourished in mind and body. Lindeiner-Wildau and those above him made an effort to follow the convention, though the quality and quantity of food supplied to the prisoners would often fall short of the standard. By appearing to at least try and play by the rules they hoped the prisoners would do likewise, and develop a cooperative attitude. It seemed a logical strategy. As the Germans would soon discover, it did not take account of the special character of the men they were dealing with.

TWO

Bill and Paddy spent the first days learning the ways of the camp and adjusting to their new circumstances. On arrival the newcomers had been treated to a welcoming address from Lindeiner-Wildau in which he let them know that 'for you the war is over'. It was a phrase they had all heard on many occasions since being captured. Previously it had sounded somewhat melodramatic and slightly absurd. Now it carried the ring of truth. The journey was at an end and they had reached their final destination. The realization produced mixed reactions. 'The prisoner's first sensation on reaching the seclusion of the barbed wire was one of relief,' wrote Aidan Crawley, who arrived at Stalag Luft III about this time. 'At last he ceased to be "on show." Having been stared at, pointed at, segregated from those around him by special guards, perhaps interrogated for long hours, he was among his own people.'[1]

A man had time for proper reflection, a chance to think back over the events that had landed him where he was. The first thing everyone recognized was that they had a great deal to be thankful for. 'It is hard to over-emphasize just how much the average pilot had been through,' wrote Bill Ash. 'Every single one of us had been through some catastrophic shooting down, parachute experience or crash landing in enemy territory.'[2] The feat of escaping from a stricken aircraft was a huge triumph over the odds. Nine out of ten aircrew in such circumstances never managed to struggle free and died ghastly deaths. Once on the ground there were more dangers to contend with: trigger-happy troops or angry civilians catching a first sight of the men who were dropping bombs on them. It seemed to Richard Passmore, who had been shot down in a Blenheim bomber early in the war, that 'each of us was a walking miracle – a man who should not have been alive but was. We listened to the endless succession of stories… in amazement at the huge and unimaginable – if not downright impossible – variety of ways in which death had allowed itself to be cheated.'[3]

The tales were astounding. There was the rear gunner of a Whitley bomber that had crash-landed one night in Germany. When the aeroplane finally slewed to a halt the gunner climbed out of his turret and went in search of his crewmates only to find that he was alone. The intercom had been knocked out when they were hit and he had not heard the order to bail out. He had survived a landing in a pilotless aircraft.

There were pilots who had been knocked senseless and blown out of their cockpits at 25,000 feet, who woke up a few hundred feet from earth, pulled the ripcord and landed safely. Some reached the ground unharmed without benefit of a parachute at all. One man fell two miles through the air then collided with another whose canopy was just opening. He grabbed his saviour's legs and touched down with him.

But thankfulness at having cheated death did not necessarily induce a feeling of contentment and a desire for a quiet life. It took less than an hour to explore every nook and corner of East Compound. The knowledge that henceforth life would extend no further than its boundaries was devastating to men who had known the freedom of the air.

Among the prisoners were men who had entered the RAF in the 1930s, whose manner and outlook distinguished them as service professionals. By now this cadre had been heavily diluted by volunteers who joined up when hostilities started and who had no desire to stay on a day longer than the war lasted. For them war had been an interruption, not a professional opportunity.

Among them were embryonic artists, engineers, actors, musicians, financiers, lawyers and businessmen. The one thing that united them was that they were all airmen. They had joined the air force because it was not the army or the navy. To them, as to everyone at the time, the aeroplane was an almost magical invention. Above all it was a symbol of liberty, promising unfettered movement and defiance of the laws of nature, the very opposite of having to fight sealed inside the steel walls of a warship or a tank. Aircrews enjoyed a freedom of action unknown to the other services. Once on operations they were beyond the reach of the earthbound hierarchy and they lived and died largely on their own initiative. Now their horizons had shrunk to the size of a forest clearing and it seemed you could not turn around without catching yourself on barbed wire.

Once the gates of Stalag Luft III closed behind them all new prisoners acquired a new identity. They were still airmen shaped by their training and experiences and the *esprit* and traditions of their squadrons. But they were also now 'kriegies'. It was short for *Kriegsgefangenen* or prisoners of war, and the domain they inhabited was 'kriegiedom'. There was no shame in it. The terms were used freely. It was simply a recognition of the way things were.

As a kriegie a man had to learn to cope with spartan communal living. This was an officers-only compound. Many inmates had attended British private boarding schools. They told each other that camp life reminded them of their schooldays, a joke that was not that far from the truth. For those like Bill Ash who had not had the privilege of a middle-class British education, the regime took some getting used to. From now on life would be appallingly circumscribed, and defined by absences. Food would become of overwhelming importance. But, as Richard Passmore wrote, 'there were other scarcities queuing up to have their turn at us: lack of affection; lack of fulfilment; lack, and worse than any of the others, of freedom.'[4]

He might have added 'lack of privacy'. Everyone ate, washed, slept and relieved themselves within a few feet of each other. In such an environment social camouflage was soon stripped away, leaving virtues and failings alike on open display. Like boarding school, the kriegie life would bring out the best and the worst in a man. It was soon clear that everybody had something of both in them.

The air force tended to attract individualists and there was no shortage of powerful personalities among the inmates at

Sagan. They included some of the RAF's most illustrious names. Arriving in the compound, wrote Bill Ash, 'was like finding I had died and arrived in the feasting halls of Valhalla, where a previous generation of warriors were already at home'.[5] There was Bob Stanford Tuck, the quintessential fighter ace, with his clipped moustache, sleek hair and silk scarf, who had destroyed at least twenty-nine enemy aircraft before being brought down by flak on a 'sweep' over Northern France in January 1942. There was Norman Ryder, a former schoolteacher who had gone on to become a celebrated Battle of Britain pilot. And there was Douglas Bader.

Bader was short, square-headed and belligerent. He stumped around the camp on two aluminium legs, replacements for the ones he had lost when he crashed while stunt flying a decade before. The RAF had pensioned him off, but using the determination he applied to every aspect of his life he had overcome every bureaucratic obstacle to return to front-line flying. He took part in the defence of the beaches during the Dunkirk evacuation and flew in the Battle of Britain, shooting down nine aircraft. He went on to command a Spitfire wing based in Tangmere, West Sussex, and in the spring and summer of 1942 led it on many sweeps over northern France. These were essentially coat-trailing exercises of doubtful military worth and they cost the lives and liberty of many valuable pilots. On 11 August 1941 Bader's name was added to the list when he was shot down ten miles east of Saint-Omer.

The Germans knew their prisoner's reputation and treated him with due respect. His prosthetic right leg had come off when he baled out. The local Luftwaffe commander, the fighter ace Adolf Galland, gave safe passage for an RAF bomber to drop a replacement. These courtesies did nothing to soften Bader's pugnacious attitude. On his first night in captivity he climbed out of the hospital where he was being held. He was soon caught and sent to Oflag VIB near Warburg before arriving in Stalag Luft III in May 1942. By then the pattern was set. Every morning he woke up and relaunched his personal war against the Germans, constantly looking for ways to escape and goading and provoking his captors.

According to his biographer Paul Brickhill, an Australian fighter pilot and inmate of Stalag Luft III, Bader went out of his way to ensure that 'life was a series of uproars'.[6] When German squads 'strode past singing their marching songs he organized bands to whistle opposition tunes and put them out of step'. When the authorities ordered shutters on the hut windows to be closed at night, 'he wanted the camp to tear them all off and throw them into the middle of the compound'. He was systematically rude to the camp authorities. Once he was standing, arms folded, chatting to Lindeiner when the compound commander, Hauptmann (Captain) Pieber reprimanded him mildly, telling him he should stand to attention when speaking to the Kommandant. 'When I want you to teach me manners, I'll ask you,' Bader snapped. 'Until then, shut up.'

Despite his prominence Bader had no formal position of authority. The convention was that the highest-ranking prisoner took the title of Senior British Officer, acting as the inmates' commanding officer and representing their interests to the German authorities. It was a formal appointment. The SBO and his adjutant were given an office with furniture and a typewriter.

In June 1942 the position was held by Wing Commander Harry Day, lean, cheerful and hawk-faced, who at forty-two years old was twice the age of many of the prisoners. He served in the First World War in the Royal Marines, winning a medal for saving the lives of two men trapped below decks when their ship was torpedoed two days before the Armistice. Later he switched to the RAF, where he led an aerobatics display team. In the summer of 1939 he was commanding 57 Squadron. Six weeks after the war began his Blenheim bomber was shot down while on a reconnaissance mission over Germany. He baled out but his two crewmates were killed. He was thus one of the longest-serving British prisoners, well attuned to the way the system worked. He combined a warrior's credentials with a talent for diplomacy, a strong streak of common sense and an understanding of how far the Germans could be pushed.

He knew Bader of old. They had both served in 23 Squadron in the early 1930s, and Day had led the unit aerobatics team of which Bader was a member. Long acquaintance did not make relations any easier. Bader's abrasive personality and determination to exasperate the enemy regardless of the consequences made friction inevitable. Bader's proposal to tear down the hut shutters sparked an early clash. According to Brickhill it provoked 'a violent argument... Day himself had a streak of the fiery rebel and would have loved to have torn the shutters off, but he also had the job of keeping the Germans reasonably placated so the prisoners could retain privileges to help escape work.'[7]

It was a delicate feat to bring off. Day was as dedicated as anyone to the principle that being a prisoner of war should not be a deterrent to carrying on the struggle against the enemy by all means possible. He had shown his determination at Dulag Luft, where he was also SBO, overseeing the digging of a tunnel the entrance to which was underneath his bed. In June 1941, together with sixteen others, he escaped in what was the first mass breakout of the war. All were recaptured after a few days, but the experience did nothing to diminish his devotion to escaping.

The episode taught Day the value of organization and discipline. His next camp was Stalag Luft I, where he was again SBO. Together with a naval airman, Jimmy Buckley, who had been on the Dulag Luft venture, he formed a committee which controlled and coordinated all aspects of escaping: approving proposals, gathering intelligence and stockpiling vital materials, including clothing, food, maps and documents. This model would be used in Allied prisoner-of-war camps for the rest of the war. The approach required large reserves of patience and a willingness to submit to group discipline, which were not among Bader's more obvious qualities. Most of the prisoners backed Day in the spat over the shutters. But Bader's approach did have its supporters. 'Camp opinion divided,' wrote Paul Brickhill. 'There were the turbulent rebels devoted to Bader, who believed in riling the Germans at every chance and others, some who wanted only peace and some, the wise cool heads, who wanted a judicious amount of goon-baiting mixed with enough tact and cooperation to ensure peace for escape work.'[8]

Bill Ash and Paddy Barthropp fell into the first category. Bill regarded Bader as 'an inspirational leader who really practised what he preached'.[9] Bader was thirty-four years old, and carried a certain amount of paternal authority as well as his celebrity as a fighter ace. It was not surprising that young newcomers would want to win his approval. Soon after their arrival they joined in one of his goon-baiting pranks. The prisoners had been ordered to line up for an extra *Appell*, the roll call that the Germans conducted morning and evening to check numbers. After a long and tedious wait most of them had been counted off and only a small group remained. 'When there were only fifty or so left to count, Douglas Bader decided it would be a good idea for about twenty officers to run across to those already checked, thereby making the Germans do the whole thing all over again,' Paddy Barthtropp remembered.[10] He and Bill Ash led the charge. 'With a whoop we set off, racing from the uncounted herd to the counted one, and others joined in,' wrote Ash.[11] For a moment the guards seemed to fear that a mass breakout was in progress and reached for their guns. Then they realized that it was another goon-baiting exercise. On this occasion, however, they were not in a mood to shrug it off. They were eager to find culprits, and Bill and Paddy were the obvious candidates. The pair were arrested and marched through the *Kommandantur* then out through the front gates of the camp. Hilarity at the escapade rapidly gave way to a mounting feeling of dread. The guards prodded them forward with their rifles, across the clearing and into the woods. 'We marched deeper and deeper into the forest', wrote Ash, 'into the gloomy permanent twilight caused by the thick pine branches blocking out even the smallest rays of optimism from the sun. Each tread of a jackboot on a twig sounded like a gunshot as we marched forward with a row of guns trained on our backs...

in a clearing carpeted by pine needles, we were ordered to halt.'[12]

According to Paddy Barthropp's account they were then 'forced to our knees for what we both thought was going to be the inevitable'.[13] Bill felt 'time passing with almost glacial slowness as we waited for the end'. Paddy had 'never prayed so hard in [his] life'. Then the game was over. They were ordered to stand and marched back to the camp. The gates and the barbed-wire fences seemed almost welcoming.

They were taken straight to Lindeiner, who delivered a lecture and ordered them to be taken to the cell block. Under the Geneva Convention, prisoners were subject to the disciplinary procedures that applied to the armed forces of the detaining power. The most severe punishment permitted was thirty days imprisonment. The pair gave different accounts of the length of their sentence – Bill said a fortnight, Paddy twenty-eight days. Either way, it was their first spell in the 'cooler', a place they would both become very familiar with in their prison careers.

The cooler was housed in the *Vorlager* and had only just been completed. The walls of the cells were freshly whitewashed and the cement on the floor still smelled damp. Each one was furnished with a bunk, table and stool of newly planed pinewood, and the mattress on the bed was clean and comfortable. A small barred window set high in the wall let in noises from the outside world. After their ordeal in the forest both found the solitude and quiet soothing at first. Paddy felt 'the first two or three days in solitary were, in some strange way, rather pleasant. You hadn't the company of your fellow men in a cramped room, so there was nothing to argue about.' The feeling soon wore off. Prisoners were supposed to be allowed books and writing materials, but the Germans seem to have frequently ignored this aspect of the Convention, an omission which added greatly to the burden of solitude. For the first three days the food ration was cut to a double ration of bread and water. It was not long before the irritations of normal camp life were forgotten. 'Towards the end of your spell,' wrote Paddy, 'when you were really hungry, not only for food but also for companionship, it was a relief to be back among them.'[14]

Bill was also surprisingly sanguine about his first experience of the cooler. His tough upbringing meant he had learned to rely on his own resources and company. In all he would spend about six months in solitary confinement. Nevertheless the experience always tested his mental resilience to the limits. He was fortunate in being able to take refuge in an inner life; this helped him emerge with his sanity intact from an ordeal that disturbed the minds of other men.

The day came when the key turned in the lock and they were led through the *Vorlager* and back into East Compound. It was not long before they bumped into Bader, whose stunt had landed them in the cooler. According to Bill, 'Paddy expected at least a pat on the back. Instead [Bader] asked us where we had been as he hadn't seen us around. Luckily he then smiled before we both exploded.'[15]

The rebel's days in the camp were numbered. Under Bader's constant goon-baiting, Lindeiner's patience snapped. Sometime in July Bader was summoned to be told that he was being sent to Colditz, the castle in Saxony reserved for the most troublesome prisoners. Bader's crime was less that he was an ardent escaper, though he was certainly eager to be included in any project, than that he was simply too much of a nuisance. Both his detractors and his supporters lined up to see him go. As expected, he put up a bravura performance. Forty guards stood ready to conduct Bader from the camp. As he was escorted out he paused then walked down the line of guards, carefully examining each one as if he was holding an inspection. The kriegies hooted with laughter. He stumped away on his tin legs with the cheers of his comrades echoing behind him.

Bader's grandstanding was one way of showing defiance. Others believed that the most effective way of resisting the Germans was to organize a successful escape. Work had begun almost as soon as the first prisoners arrived, directed by an escape committee founded on the one that had been created at Barth. It was led by Jimmy Buckley and overseen by Harry Day. Day was replaced in June by Group Captain Herbert Massey, who arrived at Sagan after being shot down during the second of the 'thousand bomber' raids instituted by the new chief of Bomber Command, Arthur Harris. Both were convinced of the value of escape attempts, and according to the private history of the camp produced by the RAF after the war, an astonishing sixty or seventy tunnels were started during the course of the summer. The would-be escapers, though, were up against a security apparatus that was determined that the camp should be 'escape-proof'. Most of the tunnels were 'very shallow and were discovered before [being] completed'.[16] A more ambitious one was under construction for six months before the ferrets discovered it.

Sagan posed particular problems for tunnelling. The layer of sandy topsoil was deep and well drained. Excavating it was easy, but it was conspicuously yellowish in colour and disposing of it without alerting the ferrets was a huge problem. Then there was the question of where to dig. The barracks provided an obvious starting point. At first the space beneath the huts was blocked off by wooden skirting, designed to stop cold draughts whistling through in winter. But the Germans soon discovered that the boards would also shield any tunnelling operations from the eyes of the security staff, and had them removed.[17]

These setbacks depressed the spirits. 'Morale became very low,' remembered Henry Lamond, a 36-year-old Flight Lieutenant from New Zealand.[18] It was Lamond, together with two other inmates, who eventually came up with a viable means of circumventing the German precautions. The three had met after Britain's calamitous withdrawal from Greece in the spring of 1941. In late April he was piloting a Sunderland flying boat alongside Flight Lieutenant Bill Goldfinch, helping evacuate British forces from the mainland. Landing off Kalamata to pick up evacuees, they hit an underwater obstacle and sank. Six of the ten-man crew were killed. The pair spent several hours clinging to a piece of wing before being picked up by Greek fishermen and taken to hospital. Shortly afterwards the Germans arrived and they went into the bag.

During a spell in a holding camp on their way north they met Flight Lieutenant Jack Best. A farmer in Kenya before joining the RAF, Best had been captured after crashing into the sea off southern Greece. All three were sent to Stalag Luft I. Bill Goldfinch had been a civil engineer before the war. With the other two he devised a novel approach to tunnelling, but there was no opportunity to try it out before they were all moved to Sagan.

A conventional tunnel was one that led from an entrance to an exit, dug deep to avoid detection and requiring timber to shore up the walls and ceiling, and ventilation to prevent carbon monoxide poisoning and possible suffocation. Goldfinch argued for something which quickly became known as a 'mole' tunnel. A man or men would burrow under the earth, shifting earth past their bodies, packing it behind them and sealing themselves in. In this way, the tunnel would always be moving forward with them. Apart from the initial displacement of dirt needed to get the tunnel going, there was no problem with disposal. It was true that, without shoring, the tunnel might collapse. But as the intention was to work only eighteen inches below the surface, the risk of disaster was greatly reduced. Nor was ventilation needed. Air holes bored at regular intervals would enable the mole-men to breathe. The amount of time that men could work in such conditions was obviously limited. A mole tunnel would also have to be a rapidly executed 'blitz' tunnel – started close enough to the wire to make the feat physically possible.

Goldfinch, Best and Lamond took the plan to Jimmy Buckley and the escape committee, who gave it their blessing. All they needed now was a spot from where they could begin digging. An ongoing problem plaguing the compound bathhouse seemed to offer an opportunity. The waste water collected in pools that never seemed to drain away. The trio decided to approach the Germans to volunteer their help. 'Bill Goldfinch... had already gained a good reputation with the camp staff [offering] advice about drainage and water problems,' Lamond recalled, 'so that when it was suggested that he be allowed to work on a soak-away to get rid of the mess caused by the flood they not only consented but also provided a shovel.'[19]

The plan was to first dig a 'starter' tunnel – an approach shaft that would get them to the point where they could begin the final blitz. The Germans agreed that the soakaway be dug at a point which was about 150 feet from the outside fence. The starter tunnel was to be fifty feet long. They would then have to burrow more than a hundred feet to be sure of getting beneath the wire. Even with three men the task seemed hugely ambitious.

The first part was relatively easy. They dug the soakaway pit deep enough so they could work at the starter tunnel out of sight of the watchtowers. The spoil from the tunnel was mixed in with the soil from the pit. 'There were a few hitches when guards came to inspect progress,' wrote Lamond. 'The worst of these was when I was in the starter tunnel and Jack Best was in the soakaway. He saw a ferret coming, shouted at me to stay still while he endeavoured to close the entrance, which he did not have time to do, so he had to squat in the hole wiping his brow and saying "*sehr heiss*", which he hoped meant "very hot" and was sufficient excuse for him to be squatting and not working.' A German-speaking kriegie then moved in to divert the ferret and Best breathed again.

The whole enterprise trusted greatly to luck. They made few preparations for life on the run once they had broken out. None of them could speak German or any of the languages of the hundreds of thousands of workers drafted into Germany from conquered territories, which would make them very vulnerable if they travelled on trains or buses. At first they decided they would walk to freedom, following railway lines by night and lying up by day. Then they came up with a better idea. There was known to be an aerodrome somewhere to the west of the camp. If they could reach it they might steal an aeroplane and fly to Sweden, the nearest neutral territory.

On 21 June 1942 – the longest day of the year – they were ready to go. They travelled very light – trousers, sweater and shoes, bottles of water and a few specially made high-energy food bars.

They turned up for the evening *Appell*. Then they returned to their hut, where there comrades donated their rations to give them a special farewell supper. As it was still broad daylight they were allowed to return to work on the soakaway. When they were sure the guards had lost interest in them they unblocked the entrance to the starter tunnel and climbed in. Another prisoner sealed the hole behind them.

Bill Goldfinch led the digging, with Lamond behind and Best in the rear clawing back the soil. They worked in darkness. Kriegie ingenuity had already devised a makeshift lamp using a margarine-filled tin and a wool wick, but they could not risk the light being seen through the air holes when dusk fell. They had already decided that it would be impossible to dig fast enough to get under the wire in a single night. Even so, they were disappointed at their slow progress. 'Perhaps we were tired before we went in,' wrote Lamond. 'Perhaps the quality of the air was not very good… we had to rest often.' Exhaustion set in. It was midsummer's day but the earth was cold and they slept huddled together. In the morning their friends watching from the huts were alarmed to see wisps of condensation rising from the air holes, but mercifully the guards did not notice.

At the first *Appell*, arrangements had been made to rig the count so their absence was not noted. Throughout the day they toiled away while the life of the camp went on as usual above them. In the early evening a dog began to sniff at one of the air holes, but its handler called it back. They passed under the final fence around midnight but waited for two more hours until the camp was at its quietest. Goldfinch was just breaking through the crust of earth above him when he heard German voices. It was the guards having a chat as they passed each other on their tour of the outer perimeter. Once their footsteps faded he punched through the soil and they dragged themselves from the tunnel and ran to the cover of the forest. 'The initial reaction was one of how glorious the fresh air tasted,' wrote Lamond, 'and the next, on looking back into the compound, was a tremendous surge of exhilaration.'

They were soaked in sweat and dirt but had used up their water supply. They found a pool near a railway line, sluiced themselves down and slaked their thirst. Then they stripped off their tunnelling togs and buried them, dressed and took their bearings. The aerodrome where they hoped to steal an aircraft was meant to be somewhere beyond the railway. The night was short and they had no map but they found it just before dawn. There were no aeroplanes to be seen. They crept around the boundary to where a trailer for transporting gliders was parked, climbed in and immediately fell asleep.

It was a very hot day but they slept through most of it. When they emerged at dusk there were still no aeroplanes to steal. Reluctantly, they fell back on the original plan. They returned to the railway, which ran north out of Sagan towards the Oder river. There they hoped to steal a boat and row the two hundred miles downstream to Stettin, then out to sea, where with any luck a Swedish ship would pick them up. It was, as Lamond admitted, 'not a very hopeful plan but something to do'.

Walking down the railway track was not nearly as easy as it sounded. The sleepers were spaced just short of a comfortable stride and the ballast made a lot of noise under foot. They only had a few of hours of darkness before they would have to find somewhere to lie up during the long day. Water was difficult to come by. They were forced to drink from pools covered with scum. The escape rations they had been issued with were soon gone. They were reduced to gnawing raw potatoes.

After five days trudging down the track, sleeping in haystacks and woods, they reached the river. The banks were deserted and they found a heavy, flat-bottomed boat equipped with oars which they managed to wrench from its moorings.

'It was a very clumsy outfit and [it] took some time to learn to control it,' Lamond remembered. 'There were many barges going up and down the river and some of their crews shook their fists at us, so presumably they were not very happy with our sea-manship.' After a few hours they moored in a reedy backwater, intending to rest before setting off again at nightfall.

They were sound asleep when a policeman arrived and arrested them for stealing the boat. The escapers had not bothered to prepare a cover story. It took no time to discover their identities. A week later they were back in Stalag Luft III. They were welcomed back as heroes. They might have failed in their ultimate objective of a 'home run' to England, but no one had really expected them to succeed. What they had done was equally valuable – they had transformed the psychological landscape of the camp. Until then, the kriegies were becoming inclined to accept the Germans' confident assessment that the camp's design and procedure made escape impossible. That premise had been exploded. 'Our success changed the atti-tude... completely,' said Lamond. 'Morale was restored. POWs could gleefully taunt the staff that their escape-proof camp was not escape-proof after all.' For Goldfinch and Best it meant the end of their stay in Stalag Luft III, and they were packed off to Colditz. They left behind an example of what tenacity and ingenuity could achieve, one that inspired all those determined not to spend the rest of the war behind the wire.

THREE

The picture of Allied POW camps that has come down to us from books and films has tended to obscure the fact that only a minority of prisoners were ever interested in escaping. Bill Ash wrote that 'as a result of their experiences of crash and capture, most… were understandably not overly keen on pushing the odds even further by escaping in the heart of Germany.' Though every kriegie might dream of escape, and most were willing to help others to get away, 'the chances were so slim of making it home and the dangers of being shot before you were out of the camp perimeter were so great, that most decided to wait it out.'[1]

The proportion of would-be escapers to those who accepted their fate is difficult to establish with precision. The RAF's history of Stalag Luft III lists 138 men who had some involvement in escape activities in East Compound during the thirty-four months of its existence.[2] Many of them were engaged in ancillary roles such as acting as lookouts or forging documents, rather than digging tunnels. The document records that about

1,850 prisoners passed through the compound in that time. That means that more than 90 per cent of kriegies were content to wait out the war to its end. The RAF's internal history of Stalag Luft VI at Heydekrug, a camp for NCOs, estimates the proportion of escape-minded prisoners at only 5 per cent.[3]

Bill Ash put the figure somewhat higher, but pointed out the significant variations in the degree of commitment. 'There cannot have been a single POW who did not think about escaping,' he wrote. 'Yet... maybe only a third in an average camp would have been actively involved in escaping-related activities. Most of the other two-thirds would assist if possible behind the scenes and undergo some hardships to help.' The majority of pro-escapers did a vital job 'keeping an eye on the guards over long, dull shifts... or helping to prepare anything from documents to clothes and maps or digging implements'. But he reckoned 'maybe only 5 per cent were committed to getting outside the wire at all costs.' And of those, one attempt was usually enough. For the 1 or 2 per cent who remained, 'escaping became a way of life.'[4]

At the other end of the spectrum were those whose experiences had 'so scarred them that keeping their heads down and surviving the war was all they could manage'. The reluctance of men who had already cheated death to dice with it once again is understandable. At the beginning at least, inertia was strong and the attractions of camp life powerful. Inside the wire you were out of the firing line for good. Your captors sheltered and fed you. The German rations might be meagre, but if Red Cross parcel deliveries were running smoothly, you enjoyed chocolate and other luxuries that were denied to the guards. The daily

than a handful of men was automatically reported to the high command. Thousands of men were turned out of barracks to comb the countryside for the escapers, diverting them from other tasks. If a man succeeded in making it home, he would not only return to fill a place in the ranks. He would also be able to provide valuable intelligence on areas he had passed through that was unavailable from photographic reconnaissance, as well as information on the outlook and morale of the enemy.

These arguments did not carry much weight with some of the kriegies. 'There were those who just wanted a quiet life,' wrote Bill Ash, 'people for whom any of us escapers were at best a necessary evil.'[7] The objection was that the activities of the few could make life worse for the many. Though the Geneva Convention forbade collective punishment, the camp history reported that 'mass reprisals were instituted against the whole compound when escape attempts or escape activities tried the patience of the German authorities too much.'[8] The penalties were not very harsh. They included closing the theatre, forbidding visits of theatre shows from other compounds, and stopping inter-compound games. In response to an escape bid in 1942 there was an attempt to stop the issuing of Red Cross parcels. The ban ceased after a complaint was made to the International Committee in Geneva, which intervened with Berlin. The result was a flood of goodies in time for Christmas.

Whether military considerations were foremost in the minds of many determined escapers is open to question. Bill Ash would never describe the impulse that drove him in such utilitarian terms. His motives were complicated. They mixed the personal and the political. At times he would describe it as something beyond his control. 'Escaping is quite addictive,' he wrote, 'and, like all addictive drugs, extremely dangerous.'[9]

It was something he had felt ever since arriving at Dulag Luft, the doorway through which airmen passed on their way to a permanent camp. The processing began with a long interrogation. The Luftwaffe's intention was to extract what information they could from their enemies, but despite the dire warnings about the subtlety and skill of the interrogators issued in the official instructions, their techniques seem to have been often quite amateurish. The man who questioned Ash claimed to be a Red Cross official and had insignia to prove it. Unfortunately the effect was spoiled by the jackboots sticking out from under his coat.

Bill confined himself to name, rank and number, but the questioning nonetheless went on for some time. In between sessions, the prisoners were held in solitary confinement. It was not the first time he had been placed in a cell on his own, but on this occasion the experience shook him profoundly. Later he would describe how he was swept by a feeling of 'utter depression'. He felt a sense of shame at being taken captive. The word 'caitiff' kept swimming into his head. It was an archaic term for 'captive', but it also meant 'base and cowardly'.[10] In his frustration he slammed his fist into the cell wall, bruising his knuckles and drawing blood. He was disgusted at himself for letting himself be shot down before he could inflict any real damage on his enemy. Most of all he felt guilty for failing the many French civilians who, risking imprisonment, torture and death, had helped him after he was shot down.

Of the several motives that drove Bill Ash to attempt escape over and over again, the feeling that he was in some way fulfilling a duty to his French saviours was a strong one. The story of the weeks between crash-landing and capture make it clear why he felt this sense of obligation so powerfully.

He had been shot down on the afternoon of Tuesday, 24 March 1942, on his way back from a mission escorting six Boston bombers tasked with attacking the power station at Comines, in the Pas-de-Calais on the border with Belgium. After the war Bill would give several accounts of his subsequent wanderings. The first occasion was when he, like all returning prisoners of war, was questioned by an officer of IS9, the British intelligence service charged with maintaining contact with the POW camps. The details are very sparse and it is essentially a list of names of French civilians who helped him – some of whom did not appear in his subsequent memoirs. The full story of what happened after the crash-landing emerges from various sources. As we have seen, he was helped by a woman who gave him a jacket and trousers. Her name, although he did not know it at the time, was Pauline Le Cam, and she would pay a high price for her bravery.

After he left her house, and after the incident with the open sewer, he spent several days living rough, then he knocked on the door of a small bar and restaurant in the hamlet of Neuville, about fifteen miles south-west of where he crashed. It was run by the Boulanger family, who hid him in their cellar. This act put them at great personal risk. The place was sometimes visited by Germans, and once a staff car stopped outside and a party of officers came in for a meal. He was looked after by the owners' daughter Marthe Boulanger, a clever and practical 16-year-old. They tried to teach each other English and French and he entertained her with stories about the bright lights of London and his Texas upbringing.

One night word arrived that the Germans were coming to search the village. Marthe and her brother Julien led him across the dark fields to the home of a local flour-mill owner called Emile Rocourt, a few miles away near Alquines. Rocourt appeared to have a good relationship with the German occupiers. But in fact he and his brother Gaston were kingpins of the local resistance network, and he looked after Bill until the danger passed. At the end of April Bill was taken again to the Rocourt house, where a man was waiting for him. He was small and dark and quiet, and gave his name only as 'Jean'. Ash would learn later that he was Jean de la Olla, an Algerian-born 37-year-old, who worked for the 'Pat Line'. This was the escape network set up by Albert Guerisse, a Belgian military doctor whose alias was 'Pat O'Leary'. The organization had successfully passed Allied prisoners to the south of France for onward passage to Gibraltar and Spain. It had almost been destroyed by the treachery of a British soldier and conman called Harry Coles, who had gone over to the Germans. La Olla had been sent north by Guerisse to revive the network and this was one of his first missions.

He escorted Bill to Lille and left him with a single woman whose name Ash never learned. There were visits from a young woman and her brother, an easygoing young man who played the latest hits such as Rina Ketty's 'J'Attendrai' on his guitar. Bill was shocked to learn that he was on a Nazi death-list, liable to be arrested and shot in reprisal if the resistance mounted an operation in the area. Bill tried to persuade him to come with him when they moved on. The boy explained that there was no point. If he escaped, his sister would take his place on the Germans' list.

After a week, Jean reappeared. He took Bill to Paris and left him with a young married couple, Joseph and Giselle Gillet, who lived in an apartment on the Avenue du Général-Laperrine near the Porte Dorée on the eastern side of the city. Joseph had been a fighter pilot until the French defeat. They put Bill up in a bedroom, where he was to stay until a courier arrived to take him on the next leg of his journey to Angoulême in south-west France, a step nearer the Pyrenees. Despite the risk, Bill was soon slipping out to explore Paris. He went for walks in the Bois de Vincennes opposite the flat, and swimming at an indoor pool near Denfert-Rochereau. Sometimes Joseph and Giselle went with him to the cinema or the zoo. Early one morning in the middle of May the flat was raided. After the war, when questioned about his experiences by IS9, he told his debriefer that 'a Frenchman living in the same block of flats informed the Germans of my presence'.[11] He was dragged out of bed and driven away to a headquarters building near the Opéra. Joseph and Giselle were taken off separately and he never saw the couple again.

He was taken into a basement and locked into a room. After an hour, two soldiers took him upstairs to an office. A grey-haired man in civilian clothes, who he assumed to be a Gestapo officer, sat behind a desk. The man motioned for him to sit down on a small chair in front of him while the guards withdrew to the door. Speaking in halting French he told his story, making no mention of those who had helped him along the way and doing his best to shield Joseph and Giselle. He explained that they were simply Good Samaritans who had found him destitute on the street and taken him in.

The Gestapo man behind the desk told him to speak English. He seemed businesslike and, at first, reasonably polite. He suggested he stop worrying about the couple and start trying to convince him that he was who he said he was. Ash repeated the date and place where he was shot down. Surely they would have a record of a smashed-up plane being found at Vieille-Église with no one in it? The man replied that this did not prove that he was the pilot. He had been picked up in Paris and in civilian clothes. He might equally be a spy who had been dropped in subsequently. Bill could not help pointing out that, with his poor French and non-existent German, he was hardly spy material. The interrogator produced a pen and paper. The only way he could prove his identity, he said, was to write down the name of every person he had been in contact with since he left his aircraft. Ash made a brave joke, claiming with some justification that he had always been terrible remembering names. The fake civility evaporated. The man rose and left him to the guards. One jerked him to his feet and pinned his arms while the other punched him in the face. The next blow drove the breath from his lungs, leaving him sick and gagging for breath. The soldier paused to wrap a handkerchief round his knuckles, then resumed punching him in the face.

He began to lose consciousness. Then a hand grabbed his hair and wrenched his head back. The grey-haired man was back. Bill described what happened next in an account published thirty-six years later:

> He placed an official-looking form on the desk and invited me to have a look at it. One of my eyes was almost completely closed and I could not focus very well on the paper which was in German anyway, so I asked him what it said. 'It's from the Kommandantur and it says that if the person calling himself William Ash fails to provide satisfactory proof of his identity he is to be executed by firing squad at 6 a.m. on June 4th.'
>
> 'What's today?'
>
> 'June 3rd.'[12]

The interrogation continued. They wanted to know whether he had ever met someone called Monsieur Jean. They seemed to know all about la Olla's activities, but Bill denied any knowledge of him. Eventually they took him back to his cell. It was still morning. They left him alone for the next eighteen hours. His mood swung between despair and defiance. He tried to convince himself that they were bluffing. If they were not, he could save his life by offering up a name or two. Even as he thought this, he knew he could not betray people who had risked their life for him. He remembered that Dostoevsky, a hero of his, had been sentenced to death by the Tsar. He had always wanted to be a writer. Only now he would not be able to make use of his experiences. He tried to imagine the firing squad, 'thinking that I must steel myself to be very steady and self-controlled when it happened, and then I remember thinking why in hell should I? Who was ever going to know whether I had died well or not and it certainly was not going to make the slightest difference to me how I had gone.'[13]

In the morning the hours passed and no one came. His hopes began to rise. Convention had it that you were shot at dawn. Yet the day was well on and he was still alive. About noon a guard appeared with black bread and sauerkraut soup. Surely they would not waste food on him if they were about to shoot him?

Later the guards returned and led him back upstairs. The grey-haired Gestapo man was waiting and this time he seemed relaxed, almost playful. He began talking about time he had spent in London, before the war. He remembered the steaks at Scott's restaurant in Mayfair. Had Ash ever eaten there?

There seemed no reason not to play along. No, he hadn't, he replied. But he was fond of Lyon's Corner House, just off Piccadilly Circus, where at the salad-bowl counter you could eat all you could manage for five shillings.

The man smiled and pushed a box of cigarettes across the table towards him. Bill didn't really smoke but something made him take one.

> Then suddenly his manner changed and he shouted at me. 'You'll never see London again! They'll see it.' He pointed at the two soldiers. 'They'll be in England living off the fat of the land, and do you know where you'll be?'
> I did not like to say.
> 'Dead. You'll be dead unless you give us some names.'[14]

The Gestapo man nodded at one of the guards, who slapped Bill across the face, knocking the cigarette from his mouth in a shower of sparks. So it went on. A sort of rhythm was established. Blows, then questions and entreaties to see reason. They had already picked up most of the people who had helped him. Why not just confirm their names and corroborate his own story in the process? Through the pain, he heard himself replying logically. Surely if they had really arrested his helpers, then they would have told the Germans all about him? They stopped when he was almost unconscious and dragged him back downstairs.

The next day was the same, and the day after. Later he could never work out how long it went on. Initially he thought a week, later ten days or even a fortnight. Then one evening he heard shouting outside his cell door. He had become something of a connoisseur of German bellowing and felt that this display 'had the quality of equals screaming at each other rather than one of the *Herrenvolk* bawling out an *Untermensch*'.[15]

Soon after, the door was opened and he was led out. A man in Luftwaffe uniform was arguing with the Gestapo man. 'What it turned out to be was an emissary from the Luftwaffe dressing down my interrogator for not informing them of the capture of someone claiming to be RAF and insisting on questioning the prisoner himself.'[16] He was the subject of a demarcation dispute. As far as the Luftwaffe was concerned, any shot-down Allied airman belonged to them, to be pumped about dispositions, equipment, anything that would add to their intelligence picture. There was a further consideration. There were hundreds of Luftwaffe aircrew in British prisoner-of-war camps. If it was learned that Allied fliers were being tortured and beaten, the assumption was that reprisals would follow. The Luftwaffe won the argument. That night, under guard, Bill was taken to the Gare de l'Est and put on a train to Germany.

He was very lucky to be alive. He knew that Giselle and Joseph were perhaps not so fortunate. In his post-war intelligence debrief he told the IS9 officer that they had been 'sentenced to be shot by [the] Gestapo' but that their 'actual fate was unknown'. By then he also knew that Pauline Le Cam from Vieille-Église had 'served three years in a concentration camp for assisting me'.[17] The encounter with the Gestapo had dispelled any inclination he might have had to empathize with his enemy, who he had 'come to hate with a passionate intensity'.[18] He could feel satisfaction that he had not betrayed any of those who had risked so much to help him. As he left France behind he had learned enough about the Germans to fear the worst if his helpers were discovered. He had to find a way to damage the enemy. It seemed the only means at his disposal was to try and escape.

FOUR

Bill had listened to lectures on escape and evasion during his training. One thing he was told was that the sooner you tried to get away, the better were your chances of success. The journey into captivity offered many opportunities. It usually involved travelling by public transport accompanied by guards who needed to eat, sleep and use the toilet. But to take advantage, you needed to be alert, fit and optimistic. Bill was weak and bruised from constant beatings. His normally buoyant spirits were flat. 'For me this was one of the lowest periods of the war,' he wrote later.[1] At Dulag Luft his feelings of frustration and guilt had deepened. But his natural *joie de vivre* and his tendency towards action over melancholy reflection soon asserted themselves. His revival owed something to having met Paddy Barthropp.

Paddy was one of The Few, but there were few like Paddy. He had seen a lot in his twenty-one years. His mother died giving birth to him in Dublin on 9 November 1920. His father, he wrote, 'was totally grief stricken and resented my very existence almost up to the time of his own death in 1953'.[2] It was typical of Paddy to add: 'I never blamed him.' Elton Peter Maxwell D'Arley Barthropp was a successful racehorse-trainer whose patrons included the Duke of Westminster and the Aga Khan. He was also a compulsive gambler. After his bankruptcy forced Paddy's departure from Ampleforth College, a Catholic private school run by Benedictine monks in the wilds of Yorkshire, he pulled strings to get his son an engineering apprenticeship at the Rover works in Coventry. Like most young men of his generation Paddy was fascinated by aeroplanes. After a visit to the annual air display at Hendon in London, he decided to apply for one of the short-service commissions the RAF was offering. After one failed attempt he was in, and flying a Spitfire in time to take part in the Battle of Britain. Paddy liked girls and parties and resented authority, yet he retained a curious innocence and felt a strong sympathy for the underdog. These were attributes that he shared with Bill Ash.

He managed to get into trouble as soon as he got to Dulag Luft. His interrogator was a Major Binder, who had been a well-known racing-car driver before the war. Binder was charged with pumping Paddy for information about the new carburettor recently fitted to some Spitfires to overcome the loss of power they suffered when rolling out at the top of a climb. 'It didn't take me long to convince him that I hadn't a clue,' Paddy recalled.[3] The major seemed relieved. He suggested that the two of them go off for lunch at a tavern in the woods beyond the camp. All Paddy had to do was give his parole that he would not try and escape. Ignoring all the RAF's stern warnings against fraternizing with the enemy, he accepted.

Lunch was a great success and went on a long time and they both ended up in the German-officers' mess for supper. When a senior British officer at the camp heard about this he gave Paddy a rocket. Paddy didn't mind. All in all 'it was well worth it'.

Their time at Dulag Luft was brief. The regime was relaxed, controlled by a 'permanent staff' of British officers who worked with the Germans. Their job was to explain the system to the new arrivals, issue them with clothes and prepare them for their onward journey. Over time they had assumed status and privileges. They messed separately from the transients and ate better food. Some of the newcomers, most of whom had just come from grappling with the Germans in the skies over occupied Europe, found their willingness to cooperate with the system surprising, even sinister. In time they would learn that this was a misjudgement.

Some of the staff gave off an air of weary superiority. They knew the way the system operated, what was possible and what was not, and were not gentle in puncturing naïve illusions. It seemed to Bill that, having resolved to escape, he should try and do so as soon as possible. When he approached a senior officer and asked him how he should proceed he got a cool response. 'Not from here, old boy,' he was told. 'Wait till you get to the main prison camp... It's all properly organized there.'[4]

Paddy shared Bill's determination. His motives for wanting to escape were unclear, perhaps even to himself. His complete lack of pomposity prevented him from attempting any deep analysis in the brief, hilarious memoir he left behind. The crushing tedium provided a spur, as did concern at how things would end if the war turned bad for the Germans. It was, he wrote, 'a time of boredom, a deep sense of homesickness, constant hunger and the nagging thought that in the end we would probably be disposed of'. But it was also a question of character. A spirit as free and anarchic as his could not submit to incarceration without a struggle.

From their neighbouring bunks in Barrack 64 they plotted their escape. They lived to the rhythm of fixed routines, and one day bled indistinguishably into another. They woke at eight and mustered outside with the other kriegies for morning *Appell*. Then they drifted back to breakfast before deciding how to fill the time before lunch. 'In our small room, stuffed cheek-by-jowl with normally hyperactive but now frustrated and often short-tempered young men of different interests and outlooks and nationalities, time dragged by leadenly,' Paddy remembered. 'Every hour was another sixty minutes to kill.'[5] Bill found it quite easy to keep himself occupied. Until now he had always been too busy to fulfil his hopes of being a writer. Here there was all the time in the world. He lay on his bunk, filling page after page of his first novel.

Sometimes they wandered over to the dusty sports areas behind the latrines in the south-east corner to join in whatever game was in progress. The players came from several different sporting traditions. The Brits were rugby men, the Australians played 'Aussie rules', while Bill had been brought up on American football. 'As the game progressed, the players and ball were passed, thumped, bounced and tackled in every way possible, with heated disputes about whether a goal was a try or a try was a touchdown,' Bill remembered.[6] The game was too strenuous for some of the players weakened by the poor food or the trauma of being shot down. Once, while charging down the wing, he threw the ball to a teammate who caught the pass then keeled over in a faint.

The prisoners relied on Red Cross parcels to supplement the meagre German rations. When deliveries were running smoothly, they ate reasonably well. In the summer of 1942, though, the supply was badly disrupted. Food had never mattered much back home where there was plenty of it. Even during the war the airmen had been used to three meals a day – good, bad or indifferent, depending on which station they were based in – which arrived on the table without them having to think about it. In the camp, food came to matter a great deal. It was the source of more fantasies than sex. Men savoured the memory of meals past and dreamed of feasts to come.

At this time they lived with growling bellies, never quite silenced by the meagre rations. The Geneva Convention stated that prisoners should be given the same food as was issued to depot troops. Instead, wrote Aidan Crawley, the rations were closer to 'the lowest civilian grade designed for those who were too old to work.'[7] Whether this was due to shortages or to a belief that those supplies that were available were wasted on prisoners is not clear. It meant a dismal diet of black bread, margarine, jam and tea for breakfast, lunch of soup or sauerkraut, and a supper of sausage and bread or a potato. Swedes and pumpkins featured prominently. Very occasionally the carcase of an old horse or cow would arrive. To stay healthy, a man living a prison-camp life needed 3,000 calories a day. The German rations averaged about 1,600 calories, which was only adequate if the prisoner took no exercise and slept often. Sometimes the energy value of the food dipped as low as 1,100 calories. Tobacco did something to relieve hunger pangs.

Much better, though, were the Red Cross parcels, the presence or absence of which could change the mood of the camp. The Red Cross parcel scheme dated back to the previous war, when British prisoners wrote home saying they were starving and desperate for warm clothing. It was revived when the new war came, supported by voluntary subscriptions. The aim was that, every week, a British prisoner would receive a cardboard box filled with food and comforts to supplement his rations, sent via the Red Cross in Switzerland. A typical box weighed 11 lb. and contained some – or, if they were lucky, all – of the following items: a small packet of tea, a tin of cocoa, a bar of milk chocolate, tins of pudding, beef loaf or chopped ham, condensed milk, margarine, processed cheese, sardines, jam, sugar, vegetables, dried eggs, oatmeal and biscuits. They also came with a small 2.5-ounce cake of soap. Tins of fifty cigarettes or pipe tobacco were sent separately. These were addressed to the Senior Officer of the camp and distributed equally among the prisoners.

Without the supplementary calories, the prisoners were on the edge of starvation.

The food the Germans dished up provoked constant moaning. The only person who didn't seem to mind it was Bill Ash. He ate everything, including the strange items which appeared intermittently on the menu. There was runny green cheese which turned everyone else's stomach. And there was klipfish. No one quite knew what klipfish was. It seemed to be some kind of dehydrated whitebait, which rumour claimed had been lying in a military warehouse since the last war. It looked like wood shavings and after being soaked in water for several days acquired the consistency and smell of wet dog hair. The normal method of cooking was to chop it into squares and fry it. Most of the kriegies could not manage more than a mouthful. Bill wolfed it down, happily cruising the camp asking others if he could have their leftovers. It was hard to explain to British men, who assumed that a Texan must have been brought up on steak three times a day, that he had gone hungry in his early days. 'The food is terrible,' he agreed. 'But think how cheap it is.'[8]

Boredom and hunger fuelled frustration and anger. Normally peaceable men picked fights and looked for slights. Bill and Paddy shared an inclination to try and treat the humiliations and privations of camp life as a joke. It was only at night that the mask of humour dropped. Then every man was as close to solitude as the confined space they lived in allowed. They lay in their private spaces, staring at the ceiling or the mattress above their heads, and let the ghosts of home and the past fill their minds. Some nights there was music on the air. It streamed from a wind-up gramophone belonging to a prisoner called Bill Stapleton, who had been shot down in his Spitfire over Dunkirk in June 1940. He had somehow acquired a small collection of classical discs. It was, wrote Bill Ash, 'some of the most beautiful music ever composed. It would waft out from Bill's gramophone, across the camp, making us feel just a little bit more free and a little less forgotten.'[9] Ash knew most of the melodies well. He had loved classical music since first hearing it during his days at the university, an epoch that now seemed to

belong to another century. The sounds from Stapleton's gramophone brought comfort and also inspiration. They were a link to
the world he had left behind and to which he was determined
to return as soon as possible. He dreamed of freedom. 'I do
not suppose there was one night in those three years when I
did not soar over the wire by merely flapping my arms or mole
underneath it like a mite in cheese, take off in a 'plane made of
bed boards or catapult myself over the machine-gun posts by a
huge rubber band.'[10]

With dawn, reality intruded again. How were they going
to realize their dreams of escape? He and Paddy spent many
hours examining all possibilities, no matter how hare-brained
and implausible. Most were rejected after a few minutes.
There was no point wasting time on any plan that did not bear
examination from all angles. To get support for any project
meant winning the approval of the escape committee. They
sat in council to examine the plans put before them, ruthlessly
rejecting any proposal that had not been meticulously thought
through.

The chairman, Lieutenant Commander Jimmy Buckley,
who flew from the aircraft carrier HMS *Glorious* before being
shot down over Dunkirk, was a small, crinkly haired, humorous
man with a theatrical streak, which came out in the sketches
he wrote and acted in to entertain his fellow kriegies. He also
had a gift for administration and a cool, rational mind, qualities
that Harry Day had spotted when he made him his deputy at
Dulag Luft.

No one approached Buckley and the committee without
a sense of trepidation. 'Compared to selling this hard-nosed

bunch your escape plans, getting past the guards was thought to be relatively easy,' remembered Bill. 'Almost any scheme, even one that sounds brilliant at its time of invention, starts to sound faintly demented when you pitch it to an audience who look as if they are trying you for your life.'[11]

At last Bill and Paddy came up with a proposal that they felt might pass muster with the committee. Once a week the prisoners were led in groups through the gate to the north of the huts and into the *Vorlager* for a shower. The guards counted them on the way in and then on the way out again. According to Paddy, 'the Goons would normally turn on the hot water for a couple of minutes so we could lather up with ersatz soap and later turn them on a second time for us to rinse off.'[12] On one of these excursions the pair had noticed a manhole cover set into the floor of the shower room. On lifting it they discovered it led down into a small space which housed the pipes for the mains water supply and the cocks which controlled it. There was just enough room in there for two men. If they managed to slip through the hole unobserved they could wait until dark, then sneak out into the *Vorlager* which was not patrolled at night. Then they could cut through the wire and be on their way. For the scheme to succeed the count in and out of the *Vorlager* would have to be fixed. By now the kriegies had worked out ways of fooling the guards, distracting them at a vital moment to manipulate the numbers as required.

The day came when their plan was put before the committee. They waited outside Barrack 69 where the members met, protected by a network of lookouts who stood unobtrusively at key points ready to signal the arrival of any ferrets. Then Bill and

Paddy were called in and given the chance to sell their proposal. Although they did not know it, the committee was in a receptive mood. With so many tunnels being discovered they had decided to concentrate on just one project, a well-engineered, deep-lying shaft which had its entrance under one of the barracks. They were inclined to look favourably on any scheme that did not require digging.

The committee listened in silence and asked a few questions. Then the pair were dismissed and the deliberations began. A little while later they were called back and told the plan had been approved. Bill and Paddy felt a mixture of satisfaction and apprehension. Something that had been theoretical was now real. Freedom had just inched a little bit closer. But so too had the prospect of a fusillade of bullets in the back.

The support of the committee meant they now had access to the resources of the escape organization. They were kitted out with a compass, a hand-drawn map of the area using information gathered from previous escapers and – very importantly – sustenance. If they could feed themselves during their first days on the run they would reduce the risk of discovery due to being forced to buy – or steal – food from local people. Prison camps were full of men who had acquired specialist knowledge of many subjects before they were drawn into the war. Much of this expertise could be usefully applied to escape activities. Among the committee members was a leading nutritionist. David Lubbock was married to the daughter of a prominent scientist, Sir John Boyd Orr. Together they had produced a study called *Feeding the People in Wartime*, which formed the basis for the government's rationing programme. Lubbock joined the Fleet

Air Arm in 1940 and flew in Albacore biplanes off aircraft carriers. In late 1941 he was shot down during a raid on Kirkenes in Northern Norway and was captured by the Germans while attempting to walk to Russia.

Lubbock applied his expertise to devising as balanced a diet as possible for the prisoners with whatever was to hand. He also invented a high-energy food bar – 'the Mixture' – to sustain escapers, as used by Goldfinch, Best and Lamond on their blitz-tunnel bid. He persuaded prisoners to donate to a food pool to provide the ingredients for the bars. They were made out of a fudge comprised of sugar, oatmeal, chocolate or cocoa, butter or margarine, dried milk or flour, Ovaltine or Bemax and raisins. The ingredients were boiled up then dried and cut into flat cakes. Compared with the fare the prisoners were used to it tasted delicious. The bars were stored to await issue to any prisoner or prisoners whose plan had been approved by the escape committee. Bill and Paddy were now eligible, and the food problem was solved.

But what about clothing? When on the run they would need to look nondescript. Once in the camp prisoners were issued with RAF uniform. Bulk deliveries of underwear, socks, shirts, razors, ties, tunics, trousers and greatcoats arrived from London via the Red Cross in Switzerland. In the Germans' reckoning, uniforms were a deterrent to escape, making the wearer conspicuous if they ever made it beyond the wire. This was not quite true. Half the male population was in military dress of one sort or another and the variety was so great that it took an expert to know which was which. Civilian clothing was obviously less risky though, and before long the camp tailors had learned how to transform any bit of service kit into something that would pass muster in a land swarming with foreign workers wearing often wildly ill-assorted combinations of clothes.

Bill and Paddy would not require much of a disguise. They were escaping during a hot continental summer, and a pair of trousers and a shirt were all they needed in order to blend in. With the issue of a pair of homemade shears to cut through the barbed wire of the *Vorlager* fence, they were ready to go.

The morning dawned when their turn came to use the showers. The shower party was mustered outside the huts and marched through the gate that connected East Compound to the *Vorlager*. One of the guards counted them off as they trooped through. The idea was that once inside the shower room they would lever up the manhole and drop through to hide among the pipes and stopcocks. When the session was over the remaining prisoners would march out again. The guards would then check them off again as they departed. Success depended on them being fooled into believing that the same number was walking out as had walked in.

By now many ruses had been devised to confuse roll calls. *Appells* were held morning and evening to count everyone in the compound. They took place on the sports field except in bad weather when they took place in the corridors of the barracks. Sick prisoners in possession of a chit from the medical officer were allowed to remain in their rooms where their numbers were verified. When parading outdoors, each barrack lined up in files of five and were counted by the guards, who checked them off against the list of able-bodied prisoners and absentees held by the SBO's adjutant. It all sounded very orderly, but as the camp history related, 'in practice the parade was a complete farce, purposely made so by the prisoners. They never formed up properly, but kept moving around and creating disturbances. The sick prisoners slipped from one room or barrack to another and were counted twice.' The Germans soon despaired. They 'carried out a superficial count as well as they could under the impossible circumstances, but rarely attempted to take a second count, usually accepting the count falsified by the adjutant or falsifying their own account.'[13]

When a small group of men was involved, deception was much harder. The best hope was to fake a disturbance at the time the count was being taken and hope that the escapees' absence would not be noted in the confusion. When the time came, Bill and Paddy would have to endure a long damp day among the pipes before making their way out at nightfall to cut through the wire.

Initially things went well. The prisoners lined up under the shower heads. A guard turned on the water and they began to lather up. As the place filled with steam, singing and boisterous shouting, Bill and Paddy lifted the manhole cover and slipped into their hideout. Crouched among the plumbing they listened hard. Soon they heard an angry voice. One of the prisoners was abusing one of the guards. The disturbance had clearly started, but it had gone off earlier than planned. They heard someone yelling insults about Adolf Hitler, followed by a torrent of angry German. Then the hiss of water died away. There was more shouting and the slap of naked feet. The normal routine was for the taps to be turned on twice – once to soap up, once to rinse off. It looked like there would be no second blast of water today.

As a punishment for the insults to the Führer, the prisoners were going back to the compound covered in soap.

They lined up outside the shower block to be escorted back to the compound. A few ferrets joined them. At the *Vorlager* gate one of the guards stood waiting to count them off. The prisoners began to mill around trying to confuse him into miscounting. The Germans were in no mood for further provocations. 'Their efforts at distracting or enraging were met by prods from a rifle to keep quiet,' wrote Bill.[14] The guard finished his count. A look of suspicion crossed his face and he began again. By the end of the third count he was in no doubt. He yelled a warning and the camp burst into life.

Squatting in their hiding place Bill and Paddy heard the air fill with 'the noise of running jackboots. Whistles blew, sirens blared and guard dogs barked themselves into a frenzy.' A few minutes later the door in the shower room slammed open. They clung to the hope that somehow the searchers would overlook the manhole. But then they heard the whining and snuffling of Alsatians and knew the end had come. 'Paddy and I looked at each other,' Bill remembered. 'We could shred the map to stop the searchers finding out what we knew, but our pockets were crammed with the Mixture. With minutes to go before we were caught we adjusted our plans. The best we could manage was not to let the Mixture fall into enemy hands.'[15] When the Germans finally lifted the manhole cover their torches flickered over two pale faces, smeared with chocolate, chewing with stolid determination. They emerged with their hands up. Bill dropped the last of the Mixture for the Alsatians to eat, hoping, he joked later, that they might remember this good deed if he met them on some future escape attempt. The bid for freedom had ended in farce. There was little satisfaction to be salvaged from the episode as they were led off to another spell in the cooler.

FIVE

No one remembered who first called the prison block 'the cooler', but the name captured well the chilly sterility of life in solitary. The threat of a spell alone in a cell ten feet long by four feet wide was a real deterrent. It was above all a psychological punishment: 'as near to living in a vacuum as a man has been able to contrive', was how Aidan Crawley described it. He went on: 'When the society of his fellow human beings is taken away from a man, when there is no certainty that it will be restored, when there are no books or writing materials to remind him of it or to keep the mind busy, he is left face to face with the bare bones of himself. The prospect is often terrifying.'[1]

The chatter of your fellow kriegies might drive you mad with its repetition and inanity when you heard it every day. But when you had been alone with your thoughts for a while you yearned for the comforting familial banality of the squabbles, the feeble jokes and the moaning. In later life Bill Ash would make light of his many trips to the cooler. He passed it off as little more than a minor irritation, the price you paid for being an escapologist, and something to be accepted and endured with as little fuss as possible. The ordeal must nonetheless have been a real one for him, especially when, in defiance of the Geneva Convention, the Germans deprived him of books, pencils and paper. For a would-be author, addicted to the written word, this was a severe loss.

Without the intellectual sustenance that was as essential to him as food or drink, he was forced to develop techniques for coping with the loss. He dredged his memory for poems he had learned at school. He got so good at it he could summon up not just the verses but the image of the pages they were printed on. There were only so many poems that came to mind, though, and the comfort they brought had its limits. He found other means of keeping himself sane. 'Over the coming years I would get a lot of practice at how to survive... spells in solitary,' he wrote, 'and to pass the time by living more in my own head than in the grim reality of isolation and semi-starvation.'[2]

He was fortunate to have a rich hoard of memories to unlock and examine. Until he passed through the gates of Stalag Luft III he had lived a life of extraordinary variety. One adventure succeeded another and each one took him into new realms that stretched his mind and expanded his horizons. He was not yet twenty-five, yet he had lived enough dramas to furnish several books. Or perhaps just one big one. He was the hero of his own picaresque novel, tossed here and there by capricious fate, yet always seemingly under the protection of some benign power that ensured that all was all right in the end – or at least until now.

He had grown up in poverty, suffering the humiliations of the poor. His father, also William Ash, toured Texas, Oklahoma and Kansas, hawking samples of women's hats around haberdashery stores. Sometimes Bill went with him and witnessed encounters with the owners, 'thick-set, loud-voiced men…who invariably greeted any salesman about to unpack his samples with the words: "What are you bringing that crap in here for?"'[3]

They moved houses and apartments often, as his father's income failed to cover the rent or mortgage payments. The automobiles he depended on to scrape his living were regularly repossessed by finance companies, 'like horses shot from under a cavalry subaltern in a rout'. His father took each setback with saintly grace, becoming ever gentler and quieter, until Bill was 'never sure whether he was there at all or not'.

His mother, born Margaret Porterfield, was a handsome, strong-willed woman. She filled him with her frustrated ambitions, drumming his lessons into him nightly so he passed every test at school, winning pins, badges and certificates which brought a glow of achievement to their lodgings.

There is nothing in Bill's writings to suggest that his family life was unhappy. He was affectionate towards his father, respected his mother and adored his younger sister, Adele. Early on, though, he began to run away from home. The first time was when he was seven or eight. On one occasion he got all the way from Dallas to Fort Worth before he got bored with the adventure and turned himself in to the police. Looking back, he could not decide what made him do it. 'It was not that I particularly disliked home or even school,' he wrote, 'but simply that I did like running away. It may be connected to my inability to lie in bed in the morning in case there is something interesting going on which I may be missing… It was called spring fever and I no more felt obliged to excuse it or apologize for it than I would for a cold.'4

Normal family life came to an abrupt end when he was still a teenager. Adele was sent away to live with better-off relations, and his mother joined his father on the road, while Bill was installed in a boarding house to fend for himself. Poverty did not bother him. It brought its own gifts, among them independence.

Almost as early in life as he could remember he went to work – washing cars, sweeping yards and selling the *Saturday Evening Post*. He managed to save up $200 towards his college education – only to lose the lot when, following a worldly neighbour's advice, he invested in stocks which were wiped out in the 1929 market crash. When in 1935 he arrived at the University of Texas he had to hold down at least two jobs to pay his way. He took a liberal arts course and graduated *summa cum laude*, but in a country that was still dragging itself out of the Depression this was not enough to secure him a proper post. He found a job as a cashier in a Dallas bank. Sometimes he was called on to operate the lift. One day he ran into a teacher from the university, who was shocked to find a former student in such lowly circumstances. Didn't his employers know that he had a degree? he asked. Bill replied that they did but had 'agreed to overlook it'.5

When that job came to an end he took to the road, travelling in boxcars or hitch-hiking. There were many like him, shuttling from Dallas to Chicago and Detroit and back again, in search of whatever work they could find. When he hit a new town the first thing he did was to study the small ads in the local paper, looking for church suppers, charity bazaars and parent–teacher meetings, where he could turn up and help himself to the free snacks. Then he would sign up as a door-to-door salesman for a hosiery company or suchlike, pick up his box of sample stockings and sell them for a few dollars at the local flea market. Once he got a job selling menswear in a Kansas City department store. He turned up at work in tomato-coloured ladies slacks – a leftover item of his father's stock, with a sash cord for a belt.

All this had been an education, too, giving him first-hand experience of the harshness of free-market capitalism. Yet he had also seen much to confirm his natural optimism. The people he met in hobo jungles and railroad cars were on the whole decent to each other and generous with whatever little they had.

He followed closely what was happening outside America, particularly in Europe, where democracy was being swept aside by the rise of Fascism. In Spain the legitimate government had been overthrown by nationalist rebels supported by Hitler and Mussolini. He was too young to go with the American volunteers who crossed the ocean to fight for the Republic. But by the summer of 1940, when Britain stood alone against the Nazis, he was ready.

President Roosevelt was giving what material help he could to Britain, in defiance of a strong isolationist lobby, but America was still a long way from joining the war. Memories of the First World War were still fresh, and most Americans were unwilling to get involved in another of the old world's murderous struggles. However, as a member of the Commonwealth, Canada had supported Britain from the start and Canadian squadrons fought alongside the Royal Air Force. Several thousand young Americans would volunteer for the Royal Canadian Air Force (RCAF) prior to America's entry into the war prompted by the attack on Pearl Harbor on 7 December 1941.[6] Late in 1940, Bill Ash became one of them. Looking back, it seemed to him that there was something preordained about his choice. 'It is difficult to say precisely why I volunteered for the air force so long before the US came into the war, because from the time it was obvious that there was going to be a major conflict I seemed already to have decided that as soon as it actually started I would go,' he wrote. He admitted that the dire economic conditions of the time contributed to his decision. Above all, though, it was a moral choice, 'a purely emotional response to Nazi brutality'.

'Seeing newsreels of storm troopers insulting and beating up Jewish people was... like seeing some lout bullying a smaller child – only infinitely worse because it was organized, licensed savagery,' he wrote. 'And then when my feelings were boiling with indignation, to see Western statesmen backing down before Hitler and the whole world apparently mesmerized by the naked cruelty running amok in Germany – well I was proper choked, that is all. Enlisting was simply a way of relieving the stifling sense of impotency I felt in the face of such gross inhumanity.'[7]

The journey began with a plate of stew in the Hungry Man diner in Detroit, a hangout for itinerant job-seekers. He cleaned his plate then set off for the Ambassador Bridge that led across the Detroit river and into Windsor, Ontario, where there was an RCAF recruiting office. He failed the medical for being underweight, but was told to try again. He returned to Detroit, borrowed money and spent a fortnight building himself up. When he returned he was accepted.

From now on he would not have to worry where the next dollar was coming from. The red slacks were consigned to the dustbin and he was kitted out in an elegant uniform, run up by the tailor at the Eglinton Hunt Club in Toronto, the club's premises having been taken over by the RCAF.

Before 1940, Bill had never been in an aeroplane. He started off with basic training at Elementary Flying School at Windsor, then moved on to the RCAF station at Kingston, near Toronto. There he got to grips with Fairey Battles, poor-performing British bombers which had been taken out of frontline service after being annihilated by German fighters in the Battle of France. The North American Harvard fighter trainer was a much livelier machine. It was noisy but highly manoeuvrable. Bill turned out to be a natural aerobatic pilot, coaxing rolls and loops even out of the lumbering Battles. He swooped under bridges and flew upside down for long periods, until he was totally at ease with the controls even when inverted. His confidence was all the more remarkable considering that, despite understanding the laws of physics that governed powered flight, he could never really believe that heavy metal machines could remain airborne except by some kind of magic. 'That basic incredulity is probably why I enjoyed flying,' he wrote. 'Every time I took off there was the exhilaration of something happening which I was not convinced could happen.'[8]

In the spring of 1941 the vagabond scholar Bill Ash became Pilot Officer W. T. Ash and a budding fighter pilot, on his way to Britain and the front line of the air war with the Nazis. When he arrived the Battle of Britain was over and the thrill of survival had been replaced by the realization that a long, grim slog lay ahead. Bill viewed his new home through a literary prism. For him it was a pageant in which figures he had known only through books had come to life. In London he looked beyond the bomb-scarred, blacked-out streets, ignored the modern office blocks and saw the city of Dr Johnson, Charles Dickens and Arthur Conan Doyle. The people he came across in the streets and pubs were not a weary bunch of survivors but coffee shop wits, *fin de siècle* aesthetes and Baker Street Irregulars.

New pilots were finished off in operational training units to prepare for combat before joining their squadron. He was sent to No. 57 OTU Hawarden in Yorkshire, where his tutor was Joe Pegge, who had knocked down eight German aircraft in the summer of 1940. He would meet many more veterans of the epic in the years to come, and the thrill of these encounters never wore off.

On 30 June 1941 he arrived with a party of Canadians from the OTU to join 411 Squadron at its base in Digby in Lincolnshire. The unit was just a fortnight old. It was commanded by Paul Pitcher, who came from a wealthy Montreal family and was practising as a lawyer when the war broke out. He had gone to England in 1940 and seen action with the RCAF's 1 Squadron in the Battle. Almost everyone else was a novice. Bill arrived with eight others from the OTU. They included vivid, lively characters like Don Blakeslee, an Ohio-born fellow American, who like him had joined the Canadians before the US got into the war, Eddie Asselin, a fast-talking French-Canadian, and the dashing Robert 'Buck' McNair. In the air force everyone had a nickname. Bill's was 'Tex', bestowed on him back in training in Canada, on account of his origins. It did not fit his rather dreamy personality and literary interests, and he did not like it particularly, but it would stick with him throughout the war.

411 Squadron already had its own identity. The badge showed a Grizzly Bear standing upright with paws outstretched like a prizefighters' fists, above a pugnacious motto: *Inimicus Inimico* – 'Hostile to the Enemy'. Building an efficient squadron from scratch was a challenge. The Spitfires they had been assigned seemed plagued with defects and the pilots appallingly accident prone. The first crash happened on 3 July, three days after Bill's arrival, when an aeroplane was damaged after the undercarriage collapsed on landing. Two days later, Bill was forced to land at a neighbouring airfield after his engine overheated. On the same day one fighter crashed into another while taxiing. By the end of the month the Grizzlies had their first fatality – a sergeant pilot called R. M. Murray, who plunged into mudflats on the Lincolnshire coast while on a training flight.

One of the most spectacular mishaps concerned Bill and Buck McNair. As Bill told the story, they were coming in to land at Digby in a Miles Magister open-cockpit two-seater trainer, with Bill at the controls, when McNair decided on a whim to make a practice parachute jump. Bill was against the idea and continued his descent. Buck nonetheless managed to drop out and descend unharmed to the ground. A rather different version did the rounds. According to this account, Bill had decided to engage in some impromptu aerobatics, Buck's harness was not properly fastened and while they were flying upside down he tumbled out.

Pitcher kept his men hard at it with a daily diet of mock scrambles, cross-country navigation exercises, and cloud and formation flying. On 27 August, the Grizzlies were at last declared to be fully operational. In September they began flying convoy patrols and occasional aggressive 'sweeps' over northern France, looking for targets of opportunity and daring the Germans to come up and fight. At first nothing much happened. Then the tempo picked up. On 27 September one of the pilots managed to bail out after being hit over the coast by 'friendly' anti-aircraft fire. A little later Buck McNair was shot down over the French coast, and was very lucky to be picked up by the Air Sea Rescue Services. For the rest of the time the work was surprisingly boring. They conducted frequent dusk patrols looking for German aircraft that rarely appeared, or cruised back and forth over convoys butting through the grey corrugated waters below.

Away from operations, Digby was a pleasant place from which to fight a war. It was buried in the Lincolnshire countryside but the food on the station was good and the pubs of Lincoln were only a dozen miles away. There was also the opportunity of romance. Bill managed to date the daughter of the station commander at nearby Kirton-in-Lindsay, until she switched her affections to another pilot. As Canadians fighting for the old country, 411 had great propaganda value, and there were occasional VIP visits. One day the Canadian prime minister, William MacKenzie King, came to the station. He was photographed alongside Bill sitting grinning in his cockpit.

In November they moved south, to Hornchurch in Essex. London was only a forty-minute Tube ride away. While his comrades headed to the bars, theatres and cinemas, Bill was more likely to seek out a concert. The authorities put on recitals to maintain civilian morale. If flying was scrubbed, as it frequently was during December and January, he was able to make it into town in time for one of the lunchtime concerts given at the National Gallery by distinguished performers like the pianist Myra Hess. At one, he spent more time looking at the pretty young cellist than listening to the music. He sent her a bouquet of flowers but never managed to introduce himself.

This was a rare failure. The poor boy from Texas found London hospitable and welcoming. There were organizations like that run by Lady Frances Ryder, set up 'to assist officers who had no friends or relations in the United Kingdom' and ensure they were 'well acquainted with the homes of England and those who dwell in them'. Candidates were invited to tea in Cadogan Square and vetted for social suitability. Bill had attended one such demure gathering when he first arrived in the capital and later met one of the young ladies who helped out there. He persuaded her to look through the files and found out how he had been rated. She reported that he was judged to have 'nice American manners... can go most places'. He was delighted. It was 'like being mentioned in despatches'.[9]

The verdict seemed justified when he was taken to a function by Walter Elliot, who was related to some friends of Bill's parents in Dallas. Elliot was a Scottish farmer's son who had risen high in the Conservative Party, serving as Minister of Health under Neville Chamberlain. The guest of honour was Queen Elizabeth and Bill was introduced to her. He had already met her husband King George VI when he visited Digby. On one of his social outings he found a proper girlfriend. Patricia Rambaut was beautiful, intelligent and well connected, and did her bit for the war effort by joining the WRNS. They were just beginning to get know each other properly when he was shot down. They wrote to each other loyally throughout all the years Bill was a prisoner, and the thought of seeing her again was one of the hopes that sustained him in the dark hours.

He enjoyed these brushes with the high life. But he had come to Britain to fight, and for much of the time he felt he was not doing it well enough. Until his last day in the air he was never certain that he had shot anything down. The closest he came to a confirmed 'kill' was one evening in November 1941, when at the end of a dusk patrol he and his wing man were vectored onto a pair of Junkers 88 bombers which were heading out across the sea for home. He was still firing when they disappeared into cloud. The radar plots disappeared at this point, so it was hoped that they had both been destroyed, but that was not sufficient confirmation and it was not even counted as a 'probable'.

Bill often worried whether he had the level of aggression needed to be a good fighter pilot. Once he was returning from a sweep over Holland with Wing Commander Derek 'Cowboy' Blatchford when they saw a formation of unusual-looking enemy aircraft below. They dived down and identified them as trainers, presumably piloted by greenhorns. The aeroplanes were unarmed and Bill hesitated to open fire on such easy targets. He was spared further agonizing when he and Blatchford were bounced by six Messerschmitt 109s, which chased them halfway across the Channel before turning back.

In early 1942 Britain was not losing the war. It was not winning it either. Each sign of progress was soon countered by a dispiriting setback. On 12 February the squadron was scrambled to escort bombers sent to intercept German warships which were making a daring attempt to reach home ports from their stations on the French Atlantic coast via the English Channel. Bill and his comrades had rehearsed such an attack in exercises, in coordination with a force of Beaufort fighter-bombers. When they made the rendezvous they were alarmed to see that the strike force consisted of six Swordfish torpedo biplanes whose antiquated appearance earned them the nickname 'stringbags'. The gallant Swordfish were all shot down. Of the 675 RAF aircraft involved in trying to locate and stop the warships, only a handful engaged their targets, which escaped virtually unscathed. The 'Channel Dash', as it was known, was a triumph for the German navy and a humiliation for Britain. The *Scharnhorst*, *Gneisenau* and *Prinz Eugen* all made it home and a great opportunity to tear the heart out of the German surface fleet was missed.

Bill's air war reached its end on 24 March 1942. The sight of the mist lifting from the airfield that morning had cheered the squadron up. For three of the last five days heavy rain had put the runway out of action, and the pilots were restless and bored. There had not been many opportunities to get to grips with the Germans recently. More often than not the skies over southern England were blanketed in low cloud that dumped rain onto the waterlogged fields. Since moving, on 6 March, from Hornchurch to Southend, a forward base on the Essex coast, they had only flown three missions, and two of those had

been convoy patrols, droning back and forth over Channel ship-
ping, waiting for something to happen.[10]

At 11 a.m. the pilots were called to a briefing. They trooped out
of the crew room, along neat paths that ran between red-brick
accommodation blocks and offices laid out like an architect's
maquette, to the briefing room, and sat down on folding chairs.
The rafters were soon smudged with a blue-grey pall of smoke
generated by some of the 25,000 cigarettes sent down as a present from RCAF Headquarters a few weeks before. The rumble
of chat and banter faded as the door opened and an officer
strode down the aisle and onto a low platform at the front. He
was slim and not very tall, a good build for the confined space of
a fighter cockpit. Squadron Leader Stan Turner had been born
in Devon on the edge of Dartmoor but brought up in Toronto,
where he joined the auxiliary air force. He returned home at the
start of the war to join the RAF and had been in the thick of the
action in the Battle of France and the Battle of Britain. Turner
had just taken over after his popular predecessor was posted
back to Canada, and was trusted and well liked.

He removed his pipe and turned to the blackboard behind
him. It was covered by a map of Northern France. The pilots
knew it well by now: there were the chalk heights of Cap Gris
Nez poking into the Channel towards the White Cliffs of Dover,
twenty-two miles across the water; above them the quays and
warehouses of Boulogne and Calais; and behind, the drab working towns of the Nord, among them Saint-Omer, where the
German fighters were based.

Turner announced that today's action was a 'circus'. This was
the code word for a short-range bombing operation accompanied

by a fighter escort. The target was the power station at Comines, a town about twenty miles behind Dunkirk, straddling the river Lys on the Franco-Belgian border. They filed out and returned to the crew room to pick up their helmets, parachutes and Mae Wests. As the pre-combat ritual progressed they seemed to have less and less to say to each other. The slightly hysterical good spirits that buoyed them up as they left the briefing had subsided to be replaced by a low hum of apprehension. By the time they boarded the shooting brakes that took them out to the dispersal areas where the aircraft were parked, most had lapsed into silence.

The wagon dropped Bill off on the concrete apron where his Spitfire stood.

Like every 'fighter boy' he adored his Spit, and it had been love at first sight. It was 'small and so beautifully shaped, like a platonic idea of what an aeroplane should look like. Particular features were the gracefully curved elliptical wings and the long nose accommodating such a powerful in-line engine. Long noses, whether on borzois or members of the British upper class, always seemed very aristocratic to me.'[11]

Pilots claimed that flying a Spitfire was like flying an extension of yourself. The thing fitted round you like a second skin, and in the air it reacted to your desires almost as soon as you conceived them, climbing and banking, swooping and twisting as if flesh, blood and metal were operated by the same synapses.

The ground crew stood back as he clambered onto the wing root and swung himself into the cockpit. He smiled and gave the thumbs up. He pressed the starter, the engine barked and the five exhaust stubs each side of the nose farted plumes of dirty smoke. The needle looped round the rev counter and he eased off the brakes, feeling the power of the 1,200-horsepower Merlin sweeping him forward. The steep upward inclination of the fuselage meant that he was looking at the sky and he had to use the rudder to swing left and right to see where he was going.

He briefly touched the matchbox that he had stuck beneath the instrument panel for good luck. The light on the control tower flashed green. He pushed forward the throttle and felt power surging through the airframe, then, as he eased off the brakes, the *thwock, thwock, thwock* of tyre rubber hitting the paving. And then came the moment that never failed to delight, when the wheels kissed the runway goodbye and the ground dropped away, and despite the engine's roar and the clanking of the retracting undercarriage and all the other evidence of mechanical contrivance, it felt that somehow a miracle had just occurred. They climbed over the mud-stained water where the Thames met the sea, through the clag and into the clean air above. Over the radio telephone Turner gave them their course for Comines, about forty minutes' flying-time away.

He could not recall the details of the operation itself. He could never forget what happened on the way home. He was flying alongside Turner, and as they approached the French coast he glanced over to see if he had lit his pipe yet, a sign that they were out of danger. 'He hadn't,' Bill remembered. 'A garbled crackle over the radio from someone in the squadron called urgently for my section to break formation. I did a tight 180-degree turn, thanking my lucky stars that I had done so much aerobatic flying in my training.'[12]

From the lower edge of his field of vision he glimpsed the stubby outline of a Focke-Wulf 190, banked over on one side as it pulled away some distance below. He was in a perfect attacking position. One of the Spitfire's few faults was its fuel-supply system, which momentarily cut the flow of petrol to the carburettor when the engine was tilted at too sharp an angle, causing it to falter for a second or two. To keep the petrol flowing he had to throw the Spit into a three-quarter roll. The manoeuvre cost him height but it didn't seem to matter. To his delight he rolled upright directly behind the German at a range of just two hundred yards. He pressed the firing button and cannon shells sprang out in a wavy line to explode in a row along one of the Focke-Wulf's wing roots, sending bits from the engine cowling spinning away. In a few seconds the fighter was screaming downward trailing a banner of smoke.

Jubilant, Bill pulled up and looked for the rest of his squadron. By now they were specks in the distance. To the left he saw another Spitfire straggler. The pilot seemed oblivious to the grey-green Messerschmitt 109 closing on him like a hungry pike. Bill shouted a warning over the radio and boosted the throttle, swinging round to bring himself onto the attacker's beam. He followed the Messerschmitt round, holding his fire as he manoeuvred. Shooting at a small fast target at constantly changing angles and distances was a complex business. Simply firing straight was futile, as the target would be hundreds of yards ahead by the time the bullets arrived.

The answer was deflection shooting – calculating the speed and angle of the enemy aircraft then channelling a cone of fire at a precisely judged point ahead of it, so that it flew straight into the path of the bullets. It was easier said then done, and few pilots found it came naturally. It was much better to approach the target from dead ahead or behind where you could aim directly at your victim and no deflection was needed. 'I worked my way round to quarter, then fine quarter, all the time reducing my angle of deflection until I was just a hundred yards dead astern before I opened up,' he wrote. 'I could see my cannon fire hitting home along his fuselage and was glad to give the pilot something to think about other than shooting down my colleague.' He kept his thumb on the button, making sure his victim was going down. Then 'suddenly there was a juddering thump. My guns had stopped working.'[13]

He knew that he was under fire. He swung hard left, kicking the rudder so the Spit skidded through the air in the tightest possible turn, out of the stream of fire from whoever was attacking him. It was already too late, for 'the engine began to stammer and I realized I was in even bigger trouble than I had thought.' The revs were dropping fast and he could feel momentum draining from the aircraft. In addition to the man behind him he could see Messerschmitts closing on him from opposite directions.

He was down to 10,000 feet and there was virtually no pull from the propeller. The Messerschmitt 109s had been joined by a few Focke-Wulfs. They were taking their time, circling unconcernedly, taking turns to come in to finish him off. He no longer felt fear but anger and frustration. All he could do was turn to face each new attack so as to present as small a target as possible. Now and then a thud would register another hit on the body of the Spit.

He was no longer thinking rationally. 'As a Focke-Wulf screamed straight at me, guns blazing, out of force of habit or blind optimism I kept pushing my silent firing button in reply,' he wrote. He even heard his own voice, 'loud and surreal in the cockpit, shouting "Bang! Bang!" as I narrowly avoided colliding with one of my tormentors.'[14]

One way or another it was over. He had imagined this moment many times, wondering whether he would be able to remain in control of himself, but his brain was clear now as he ran through the possible endings. The fighters were heading away from him but only to wheel round for another attack. The next shell that hit or the one after would set the Spitfire ablaze and he would pass his last seconds being burned alive and praying for the collision with the earth that would end the agony. 'I only really had two choices,' he decided. 'Pick a spot to crash land or bail out.' Bailing seemed the obvious one. He was still a few thousand feet up, leaving a comfortable ceiling for his parachute to open. But he feared that he would 'provide the Focke-Wulfs with target practice on the way down.' More importantly, 'it would give the [Germans] plenty of time to have a reception committee waiting to catch me on the ground.'

He knew very well the consequences of messing up a crash landing. The Spit would somersault and crumple and he would be dead by the time the Germans arrived. But, he calculated, 'landing under my own steam seemed to offer a better chance of getting away.' That decided it. He cut the engine. For a few seconds the only sound was the swish of wind pouring over the airframe. Then came the sound of more firing, but his going too fast to be able to line up on the Spitfire as it glided down.

Ahead he could see a broad flat field flecked with dead stubble, and beyond it a Gothic-looking church. There was no power to control the flaps and he knew he was coming in too high and too fast. 'As I reached the ground, I dug a wing tip into the field,' he wrote. 'Almost instantly my plane began a cartwheel, careering over the ground. Flashes of grass and sky alternated as pieces of the plane started to disintegrate. One wing was practically ripped off and a shuddering crunch close behind told me my fuselage had probably gone too.' He finally came to a stop 'not too far from the church, which – like myself – was miraculously intact.'[15]

All this had happened only six months ago but it felt now like an event from a different life. The days in the cooler followed indistinguishably, punctuated only by the scrape of the key in the lock as the food arrived or he was led to the lavatory or out for the daily hour of exercise. When the fortnight was up, he and Paddy returned to the compound to hear some unexpected news. The more troublesome elements in the compound were being moved to a new camp in Poland. Unsurprisingly, their names were on the list.

SIX

By the autumn of 1942 the system could no longer cope with the number of Allied airmen prisoners. Stalag Luft III was supposed to hold them all but it was already bursting at the seams. As well as the officer prisoners there was now a large number of NCOs, who were held separately in Centre Compound. With the Allied air war gathering pace, it was clear that there would be many more to come and new accommodation was needed. Plans were made to add another compound on the north side of the camp. While the work was going on it made sense to move some prisoners to other locations. In the process, the authorities would be able to get rid of some of their more difficult customers.[1]

Once again, the Germans were finding that airmen captives caused them more trouble than soldiers or sailors. In theory, escape held the same appeal for everyone. It offered the chance to return home to your loved ones. It brought an end to a situation that offered only the indefinite prospect of boredom, frustration and privation, possibly culminating in violent death.

For the most dutiful, worried that they were not doing their bit for the war effort, escape provided the only means available of continuing the struggle against the Germans.

The peacetime air force demanded an advanced level of education, dedication and aptitude from candidates, and the weeding process was rigorous. Those who got through tended to be smart, ambitious and resourceful. Even in wartime, high standards were maintained, and all aircrew roles required a significant level of skill. The result was that airmen tended to be better educated than their equivalents in the other services. Most of them had chosen to join the air force rather than been sent to it as conscripts. The RAF's Bomber Command was manned entirely by volunteers. As the youngest service, the air force was eager to assert its worth and prove its mettle. In the eyes of military traditionalists, this could translate into a certain brashness, even aggression. Airmen were thus likely to be educated, self-confident and bold.

The tedium of prison life was consequently all the harder to bear. Air force men were used to operating in small groups or alone, and using their initiative, far from the control of higher authority. Added together, as one historian wrote, 'the airman then was almost the ideal escaper. Well educated, aggressive, used to working in solitude and activated by all the normal impulses that make a human seek freedom, he brought an impressive arsenal of escape skills to the prison camp in which he was incarcerated.'[2] As we have seen, not every prisoner was bent on breaking out, and those who were not viewed those who were with a variety of feelings.

The 'escapologists', though, were strongly represented among the group scheduled to be moved from Sagan to another camp, Oflag XXIB, which lay 150 miles to the north-east in Poland. They included Tommy Calnan, who had been shot down when flying a Spitfire with the RAF's photo-reconnaissance unit, and who was recovering from the disappointment of a failed mole-tunnel bid. Before leaving Stalag Luft III he had managed to steal and copy the key to the padlock on the gate between the compound and the *Vorlager*. He had it with him now, in the hope that German locks might be of standard issue and it could come in useful in Poland.

There was the escape committee stalwart Aidan Crawley, a loud, confident Englishmen, educated at Harrow and Trinity College Cambridge, a county class cricketer who in peacetime worked as a journalist and flew with other gentlemen pilots in the Auxiliary Air Force. He had been shot down over Tobruk in July 1941 and taken prisoner. Since then he had been directing all his talents and energies to escape activities. Also in the company were charming daredevils like the French Canadian Eddie Asselin, and brooding intellectuals like Robert Kee, who had joined Bomber Command from Oxford University, trained as a pilot and been shot down over the Dutch coast the year before.

They were going to Schubin, Szubin in Polish, a small market town about 150 miles west of Warsaw, where Oflag XXIB had been created out of a large school for girls, requisitioned by the Germans when they marched in. They travelled in third-class carriages pulled by a wheezing train, under the gimlet eye of the chief ferret, Feldwebel Glemnitz. It stopped and started, speeded up and slowed down, according to no discernible pattern. To one of the kriegies aboard the opportunity seemed too good to miss. Even among such eclectic company, John Bigelow Dodge was an unusual character. He had been born in New York in 1894 into a well-connected family and was related by marriage to Winston Churchill. He joined the British Army shortly after the start of the First World War, took British citizenship, fought at Gallipoli and was wounded twice on the Western Front, where he ended the war as a lieutenant colonel commanding an infantry battalion. He was recalled to the colours at the outbreak of the next war and had been captured at Dunkirk. It was never clear how he came to be incarcerated in an air-force prison. He was one of the camp personalities, known as 'the Dodger', and although old enough to be father of most of the prisoners he retained a strong streak of recklessness.

The train journey to Schubin took all day. The guards were vigilant and hostile. The prisoners were forced to remain seated at all times and guns were brandished if anybody got to his feet. They had already been told to remove their boots, which most prisoners felt ruled out any possibility of making a run for it. 'But it did not stop the Dodger,' wrote Tommy Calnan. 'In broad daylight, in full view of half a dozen guards, he leapt from the fast-moving train and disappeared into the woods amid a hail of bullets. He was recaptured quite unharmed a short time later, but his effort revived our flagging spirits and stopped the train for over an hour.'[3] Bill Ash remembered him turning to one of his guards as he was led back and remarking: 'No harm in trying!'[4]

The journey ended at Schubin station. The prisoners were marched down the main street of the village on the two-mile journey to the gates of the camp. The guards seemed strangely reluctant to let them in. The prisoners soon learned the reason for the delay. Unlike the previous camps they had stayed in, Oflag XXIB was run not by the Luftwaffe but by the Wehrmacht – the German army. As the kriegies were learning, relations between the services were far from comradely. When Glemnitz tried to escort them in and sought an audience with the camp comman-dant to brief him on the wiles of his new charges, he was refused entry. The prisoners were not his responsibility any more and according to Bill he was sent 'back to Stalag Luft III with a Wehrmacht flea in his ear'. As Glemnitz was saying farewell to some of the prisoners, 'he confided the whole sorry exchange, complimenting us by saying that if he was a gambling man he would be laying bets on a mass breakout within a month, and it would serve the army blockheads right for not listening to him.' He did 'everything but wish us luck, and we assured him that we would do our best to make his dreams come true.'[5]

Once inside the camp, the prisoners were pleasantly surprised at their new home, which after Sagan looked like an English country estate. At its centre stood the school, a handsome, classically proportioned three-storey building faced with white stucco. There was a chapel, a modern sanatorium, a small brick bungalow, a bathhouse and a stable block, all set in spacious grounds, which included playing fields and vegetable gardens. A long drive lined with chestnut trees led up the hill behind the main building, which was known as the White House. This was where the camp administration had its offices and later rooms were made available for the senior British officer and his team. The prisoners were to be housed in four main barracks built on the terraced slopes behind the school buildings. The usual barbed-wire double fencing and watchtowers surrounded the school and the barracks. But in general, as Aidan Crawley noted, the overall effect 'created a feeling almost of homeliness. Beyond the wire instead of a monotonous vista of pine trees, fields stretched away into the distance and all the business of farming could be watched every day.'[6]

After the encouraging first impressions the quality of the accommodation came as a disappointment. Two of the barracks were dilapidated and would not be used at first. The other two were single-storey buildings with pitched roofs and concrete floors. 'The accommodation, if you can call it that, consisted of lice-infested brick buildings with no ceilings and only raftered roofs to keep out the elements,' remembered Paddy Barthropp.[7] There were no partitions but each pair of prisoners was given a double-decker bunk bed and a cupboard, and two benches and a table were provided for every twelve men. They arranged the furniture so as to create private spaces down each side of the barrack, making it a little more homely. Bill dragged a few lockers to barricade off a corner of Hut 6 and bunked up with Paddy, Aidan Crawley, Eddy Asselin and a few others.

In the large space, talk echoed off the bare walls and floor, creating such a din that you had to shout to make yourself heard, and the partition gave them a quiet corner for private discussions. Each barrack had a night latrine, and a washhouse attached with boilers where food and water could be heated, which doubled as the kitchen and laundry. When the prisoners arrived the sun was still shining, but it was clear that once the Polish winter set in, the two brick-and-tile stoves at the end of the building would offer little protection from the cold. Nonetheless, noted Crawley, morale among the prisoners was 'extremely high'. The reason was simple. Even to the most inexperienced eye it was clear that Oflag XXIB offered numerous opportunities for escape. Paddy Barthropp maintained that whoever had designed the camp 'must have had a touch of British blood in him'.

The compound was small. Some of the barracks were only seventy feet from the perimeter fence, much nearer than at Stalag Luft III, and the soil was well drained and easy to work, so that tunnels could be dug at any level. 'From a point of view of escape the camp was almost ideal,' said Crawley. 'It had not been designed for any military purpose and not only were many of the buildings so placed that they created blind spots which were hidden completely from the guards in the sentry towers but the many large trees and steep banks also proved excellent cover.'[8] Tommy Calnan was even more enthusiastic: it was 'an escapers' paradise'.[9]

The Wehrmacht administration also made a favourable impression. The guards seemed anxious for a quiet life. Among their ranks were semi-invalids who had been wounded on the Eastern front, men who looked too old to be in uniform and unsoldierly types who seemed happy to be engaged in safe duties that kept them far from the fighting. Although the camp had been open since 1940, the previous inmates had been French prisoners who believed they were due to be sent back home under the armistice signed after France's defeat, and had little incentive to escape. As a result, according to the official RAF history of the camp, the guards 'continued to exercise only lax discipline until they realized that the new prisoners of war required much closer watching.' The camp commandant, Oberstleutnant von Bodecker, who had lost a leg on the Western Front and wore a monocle, 'left the administration of prisoner-of-war affairs to the Senior British Officer, except in connection with roll calls and searches.'[10] Nor did the camp security officer, who had been a Professor of English at a German university before the war, seem to take his duties particularly seriously. According to Crawley, he was 'an attractive character with a large red face and a deep husky voice. He treated the whole business of war as an absurd episode in which the one thing that mattered was to preserve a sense of humour.'[11]

Some of his colleagues took a less relaxed view. The camp adjutant was a Czech renegade, a former grocer called Simms, who showed all the zeal of the convert in his treatment of the prisoners. He was 'irascible, anti-British and vindictive', wrote Crawley. Within hours of arrival the prisoners were introduced to him at the first *Appell*. Simms was affronted by the prisoners' shabby appearance and began haranguing them. He was unpleasantly surprised when the kreigies screamed and shouted back. Simms's posturing could not disguise the fact that he was barely competent. 'Had Simms thought a little less of inflicting discomfort on the prisoners and a little more of his duties the story of Schubin might have been different.' As it was, his odious personality 'added spice to every attempt to defeat the enemy'.

There was another factor which played in the prisoners' favour. The bucolic surroundings of the camp were misleading. The area had recently seen some terrible events. It had been part of Germany until 1920 when, under the Versailles treaty, it was granted to Poland. It was home to a large minority of ethnic

Germans. In September 1939, about 250 of them were killed in the town of Bromberg – Bydgoszcz in Polish – about twenty miles to the north of the camp. The circumstances would be endlessly disputed, but it was clear that some had been victims of massacres. The SS, Wehrmacht and local German Selbstschutz ('self-defence') units responded with a series of atrocities, killing hundreds of Polish hostages before going on to murder up to 3,000 Jews and Poles deemed to be members of the intelligentsia. The terror unleashed by the Germans had failed to cow the Poles. 'That meant,' wrote Bill, 'that if we got out and managed to knock on a door we were just as likely to be helped as not.' This was 'in stark comparison to Luft III in the heart of Germany, where every Nazi boy scout was on the lookout for escaped flyers and every blonde-haired apple-cheeked lass would sooner stick a... dagger in your ribs than help you.'[12]

This assessment turned out to be largely true. There was inevitably much contact between the camp and the local population. Some of the guards were Polish. Local people came in every day to maintain the infrastructure, carry out repairs, wash, cook and clean. Through them the escape organization could establish links with families who were prepared to shelter escapers and with the local underground.

Any Pole caught offering even the slightest assistance to a prisoner faced certain death for himself and possibly his family. Yet in Crawley's experience, 'of the dozens of Poles with whom the prisoners at Schubin came into contact only one proved unreliable. All the others, including many women, helped in every way they could.'[13] The prisoners knew that beyond the wire were friends. It was a further boost to their spirits.

The Stalag Luft III arrivals were joining another contingent of about two hundred RAF officers who had been transferred to Schubin from Oflag VIB at Warburg in north-western Germany. Added to the numbers were about eighty-five Army NCOs who had been in Warburg but had volunteered to move. Ostensibly they were going to serve as orderlies to the officers. Their real motive was that they believed the new camp would offer a better chance of escape. Another fifteen NCOs arrived with the Sagan party.

As it was, it was the orderlies who achieved the first successes. They were housed in the stable block which had been converted into a barracks. Under the Geneva Convention, officers were not required to work. NCOs could be used as labour by the 'detaining power'. Fatigue parties were regularly sent out of the camp under escort to deliver swill to the pigsties on the estate or collect fuel. Larger groups were taken into Schubin to collect bread and Red Cross parcels from the railway station. At the end of October an army corporal and an RAF warrant officer both managed to get away from work parties, but both were soon recaptured. Six weeks later Sergeant Philip Wareing of the RAF made another attempt. His story gives an idea of the fortitude, stamina and copious good luck that was needed to bring off a 'home run'.

Wareing was a Spitfire pilot with 616 Squadron and had been shot down over Calais in August 1940. On the afternoon of 16 December he was sent with other prisoners by lorry to Schubin station to collect a delivery of bread from a wagon in the sidings. As they loaded the truck, someone dropped a loaf on the line. Wareing went to pick it up, then ducked under a railway wagon and ran off. It was about 5.30 and in the darkness no one saw him go. Wareing had always intended to slip away if the chance presented itself. He was dressed in a pair of dirty and faded army trousers, an RAF tunic with all the badges removed and which could pass for a civilian garment, and a cloth cap, an outfit that would not stand out in shabby wartime Poland. By the following afternoon he had covered the twenty miles to Bromberg, where he stole a rickety bicycle and pedalled and walked to Graudenz (Gruziądz), a town on the Vistula river. Gossip in the camp suggested that some British soldiers had managed to board ships at Graudenz bound for Sweden, but when Wareing reached the river there were no big ships to be seen. He would have to press on to Danzig (Gdansk), seventy miles away. He did not dare try and take a train. Instead he stole a new-looking bicycle and set off northwards. To get there he would have to cross the Vistula. There was a checkpoint on the bridge but Wareing blithely rode round it while the guards were checking the credentials of two soldiers.

He arrived in Danzig on 19 December and spent all day dodging policemen and trying in vain to get into the docks. Early the following morning he finally wheeled the bike into the port area. He saw three or four ships were flying the Swedish flag and two flying the Blue Peter, the latter a signal that they were preparing to sail. Sentries were posted on the quayside beside the ships so he hid himself and the bike between some stacks of timber. He waited there until he saw the guard being changed and walked to the last ship on the dock. It was taking on a cargo of coal but there was a lull in the loading. He ran up a gangplank and dropped into the hold. There he stayed for the next twenty-four hours. Once a work party of Russians escorted by German guards appeared to trim the coal. One of the Russians saw him, hiding behind a pillar. He whispered '*Angliski pilot*' and the man kept quiet. He slept that night in a hole he had dug in the coal. The following morning the Germans searched the ship and one shone a flashlight into the hold, but Wareing was well concealed. At 9 a.m. on 21 December he heard the anchor chain rattle and then the shuddering of the engine, and the ship moved away from the pier. For the next two and a half days he stayed in hiding, eating nothing and coming out at night to warm himself against a boiler pipe. Half-starved and black with coal-dust he left his hiding place in the early hours of 23 December and was spotted by a member of the crew. When the ship reached Halmstad early that afternoon he was handed over to the Swedish police and taken a few days later to the British legation in Sweden. A short time later he was back in Blighty, where he was awarded the Distinguished Service Medal for his pluck.

The black farce of the shower-room escapade had only sharpened Bill Ash's determination to get away. The casual set-up at Schubin seemed to promise every chance of success, and he was 'intoxicated by the opportunities'.[14]

The camp arrangements, so much less constricted than at Stalag Luft III, opened up possibilities for the quick-witted which required none of the tedium and effort of tunnelling. The access which the NCO fatigue parties had to the town seemed particularly promising. Of Bill's numerous escape attempts, his next one was more a caprice than a serious effort, carried out with little planning and no preparation. The chances of success were small. The prime purpose seems to have been to satisfy his nagging urge to break free, which he admitted amounted almost to a mania. It came about when Bill persuaded an army private to allow him to take his place in a group that was being sent to Schubin station to unload a goods train.[15] He got to work, biding his time and awaiting his chance. It came when the guards were looking the other way. 'I managed to roll myself under the train,' he wrote. 'Looking up at the sooty, oil-smeared wheels I prayed that the train wouldn't move and rolled as quickly as I could to the other side of the line.'[16]

He looked up. In front stretched about half a mile of open ground, devoid of cover, but beyond it lay a wood. He hesitated for a moment. There was a great deal of open terrain in which even a bad shot could pick off a fleeing prisoner. But 'the woods were calling me. It was too tempting and I set off like a grey-hound.' A few seconds later he heard shouting behind him, and what he hoped were warning shots whistled over his head. The German officer in charge of the work detail calculated Bill's chances of reaching the distant woods and decided to take pity on him and ordered some soldiers mounted on pushbikes to head him off. 'There are few experiences more depressing than racing as fast as you can for an unattainable target while your enemies overtake you in a leisurely manner and are waiting for you, guns at the ready, just in front of your objective,' he remembered. If they had expected him to come quietly they were mistaken. Having come this far he 'decided [he] might as well really go for it', He tried to charge through them as if he was 'an American footballer, determined to score the win-ning touchdown', He was brought down with a rifle butt to the face. The guards then punished his defiance by administering a severe beating.

Back in the camp he was taken off for his first spell in the Schubin cooler. Bill seems to have known his attempt would end in failure. One preparation he had made was to tape a small metal file to the inside of his leg before setting off. Following the beating, the guards had not troubled to search him too closely.

Over the next few days, he sawed away at the three thick iron bars set in the small window. He disguised the marks with a paste made from his bread and water rations, mixed with dust from the cell walls. 'Each day I was able to cover up my handiwork with Reich bread putty and, when the coast was clear, continue with my sawing,' he wrote. After a week he had cut through one bar. It seemed unlikely that he would finish before his sentence was ended. It turned out to have been wasted effort. For no apparent reason he was moved to a new cell. While cleaning out the old one, a guard noticed his efforts on the bars. He was searched and the file, so blunt by now as to be almost useless, was taken from him. He was then sentenced to another two weeks in the cooler.

He was released one lunchtime. Two friends of his, Mike Wood and Bill Palmer, had prepared a feast for him from their Red Cross parcels to make up for all the bread and water. Both belonged to the fraternity of escapologists with several failed attempts behind them. As Bill ate, they explained that they were making another bid that night, and outlined their plan. At the end they asked him if he would care to join them. 'I really could have done with a rest,' he recalled. 'But the one thing time in the cooler does for you is to make your priorities very clear, and mine was escape.'[17] His mind was soon made up: '"Well," I thought. "What the hell."'[18]

As soon as it was dark they slipped out of the hut and sheltered in a dip in the ground which Wood and Palmer had identified as being out of sight of the watchtowers and shielded from the searchlight and arc lamps that lit up the camp at night. Then they wriggled through a vegetable patch, one of several cultivated by the kriegies, towards the wire. 'I found myself trying to huddle under a potato plant that was about six inches tall, and I began to wonder why I kept on doing such stupid things, reasoning that I would probably have another month in the cooler to figure it out,' he wrote. Then Bill Palmer clamped a pair of homemade shears around the first line of barbed-wire fencing and pressed hard. The wire was 'stretched so tight that it went off like a gunshot… whipped around and nearly caught us. An incredibly loud twang, like the first note of a crazed bluegrass banjo solo, filled the air.' The three scuttled away in different directions as sirens sounded and guards ran towards the noise. Wood and Palmer were soon discovered, but for once Bill's luck held. He lay in the cover of the vegetable patch a few feet from the boots of the guards. Satisfied that there had been only two escapers they eventually departed and Bill 'crawled very slowly back to our hut and fell into a long sleep'.[19]

The wealth of opportunities brought a profusion of attempts. Within a fortnight of arriving, Tommy Calnan had devised a shallow 'blitz' tunnel by which they would burrow out in a single burst of digging. The prisoners' vegetable patches around the inside of the rail that defined no-man's land provided a good place to start digging. 'In September the asparagus ferns grew tall and bushy and were covered with pretty red berries,' he wrote. 'My plan was to dig a short vertical shaft behind an asparagus bush and then to mole out.' He would carry out the operation 'in broad daylight, right under the nose of the sentry'.[20]

He recruited Ian Cross and Robert Kee to join him. The two were unlikely best friends. Cross, a squadron leader with 103 Squadron was 'built like a small bull, compact and muscled', as if he had been genetically designed for tunnelling. While normally good natured and extrovert he had a hair-trigger temper. Kee was 'studious, vague and entirely non-athletic'. He was known as the most argumentative man in the camp and in Calnan's opinion treated escape as a form of recreation from more serious occupations such as studying Russian.

One morning the trio arrived in the vegetable garden armed with crude homemade tools and began hoeing between the long rows of asparagus, raking the sandy earth into ridges. The guard outside the fence barely gave them a second look, even when they neared the fence. Calnan could barely believe their luck. They would never have got away with it in Stalag Luft III.

He started to dig the vertical shaft from behind a sheltering asparagus bush about twenty feet from the wire, while the others hoed and kept watch. After three days it was four feet deep. They now began to burrow horizontally towards the wire. As they were working mostly in full sight of the guards, progress was slow. Eventually they had cleared fifteen feet of tunnel. A little further and they would be able to seal themselves in and 'mole' out in one night.

Then the run of good fortune ran out. Calnan was digging at the face with Cross behind him, pushing soil out to Kee who scattered it around the vegetable patch whenever the guards were not looking. His hand closed around a large piece of paper buried in the dirt. As he groped his way forward he began to suspect the tunnel was passing under an old rubbish dump. This was bad news. It meant the earth over his head would be unstable. Sensibly, he inched his way back. Then 'an enormous weight hit me everywhere at once and I was completely unable to move my head, arms or body,' he wrote. 'As I drew my first terrified breath I inhaled so much sand that I almost choked.' He tried to twist free but he was crushed by the weight of the earth. Only his legs remained loose and he kicked them violently to attract Cross's attention. He felt hands grasp his feet and start hauling but it was no good. He was stuck fast under tons of sandy soil, fighting a losing battle to control his breathing, which was now coming in panicky gasps. Soon he was 'panting like an exhausted dog and taking in more and more sand with each breath'. A terrible thought struck him: 'I realized that I could survive for very few minutes and that they were going to be long, painful minutes.'

It was the second time in his life that he had contemplated his own imminent death. The first had been on a clear winter's day, 30 December 1941, when his aircraft had been hit by flak over the Normandy coast and with burning aviation spirit spraying his face he had tipped his Spitfire over and tumbled out into the air at 29,000 feet, only to realize that he was miles out to sea and certain to drown. An onshore wind had saved him then. Could anything rescue him now? His mind was surprisingly clear. He felt only 'sad because of all the things I had not yet done, sad because it seemed so futile and meaningless that my life should end under a rubbish dump in an asparagus bed in Poland.'

Then he heard the sound of spades hitting the ground above. Cross had scrambled out of the tunnel and alerted a kriegie rescue squad. It could not arrive soon enough, for Calnan was reaching the end of his endurance. 'I was now snorting sand in and out of my nostrils at an incredible rate,' he remembered. 'It was an entirely involuntary reflex action induced by breathing carbon dioxide.' A spade hit him in the middle of the back and hands grabbed his legs. With a 'one, two, three, heave!' his rescuers hauled him free. He lay gasping in the asparagus bed surrounded by German guards. He had turned a dull blue colour and for the next three days coughed up blood and sand. But in a week he was completely fit and ready to try again.

The Germans were learning that they could never afford to relax. In December a van arrived at the camp carrying equipment to put on a film show. The van had a sagging canvas roof which attracted the attention of one enterprising British officer. While others distracted the guards he hopped onto the hood. It was dark when the film show ended and he was driven out through the gates to freedom. It did not last long. He was caught loitering round a nearby airfield, trying to steal an aeroplane, and sent back to Schubin.

These attempts were good for morale and kept the Germans busy, but they were essentially individual efforts, lacking in resources and organization and therefore all the more likely to fail. The 450 air-force prisoners from Warburg, who had arrived at Schubin a few days before the first Sagan contingent, had their own escape organization and way of doing things. The camp history notes that initially 'there was a certain amount of disagreement' between the two groups about how to approach breaking out.[21] It came to an end in November 1942 when a second group of about a hundred officers was transferred from Stalag Luft III to Schubin. Among them were Harry Day and Jimmy Buckley, who as senior British officer and head of the escape committee respectively had supervised the escape effort at Sagan. With their arrival came a more systematic and long-term approach. It started with the establishment of a new escape committee, along the lines of the set-up at Sagan. The members would vet proposals and accept or reject them. They would maximize the skills available among the camp personnel to provide technical expertise, food, clothing and documentation to those whose plans were given official backing.

Somewhat to his surprise, Bill Ash was selected for membership of the committee.

His fellow members included Charles Marshall, who had been forced to bale out over Essen in April that year, his friend Bill Palmer, Aidan Crawley and Eddie Asselin.

Bill felt uncomfortable being in a position of authority, standing in judgement on other people's dreams of escape. He justified his acceptance of the role to himself on the grounds that he planned to get away as soon as possible and would not feel the weight of responsibility for long. With Day's arrival, though, it became clear that opportunistic attempts, cheering though they might be, would not get official encouragement. Day and Buckley favoured well-planned, large-scale projects aimed at freeing the maximum number of prisoners. And these would take time.

The balmy autumn turned into a savage winter and the shortcomings of the barracks were laid bare. 'We were assailed by a novel version of the biblical plagues,' Bill remembered. 'The main ones being famine, pestilence and ice.'[22] Food – its presence or absence – was one of the great determinants of the mood of the camp. Schubin was a long way from anywhere and Allied bombing sometimes disrupted the flow of Red Cross parcel deliveries, causing supplies to halt for weeks or even months, so that contents had to be rationed.[23]

On a parcel-less day a prisoner might breakfast on a single slice of black bread smeared thinly with margarine and jam, washed down with weak tea. For lunch there would be watery cabbage soup. Supper frequently amounted to no more than bread and a few potatoes. There was no fresh milk and other vegetables came from the prisoners' gardens.

Prisoners were naturally prone to any infection going. Jaundice was rife and to add to their tribulations the huts were infested with lice and bedbugs. Above all it was cold. The wind whipping in from the Baltic sliced through the walls and ceilings of the blocks, turning them into iceboxes. The ground froze and the football pitch now served as an ice rink for the kriegies, who glided around on skates which arrived in a Red Cross consignment. Tommy Calnan remembered the winter as 'the coldest I have ever experienced. Instead of undressing to go to bed, one dressed. Double and triple layers of underwear, all one's sweaters, two or three pairs of socks, covered by all the blankets and greatcoats one possessed.'[24]

The barrack stoves failed to make a dent in the all-pervading chill. Before long everything that could be burned had been.

The prisoners' made themselves as comfortable as they could. As the Germans began to adopt countermeasures to thwart escapes, the prisoners sometimes found themselves turned out of their barracks and forced to move to one of the empty ones for long periods while their quarters were searched for signs of suspicious activity.[25]

Day used all his considerable authority and powers of persuasion to try and improve the kriegies' lot. Lindeiner-Wildau at Stalag Luft III could be relied on to give him a sympathetic hearing. Oberstleutnant von Bodecker, the camp commandant at Schubin, was less obliging. Their first encounter had not been a success. According to Crawley, Bodecker 'tried to make Day stand at attention while in his presence, barked at him in German, and told him not to speak unless he was spoken to.' Finally, during one encounter, 'Day, without losing his temper, told the Kommandant that they were of the same rank in their respective forces, that he had served his king and country for twenty-five years and was only doing his duty by making complaints about the camp, which was no better than a pigsty.' He then saluted and walked out. He arrived back in the compound 'shaking with rage', just as the prisoners were being dismissed from a roll call. He halted them and told them of the commandant's rudeness. 'He hopes to retire as a general,' he declared. 'But he won't. We'll break him.' Thus began a protracted battle of wills between the RAF and the Wehrmacht.[26]

The German military mindset, the prisoners had discovered, was complicated. By now the Wehrmacht had carried out its share of the routine atrocities that accompanied the campaign in the East, and if this had caused individuals concern from time to time it did not seriously affect operations. Soldiers mainly hesitated if there was doubt whether their actions were covered by an order or official pronouncement. What mattered was not what they did so much as whether they were authorized to do it. The commandant felt constrained by the Geneva Convention and, under pressure from Day, would grudgingly respond to his demands. One day the prisoners were offered some moth-eaten greatcoats, apparently taken off the Polish cavalry. On another there was a consignment of clogs from France, similar to the ones Bill had foolishly chosen as part of his peasant disguise after he was shot down. The kriegies found it impossible to walk in them, but they burned splendidly in the block stoves.

The prisoners' spirits sank with the dwindling sun. They clung to the hope provided by odd bits of cheering news that they heard on the camp's clandestine radio or gleaned from the German newspapers that circulated in the camp. The radio was assembled by Flight Lieutenant L. B. Barry, who arrived in Schubin in October. He managed to obtain two radio valves and some wiring from a Polish worker. Ingenuity provided the rest. He and his helpers made capacity condensers from tinfoil and margarine-soaked paper, solder out of molten silver paper, flux from resin, and the sensitive parts of the headset from old Gillette razor blades. The set was hidden under the stove in the medical officer's room in the camp sick quarters. By November they were able to listen in to the BBC. The news was improving. A month earlier, Montgomery and the Eighth Army had smashed Rommel's Afrika Korps at El Alamein. The bulletins were taken down in shorthand and transcribed for circulation. 'The dissemination of news every day was of very great value in keeping the standard of morale high,' the official history records.[27]

Letters from home could be the greatest tonic, a physical link with the world the kriegies had left behind and a reaffirmation that love and familiar joys were waiting if they could only hang on. They could also bring sickening news. One of the hardest things for a prisoner was to be told that someone he loved and relied on no longer loved him. As the war progressed and absence grew longer such letters became increasingly frequent. They were known as 'mespots', a hangover from the First World War when extended service in Mesopotamia had ruptured many an engagement and marriage.

It was impossible to keep the news secret. In Stalag Luft III some decided the best thing was to give it maximum publicity, pinning up their mespots to the camp notice board. 'The effect was oddly therapeutic,' wrote Richard Passmore. 'All your friends understood and sympathized – at times they even found cause for laughter and this… wryly infected the victim.'[28]

The content of some of the letters, no doubt embellished in the retelling, entered kriegie legend. One allegedly ran: 'When you were reported missing I went round to see your widowed dad and we got on very well. Now I have to tell you that last week he and I were married. I hope you don't take it too hard. Yours truly, Mum.' Another announced: 'I am sorry to tell you that I have been living with a soldier. He doesn't get paid very much so I wonder whether you could see your way to increasing the allowance.'[29]

For anyone in a fragile frame of mind, the weight of camp life was heavy, sometimes unbearably so. Among them was Flight Lieutenant Robert Edwards, who had been traumatized by the crash that preceded his capture. Bill Ash watched his deterioration with concern. As the weeks passed in Schubin he became 'less and less stable… his unhinged arguments and nervous tics could be irritating to men already cooped up and spoiling for a squabble, but he was harmless and most of us did our best to look after him.'[30]

No one took much notice when on 26 September 1942 he announced that he was 'fed up with this place'. Shortly after, he strolled over to the warning wire, which as at Sagan stretched inside the perimeter fence, and stepped over it. He walked calmly to the barbed wire and in broad daylight began to climb. It would have been easy enough to pull him down and drag him off to solitary. Instead the guard called a single warning. The incident was witnessed by Bill Ash. Edwards 'climbed on feebly, not getting very far up the wire. The nervous guard aimed low but shot him in the groin and he dangled briefly on the wire like a broken doll before being taken down.' He was taken immediately to the camp doctor but died of his wounds.

The incident brought a crowd of angry kriegies to the edge of the forbidden zone. 'One particularly vicious guard known as the Blonde Beast was all in favour of mowing us down too,' Bill remembered. 'But some of the more moderate guards cooled the situation and we were spared.' Instead he was grabbed and marched off to the cooler for shouting and raising his fist at a guard.

Years later, when watching the film *The Great Escape*, he sat up when on the screen appeared what he describes as 'a similar

The dashing aviator: the formal portrait Bill sent home in 1941.

Above: Bill, aged seven or eight, with his beloved sister Adele at home in Dallas in 1925.

Left: Underneath the surface insouciance Bill was an outstanding pilot. His seriousness shows through in this image, perhaps taken during training.

Above: Bill at the controls of his Spitfire in late 1941.

Left: Canadian Prime Minister Mackenzie King greets Bill during a visit to 411 Squadron.

The squadron at Digby with Bill seated on the far right.

At dispersal, waiting for action, Digby, late summer 1941. Bill is on the far right, looking up.

'Hostile to the Enemy': 411 pilots in Mae Wests just before or after an operation. Bill is fourth from left.

Above left: Squadron Leader Stan Turner with trademark pipe. *Above right*: Bill is entertained by a line-shooting Buck McNair.

The church at Vieille Église today, behind which Bill crash-landed…

…and the house where the Boulanger family who sheltered Bill once had their *estaminet*.

Personalkarte I: Personelle Angaben

Beschriftung der Erkennungsmarke

Nr. *757*

Kriegsgefangenen-Stammlager: **Stalag Luft 3**

Lager: *Stalag Luft 2*

Des Kriegsgefangenen

Name: *ASH*

Vorname: *William Franklin*

Geburtstag und -ort: *30.11.17 Dallas, Texas*

Religion: *Prot.*

Vorname des Vaters: *William*

Familienname der Mutter: *Porterfield*

Staatsangehörigkeit: *USA [will aus Kanadier goûten]*

Dienstgrad: *P/O. F/Lt*

Truppenteil: *RCAF* Kom. usw.:

Zivilberuf: *Schriftsteller* Berufs-Gr.:

Matrikel Nr. (Stammrolle des Heimatstantes): *J4787*

Gefangennahme (Ort und Datum): *b. Paris 17.5.42*

Ob gesund, krank, verwundet eingeliefert: *ges.*

Lichtbild

Nähere Personalbeschreibung

Grösse	Haarfarbe	Besondere Kennzeichen:
1.83	*braun*	

Fingerabdruck

Name und Anschrift der zu benachrichtigenden Person in der Heimat des Kriegsgefangenen

1/ *Vater: Mr. W. F. Ash, 3211 Oliver St. Dallas, Texas, USA.*

2/ *c/o. Lloyds Bank, 6 Pall Mall, London S.W.*

Beschriftung der Erkennungsmarke Nr. Lager: Name:

Bemerkungen:

Personalbeschreibung

Figur:

Größe: *1.83*

Alter: *26 J.*

Gesichtsform: *schmal*

Gesichtsfarbe:

Schädelform:

Augen: *blau*

Gebiß:

Haare: *braun*

Bart: —

Gewicht: *72* kg

Besondere Merkmale: —

Deutsche Sprachkenntnisse: —

Kr. Gefg. OKW Nr.

25.3.42 mit Wirkung vom

25.3.43 zum *F/Lt*

Sagan, den _____ 19___

The cover of Bill's prisoner-of-war file at Stalag Luft III. The bruises from his beating at the hands of the Gestapo in Paris are still clearly visible.

Left: An angelic-looking
Paddy Barthropp.

Below: Sketch map of
Stalag Luft III, scene of
'The Great Escape'.

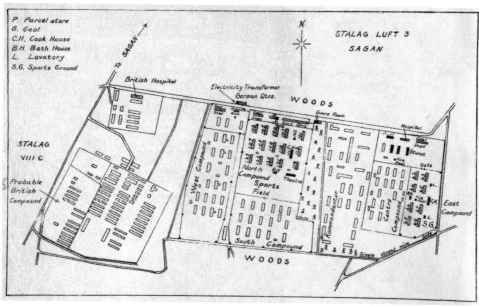

tragic moment in which an officer is shot down on the wire and a protesting American is led away to the cooler'. There is no record of such an incident happening at Stalag Luft III where the film is set, 'but the real life tragedy at Schubin was burned into the minds of anyone who saw it.'

One of his jailers was the 'Blond Beast', who made a point of taking Bill's shoes away each night to further reduce the already non-existent chances of escape. The first time he came to collect them he asked Bill who he thought was winning the war. He replied 'we are' and was rewarded with a backhander to the face. The next night he repeated the question and this time Bill diplomatically gave what he thought was the right answer – the Germans. It made no difference: the Blond Beast struck him again. The routine went on night after night.

The cell had a window set high in the wall, and to relieve the boredom he sometimes hauled himself up for a glimpse of life outside. It looked out on the main road that ran in front of the camp. One day he heard unusual noises drifting through the window. It reminded him of something from his Texas childhood: the sound of cattle being herded. When he looked out he saw not cows but a crowd of about two hundred young women. German soldiers and members of the Selbstschutz local militia were driving them along with sticks and whips towards the railway station. Whether they were Jews or young Poles being deported to forced brothels on the Eastern Front he never learned. The sight brought back all the anger and revulsion he had felt when watching cinema newsreels of storm troopers beating Jews and Communists. 'Something inside me snapped,' he wrote. 'The year of abuse, captivity, beatings and a thousand tiny humiliations boiled up into one overwhelming desire to fight back and defend these poor women.'[31]

Through the barred window he 'screamed at the fascists herding the women, shouted and cursed, throwing every vile word I could at them'. Some of the women looked up and he liked to think later that his outburst had somehow brought them a little comfort. His shouts soon brought the guards running, and they tried to pull him down from the window. 'I was so enraged that I hardly felt the blows raining down on me and the gun butts smashing my hands until I finally let go of the bars and fell to the floor, where the kicking continued,' he wrote. Before they left him they nailed boards over the window. He lay in the darkness on the cold concrete floor. His face ached and his back and stomach throbbed. But he was glad for what he had done.

SEVEN

Soon after emerging from the cooler Bill was able to channel his anger and energy into a new escape project. He could claim some credit for coming up with the idea. One of the most significant buildings in the kriegies' lives was the main latrine, known in German as the *Abort*. It was a long, low, brick structure, which stood in isolation a hundred yards from the nearest barrack block. In the mornings it was a busy place, a forum where the kriegies met to do their business and swap the latest 'gen' gleaned from whatever was picked up from the radio or the German newspapers brought in by the guards. The atmosphere was relaxed and convivial and they were rarely troubled by visits from the Germans. According to Tommy Calnan, it was reminiscent of a London club, even if it did not smell of old leather and expensive cigars. 'It was here that all the lavatory rumours started which flashed round the camp at the speed of sound. It was here that one first heard that there was a trainload of Red Cross parcels on the way, or that we were all about to be moved to another camp.

It was here that plots were plotted and grievances grieved over.'[1]

It was in this stimulating atmosphere that Bill and a group of his cronies were struck by a startling but potentially very promising idea. Why not use the *Abort* as the starting point for a serious, properly engineered tunnel from which a major escape of the type that Day was encouraging could be launched? After some initial preparatory work they revealed their thinking to a group of like-minded kriegies, hardened escapers who they thought could be trusted to appreciate the concept.

One day in early November they met in a discreet corner of the barrack. It was a freezing day, ten degrees below outside, and two degrees above within. They cradled cups of Red Cross cocoa as Bill and his associates explained the plan to the gathering. Those present included Edouard Asselin, a comrade from 411 Squadron who had been a star athlete at Montreal's Loyola College and played a mean game of poker. Bill found him 'immensely likeable' but also noted 'a very well-developed streak of ambition... we all had an unshakeable sense that no matter what happened, Eddy Asselin would come up smelling of roses.'[2] Also present were Charles Marshall and Bill Palmer. Marshall had been a London policeman before joining the RAF, spoke good German and was an outstanding organizer.

They observed that the latrine had many things in its favour as the starting point for a tunnel. In the first place, it was reasonably close to the perimeter fence. Its construction provided excellent conditions in which to dig undetected. The interior was divided into two areas. At the northern end was the urinal. This was a simple affair. The rear wall and part of the two side walls were tarred and a trough laid along the bottom which emptied into a pit. The rest of the *Abort* was devoted to the sit-down facilities. These consisted of a row of broad wooden benches that ran along the remaining three walls, pierced at intervals of three feet by a series of holes. The planks were made of soft pine and the holes had smooth and rounded edges so they were comfortable and easy on the anatomy. There were a further two rows, arranged back-to-back in the middle of the *Abort*. Each space was separated from its neighbour by a partition but was open at the front. There were enough seats to cater for seventy men at any time.

The *Abort* had a cement floor which extended to the edge of the wooden benches. Below lay a cesspit, the contents of which were pumped out once a month into a tank mounted on a horse-drawn cart provided by a Polish contractor. The sewage was then spread over nearby fields as fertilizer. The floor of the urinal was also cement-covered. The ground beneath it though was solid. The cesspit ended where the urinal area began.

As Bill explained, it was this feature of the *Abort*'s construction that made it such an attractive place for a tunnel. The space below the urinals could be hollowed out to make a sizeable chamber. This would be large enough to accommodate the workforce as they bored a lateral tunnel westward, deep beneath the wire.

The men could work at a steady pace, completely hidden from the eyes of the ferrets. Even better, there would be no telltale spoil from the digging to give the game away. The disposal of dirt was the tunnellers' greatest headache. Ingenious ways had been devised to disperse it, such as trickling it over vegetable patches from bags concealed beneath trouser legs, but the process was very slow and the risk of detection high. Once a ferret spotted suspicious-looking spoil, the camp's Russian slave workers would be put to work with spades and the tunnel would be uncovered. There was no such problem with the latrine project. The excavated dirt could be dumped straight into the cesspit, where it would soon blend in with the contents. Even the most dedicated ferret was unlikely to spend much time probing the effluent when the truck came to pump it away.

There remained the question of how the initial chamber was to be excavated. Bill and his team had the answer to that. Their idea was not to burrow down through the cement floor of the latrine but to make a start from the side of the cesspit. They would attack it by slipping through one of the lavatory seats next to the urinal and unbricking a hole in the pit wall big enough for a man to clamber through. From there work could begin on digging out a space big enough for eight to ten people to operate in comfort. Perhaps 'comfort' was not the right word. Nobody relished working amid the fumes of a sea of excrement. But as Tommy Calnan, who was among the listeners, immediately recognized, the plan sounded like a winner. 'It was ingenious in its simplicity. All the major risks of detection had been very nearly eliminated.'[3]

From the start it was envisaged as an ambitious project, using the latest tunnelling techniques, shored all the way with wooden planking and ventilated by an air pump. If it succeeded it could indeed channel scores of men to – at least temporary – freedom. Day was looking for a large-scale breakout. Exactly how many prisoners should be involved was a moot point. To some the notion of a mass escape was very appealing. They argued that once the tunnel was completed and 'broken' – the term used for the final stage of burrowing upwards and through the last layer of topsoil – it should be open to all comers until the Germans were alerted.

Calnan, though, was adamantly opposed to the idea. They were not attempting to break the record for the greatest number of escapers. They were trying to give those who dug the tunnel the best possible chance of getting back to England. If the last man was out of the tunnel by midnight and the breakout was not noted until dawn, then the escapers would be well clear of the area before the balloon went up. After all, only three hours train-ride away was Danzig, from where there was a chance of stowing away on a boat bound for Sweden. The argument went back and forth but Calnan won the day. 'We would, it was agreed, keep our numbers as low as possible and only take on essential workers. It was to be a private tunnel for the benefit of those who had made it and nobody else.'

Palmer raised the delicate question of the extent to which they should involve the escape committee in the project. The rules demanded that they get its backing before proceeding further. Its approval was potentially valuable. The promoters of the scheme would then get access to all the expertise and resources at the committee's disposal. The camp history records the latrine tunnel as a straightforward operation carried out under the authority of the escape organization. Tommy Calnan gave a different account. He claimed that he opposed involving the committee at this early stage on the grounds that the more people who were involved, the greater the chance of someone making an unguarded remark that would be picked up by the ferrets. 'Let's do it ourselves,' he urged. 'It's more work but it's safer.' Apparently the others agreed. All that remained was to decide on what was the bare minimum of men needed to carry out the labour. They decided finally on a figure of twenty-five.

Between them they would cover all the main elements of the project. Palmer was in charge of engineering, designing the ventilation, lighting and shoring, aided by Charlie Swain, the best carpenter in the camp. This side of the project would in time be overseen by a Fleet Air Arm officer, Lieutenant Commander Peter Fanshawe. The actual digging was the responsibility of Bill Ash and Eddie Asselin, whose band of labourers included Paddy Barthropp, Ian Cross and Robert Kee. Intelligence and security were in the hands of Aidan Crawley and Tommy Calnan.

The first phase of the work was in some ways the most vulnerable to discovery. It involved modifying one of the lavatory seats nearest the urinal and took two days. The section of bench was sawn through so it could be lifted sideways to rest against the wall. The carpenters worked in brief spells, protected by lookouts – 'stooges', in camp slang – ready to signal when a ferret came near. The result was impressive. The bench was transformed into a folding lid which opened sideways, creating a hole three feet square, beneath which lay the cesspit. The lid was released by a hidden catch and moved on hinges. Opening and shutting it took only seconds. If any German appeared in the *Abort*, one of the stooges would fold down the seat and whip down his trousers.

The underside of the bench was fitted with a handrail. By hanging on to it, a man could swing through the hole in the brick wall of the pit that led to the chamber below the urinal. As yet the breach had not been made. Tommy Calnan, who was small and light, was given the job. He lowered himself head first into the pit while two men held his legs. Then he began banging at the brickwork of the cesspit wall with a hammer and cold chisel.

It was tough work. The job was made even harder by the nauseating fumes assailing his nostrils. He managed to keep it up for a heroic fifteen minutes. After that, so much blood had drained to his head that he could no longer see properly. His thumb was already throbbing from repeated miss-hits. His grip on the hammer and chisel never slackened. The tools were precious. He knew that if he dropped them he would have to descend on a rope and fish them out of the noxious lake below.

When Tommy's time was up a succession of wall-bashers took over. They were careful not to let any of the bricks drop into the pit. They were to be saved to fashion a removable hatch that would be put in place to camouflage the entrance to the chamber at the end of a day's digging. Over the next three days they worked in short shifts to hammer out the hole. The wall-bashers were shielded by a network of stooges standing watch over every possible line of approach to the *Abort*. They could expect to get three minutes warning of any approaching German – enough time to suspend operations, replace the lavatory seat and clean up.

Then at last the final brick was removed and they were through to the hard-packed sand that lay beneath the urinal floor. Two days later they had dug out enough of it to put a man inside. The first occupant was Eddy Asselin who soon enlarged it to the point where Bill Ash could join him. A day or two later there was room for four men, so the digging could start in earnest. The twenty-five men of the escape team all took their turn. They worked in two-hour shifts – *Dienst*, as they called it, using the German word for 'duty'. The short stints enabled them to work flat out and accelerate progress. Getting into the chamber meant reaching through the lavatory hole for the handrail, lowering oneself down into the pit then raising your knees gymnastically and propelling your legs through the entrance. The first man through would then help the next in and so on. Later, diggers would have to first remove the concealing hatch before getting through.

As chief tunnellers, Bill and Eddie had to perform the feat more often than anyone. 'Entering… was a daily experience of horror as I wriggled through the hole where the toilet seat was and my face came to within a few inches of the great stinking lake of sewage,' wrote Bill. Inevitably he was reminded of his immersion in the Vieille-Église village sewer after he had been shot down. Malodorous encounters seemed to be part of his war.[4] But the essential fact of kriegie life was that if you wanted to survive, and certainly if you wanted to escape, you had to be able to get used to anything. And so it was. Fastidious men who in their previous lives would have wrinkled their noses at the prospect of wearing the same shirt two days running now barely noticed a stench that would fell an ox.

Once the chamber was big enough to hold them, the carpenters arrived to tidy up the access hole and fit the hatch door. Asselin wanted the chamber as big as possible, to maximize the number of diggers at any one time and leave space for undispersed spoil. Eventually about 500 cubic feet of dirt were excavated, leaving a large space measuring about 10 feet by 15, and tall enough for most men to stand upright in. As well as accommodating the team there was room to store all the tools and equipment.

Work could now begin on the tunnel itself. On a normal two-hour shift, two men, stripped down to their underwear, would dig using scoops made out of old tin cans and cut-down broom handles or coal shovels from the barrack stoves. They would pack the spoil in kitbags which were hauled back on ropes to the chamber and emptied. It was decided to keep digging and dispersal as separate operations. It would have been simple to just shovel the dirt through the chamber entrance and into the cesspit below. Before long though it would form a suspicious-looking mound which would be instantly spotted by any ferret who chose to inspect the pit. Far better to spread it evenly over the whole surface, where it would sink invisibly. Tommy Calnan came up with a plan to sprinkle the soil through the seventy toilet-seat holes that ran the length of the *Abort*. Aluminium jugs from the barrack washhouses would make ideal containers. In a day's work the digging teams dislodged enough dirt to fill about a hundred jugs. It was decided to leave the spoil in the chamber overnight then disperse it in an hour-long blitz each morning. Once it was over, the digging team could shut themselves in and carry on work undisturbed.

There would be four men in the dispersal team inside the chamber. One filled the jugs and passed them to a second who handed them up to two helpers hanging through the seat flap to haul them up. There were some risks. Both the hatch door and the folding section of lavatory seat would have to be open for the duration of the exercise. A full complement of stooges was needed to give warning if the ferrets showed up. Calnan was confident the operation was feasible and that the best time to conduct it would be between 8.30 and 9.30 in the morning, when the whole camp had breakfasted and, 'the British constitution being what it is', the *Abort* would be at its busiest. Even the most observant German guard was unlikely to notice that a dozen or so men who had visited the lavatory had not emerged. This was the team charged with systematically emptying the jugs through the toilet seats.

On the first day that the exercise was tested it did not go quite according to plan. Bill was at the workface with Eddie, assisted by two helpers to haul back the soil. The four-man team began filling the jugs from the kitbags and passing them up through the hole, where four more men were waiting to disperse them up and down the lines of thrones. It was the busiest time of day and all were occupied. Many of the occupants responded belligerently when told to shift so the jug could be emptied. So stiff was the resistance that Calnan was forced to think again. 'We had made the great error of not remembering that there are some moments sacrosanct to an Englishman, when he may not be disturbed for any reason,' he wrote. As a result, 'the next morning we changed our system. We increased our dispersal team to seven workers. Of these, four occupied lavatory seats through which the sand could be poured, changing their station whenever the departure of a client permitted it.'[5] The others ran back and forth, emptying the contents through whatever holes their comrades had reserved.

They had decided on a deep tunnel, running about seventeen feet below the surface. This would minimize their risk from the underground microphones, which as at Sagan had been buried in the earth to pick up suspicious vibrations. As it turned out this was an unnecessary precaution. Crawley's intelligence network soon learned that 'these microphones were far too sensitive and that the noise of the prisoners walking around the perimeter of the camp or skating on the flooded football field made it impossible for other sounds to be detected clearly.'[6] The breakout point was to be in the middle of a cluster of potato clamps on the other side of the perimeter fence, which would provide cover from the patrols that circled the camp at night. To reach this haven would mean digging a tunnel of about 150 feet.

The team's pride in their project was growing by the day and a degree of perfectionism touched every aspect of the work. The entrance to the tunnel was neat and robustly framed in timber to deal with the wear and tear of constant coming and going. By Christmas Day they had burrowed ten feet, creating a shaft two feet square. Tiny though it sounded, this was just big enough for an undernourished man to crawl along it and work reasonably efficiently at the face.

Christmas was a time for forced jollity in kriegiedom. There was something rather melancholy about the preparations, made more profound by the greetings that arrived in the mail from homes which at this season seemed particularly dreamlike and far away. This year, the kriegies of Oflag XXIB even received a Christmas card from King George VI, delivered to Harry Day with all due reverence by one of the senior guards. For weeks beforehand the Red Cross parcels were hoarded to provide a blowout on the big day. The prisoners' fertile minds had easily solved the problem of conjuring a booze supply out of nowhere, distilling spirits from raisins, sugar and the like, in clandestine Heath Robinson assemblages. The results were given fanciful names which bore virtually no resemblance to the real thing. It hardly mattered. The point was to get spectacularly, amnesiacally drunk. The Germans wisely decided to leave the kriegies to let off steam. The flavour of the celebrations was caught well in an autobiographical novel written by Robert Kee after the war.

We decided it was time to start on Jack Nopps's apricot brandy. It tasted of petrol mixed with hair oil. Jack took one gulp, said 'Lovely stuff', and went off to tune in to the King's Speech on the secret wireless which only he could operate. Soon it was dark and the Christmas evening was in full swing.

The drink made me excited and confused so that time seemed to be moving in a series of huge uneasy jerks, sometimes accelerating wildly and sometimes standing absolutely still.

First I was in a room where people stood crowded together in the atmosphere of a cocktail party.

'Of course I was in the same squadron as him for a time.'

'If I can get drunk enough on this stuff I might be able to get away with it on the next repatriation board.'

'It was one of the finest knocking shops in Cairo.'

'If only we can get a foothold around Calais.'

Every now and then people would step neatly aside while

the person they were talking to was sick on the floor. 'Awfully sorry, old boy…'

Later Nopps, now much the worst for wear, reported back on the King's message to the nation: 'He said… the prisoners of war… were conducting themselves… with great dignity.'[7]

For the select group in on the latrine tunnel, that year's festivities felt a little more authentic. The system they had evolved seemed ferret-proof, so much so that they were able to cut down on the number of stooges and employ them below ground.

They rehearsed the emergency drill so thoroughly that by the end they could close down the lavatory seat entry-point while the diggers stayed below. If they had to come up in a hurry, for an unexpected *Appell* or some other emergency, they could be out and on display, looking the picture of innocence, in less than three minutes.[8]

The work was boring, dirty and smelly, but strangely satisfying, providing a focus and a purpose that was missing from life above ground. 'The routine had become part of us, and though we often hated it and grudged the time, we felt affectionate and possessive about it,' wrote Kee.

There was something stimulating about the hours spent digging at the tiny face, tugging on the rope for the earth to be dragged away and receiving the faint answering tug from the other end, or squeezing backwards cursing to join the rope where it had snapped under the strain. When we came up to the familiar tea and the squalor and the faces it was as if we had spent the afternoon in another planet.[9]

The operation was being carried out in the most public place in the camp so every kriegie knew about it. The exclusive nature of the scheme meant that all that was required of them was to keep their mouths shut and to donate useful items to the cause. Each prisoner was asked to contribute a bed board or two, to be put into service as pit props, shoring up the tunnel's sides and roof to prevent falls. Almost all of them complied, though Bill Ash noted that some whined at this further reduction in their comfort. As a team leader he was expected to show an example. Eventually his bed was left with no boards at all and he was forced to weave a string net across the bedframe to support his mattress.

Even so, the supply of boards eventually ran out. Almost everyone in the camp was down to five slats – the bare minimum to support a mattress. It fell to Marshall to come up with a new supply. For a while he considered seeking the help of the escape committee, to use their authority to insist on a levy of one more plank from every prisoner. But that risked turning the camp against the latrine team and limiting cooperation they might need in other areas. He decided to seek a solution elsewhere. He went instead to the German quartermaster's stores. They were located in the basement of the White House, which was out of bounds to prisoners. The Wehrmacht guards had still to wake up to the full extent of the kriegies' wiles, and believed that a locked door would stay locked. But by 1943 every prison compound had one or two expert locksmiths who had learned their craft by dismantling and studying the locks and padlocks they encountered during their imprisonment. Most fixed door locks in the camps were of fairly simple design and were relatively easy to pick. 'All that was needed was a strong piece of wire about an eighth of an inch thick, one end of which was bent at right angles and the other formed into a loop to serve as a handle,' wrote Aidan Crawley. The angled end was beaten with a hammer to flatten the wire. This was then filed square and inserted into the lock. By trial and error it was then trimmed until it was the right shape to free the bolt. In Crawley's estimation, 'with a set of wire keys of varying lengths and widths, and with lots of practice most fixed door-locks could be picked in well under a quarter of a minute.'[10]

Tommy Calnan had already learned about locks in Stalag Luft III. He joined Marshall and they waited for a quiet moment when neither the quartermaster nor his staff was around. The door to the stores posed no problem. He turned the key and they walked in to 'a treasure house of valuable material. There were two rooms stacked to the ceiling with two-tier wooden bunks and literally thousands of bed slats. There were also many other items that made our mouths water.'[11]

They decided not to be greedy. If they were caught they would be in trouble not just with the Germans but with their own side as well. Despite all the goon-baiting and organized disobedience there were certain rules of conduct in the camps that the SBO and his staff insisted on. One was a ban on too-obvious thieving from the Germans. If a theft was discovered, the Germans would first report it to Day, who would be duty-bound to appeal to the culprit to return the stolen goods immediately. If they failed to do so, the Germans could impose collective punishment.

Carefully they extracted a stack of bed boards, removing

them from the back of the pile so that at a casual glance there seemed nothing amiss. There were just enough to meet the carpenters' immediate requirements. They decided that rather than stockpile supplies they would return to the stores when more slats were needed.

To do their work the tunnellers needed light. Someone had suggested they rigged up an electric bulb powered by a feeder line run off the wiring in the *Abort*. Bill Ash had been all for it, but Eddie Asselin reminded everyone that a prisoner in another camp had been electrocuted by a faulty connection while digging in a damp tunnel. Tommy Calnan also warned that the connecting wire might well be noticed by a nosy ferret, which would lead him straight to the tunnel. They fell back on the tried-and-tested fat lamps.

These were one of the many inventions that kriegie ingenuity had devised under the spur of necessity. They were simply old tin cans, filled with margarine which had been boiled up to reduce the water content, and with a piece of old shoelace or pyjama cord for a wick. They gave limited light but were easy to produce and burned little oxygen, a serious consideration if you were labouring in a stuffy hole. It was another example of how, over time, prisoners had learned how to turn mundane items into useful artefacts. For shoring tunnels they needed saws, chisels, hammers and nails. Men planning to go over or through the fence needed ladders or wire cutters. Those who attempted to slip through the gates in disguise needed keys or dummy rifles which had to look totally authentic.

Despite the SBO's desire not to provoke the Germans by overt theft, escape activity could not have gone on without a high degree of larceny. The activists stole what they could not make. There was usually construction work going on somewhere in a camp and as Aidan Crawley noted, 'it was difficult for workmen to be unceasingly vigilant against a community in which theft was a virtue.'[12] Sometimes a theft was noticed, reprisals were threatened and the items recovered. It was also likely that the guards might not report the missing item for fear of being disciplined. Furthermore in Schubin, the Polish workmen who visited the camp were almost to a man on the side of the prisoners. What the prisoners could not steal they might acquire by bribery. Some of the guards were susceptible to offers of cigarettes or chocolate or some other luxury from the Red Cross parcels in return for services rendered.

Even these sources were not adequate, and any bit of junk that in peacetime would have been overlooked as rubbish took on a potential value. 'Broken bits of iron, the bars of an old grate, old motor-car springs lying in a dump, the rims of cart-wheels or the bands of a barrel were seized upon at once and guarded almost as carefully as food,' wrote Crawley.

There was a surprising amount of metal around. Barrack huts constructed of wood were reinforced with iron angles in the corners and long bolts through the beams. The hinges on shutters if filed for long enough turned out to make excellent wire cutters. Stoves proved to have lots of promising extraneous bits and pieces and the barrack kitchens were reasonably well equipped with utensils which could be put to a dual purpose. To the seasoned kriegies' eyes there was virtually nothing which did not have some potential use to increase their comfort or aid their escape.

Making an air pump that would ventilate the shaft while digging was in progress therefore presented no problem. The design was simple and effective. It was based on an ordinary kitbag – there were hundreds lying around the camp – which was transformed into a large bellows. The bottom of the bag was attached to a square wooden board. This was pierced by two holes, each covered with a leather flap to form a valve. On the outlet valve the flap was on the outside and on the inlet valve, on the inside. The other end of the bag was attached to a round piece of wood with a handle attached. The kitbag was reinforced with wire rings sown onto the outside to prevent it collapsing, and the whole apparatus attached to a wooden frame. By pushing and pulling on the handle as if he was playing a giant concertina a man could keep a steady flow of air coursing out of the outlet valve. This was carried down the tunnel by a pipe made of old tins of Klim, the powdered milk that came in Canadian Red Cross parcels. The lid end of the can was slightly tapered so they fitted together neatly and could be extended indefinitely.

As the work advanced, the diggers' initial enthusiasm began to falter. 'The tunnel, as it grew longer and longer, passing sixty feet, became a suffocating place,' Bill Ash remembered. 'Each trip down it required a little more courage, and the need to blot out the thought of all those tons of earth pressing down on you, knowing that a cave-in would leave us trapped, breathing mouthfuls of mud and unable to go forwards or backwards.'[13] Soon it was taking half an hour to crawl to and from the face in order to spend an hour digging. The further they burrowed the more they felt the grip of claustrophobia closing around them.

Clad only in 'combination' underwear they 'felt the cold clay around us, pressing in on us and seeping into our bones until we almost became part of the tunnel.' When the margarine lamps flickered and died, which they frequently did as the air grew increasingly foul, the men lay entombed in total silence and darkness that was both awesome and terrifying.

The work provided little distraction from fearful thoughts. The digger shovelled the dirt into a canvas kitbag attached to a rope. When it was full, he tugged on the rope and a helper at the other end answered with a double tug and hauled it back. Rope was scarce and hard to manufacture and as the tunnel grew there were frequent breaks. Then a man was stationed to pull the bag back to a midway point from where another waiting at the entrance would take over.

The practice of disposing of some of the spoil through the toilet holes was soon deemed unnecessary. It could be mixed evenly into the cesspit slurry by simply poking it with a stick. The method had to be reassessed following an incident which Bill Ash witnessed after emerging into the late afternoon light from a long day's digging. He came across one of the pilots, Josef Bryks, a 27-year-old Czech whose name had been angliciscd to Joe Ricks to avoid reprisals being taken against his family. Ricks was talking to an elderly Pole, the man who had been engaged by the Germans to pump the contents of the cesspit into a horse-drawn tanker known to kriegies as the 'honeywagon'. The old man seemed upset about something and Ricks explained that he was complaining that the honeywagon was choked with sand and gravel when he emptied it after each trip. The old man was a patriot and was easily talked into keeping quiet about the discovery. Ricks even persuaded him to cooperate in a scheme to smuggle him out in the tanker after some future visit.

This plan was duly taken to the escape committee. They had some serious misgivings. If it was discovered that the old man had aided and abetted Ricks's escape he would certainly be shot and perhaps his family along with him. However if the attempt was timed to coincide with the tunnel break, then the Germans would assume that Ricks was one of the escapers and the old man would be in the clear.

As the thaw set in and the tunnel lengthened, the team's excitement grew. They went to work with lighter hearts and the cursing and grumbling as they scraped and hauled was tinged with hope. The latrine tunnel was not the only engineering project underway. Early in December, a prisoner called Dickie Edge had started a rival tunnel from beneath the wooden floor of the night latrine of one of the barracks. This knowledge introduced an extra urgency to Bill and the team's efforts. If Edge and his boys broke out first, the guards would tear Schubin to pieces looking for any sign of other escape activity. The luck they had enjoyed could not possibly last; the tunnel would be uncovered and all their work would be in vain.

The Germans sniffed the air and knew that something was afoot. But their Wehrmacht noses were nowhere as keen as those of the Luftwaffe bloodhounds of Stalag Luft III. Captain Simms tried to catch the prisoners out by ordering extra *Appells*. Instead of two, there were three, sometimes four and five a day. He also attempted to change the rules so that kriegies had to be back in their barrack blocks by 5 p.m. instead of the normal time of 7 p.m. Harry Day argued that it was essential for the prisoners' health that they spent as much time in the open air as possible. Fearing an outbreak of some contagious disease that would inevitably infect Germans and kriegies alike, Simms backed off.

This was good news. The problems with the honeywagon meant alternative means of dumping spoil had to be found. As the ground began to thaw and the ice turn to slush, the latrine team took advantage of the early dusk to disperse the evidence. 'Every evening groups of prisoners could dimly be seen walking up and down the dark side of the football field or digging methodically in the gardens,' wrote Aidan Crawley. 'At given signals kitbags full of earth were carried out and dumped in front of them to be trampled into the ground.' There was little to fear from the Germans, for at that time of the day 'the only guards in the camp were two ancient infantrymen who wandered slowly and harmlessly around the compound and were easily trailed.' Furthermore there were 'too many trees, buildings and banks to make searchlights any real danger'.[14] As they trudged back to their bleak accommodation, the escape team could warm themselves with the thought that it was all going remarkably well.

EIGHT

The tunnel was supposed to emerge in a dip in the ground about fifteen yards beyond the perimeter fence. There the escapers would be hidden from the guards who patrolled the wire at night. It was essential to know whether or not the tunnel was on track. There was only one way to find out. One day in mid February Eddie Asselin crawled to the end of the tunnel and poked a slim iron rod through the roof. Above ground, a group of observers loitered near the fence trying to see where it came out. The seconds passed and there was no sign of the rod. Then at last someone spotted it. It was not where it should have been. It was only a few feet beyond the wire and about thirty feet south of the line which led to the dip in the ground. It was apparent that the trajectory of the tunnel had wandered off track by some fifteen degrees during the digging. It was easily done. Compasses did not work below ground and the diggers had to rely on a protractor and string arrangement to calculate the angle. It was a setback but not a catastrophic one. The engineering team went back to work to find the right line to put the tunnel back on course. Bill, Eddie and the diggers stayed on the surface for a day or two while the problem was worked out.

All this activity, the burrowing and the shoring, the hauling and the pumping, represented only part of the escape effort. While some were toiling away in the darkness, others were engaged in more delicate work, doing what they could to ensure that when the escapers at last emerged they would have every possible chance of success. The truth was that breaking out was the easy bit. Staying at large long enough to reach friendly territory was the real challenge. To meet it you needed all the help you could possibly get.

The basis of success was good intelligence, and a competent intelligence officer was vital to success. At Schubin the role was occupied by Aidan Crawley. He had the perfect qualifications for the job. He spoke German, and early in the war was drafted into the Balkan section of the Secret Intelligence Service and sent to Turkey. His duties took him to Yugoslavia and Bulgaria and he was in Sofia when the Germans took over in March 1941. He managed to escape and returned to flying with 73 Squadron in North Africa. In July that year the squadron was ordered to carry out an ill-judged ground-strafing mission against targets east of Tobruk. Of the six aircraft that took part in the raid only one returned. Crawley was brought down by ground fire and crash-landed in the middle of a company of German soldiers.

While he was being escorted to Germany by train a soldier showed him a copy of the *Berliner Illustrirte Zeitung* magazine. To his horror there was a picture of himself on the front cover, accompanied by a story describing him as a great explosives expert and dangerous British spy who had been planting bombs all over Sofia before being smuggled out. Mercifully his stubble and battleworn appearance meant he bore little resemblance to the smooth fellow in the photograph.[1]

Crawley, then, was a professional, and brought considerable experience and expertise to the job. Any information that had a bearing on the kriegies' situation was his domain. By the beginning of 1943 he had managed to build up a comprehensive intelligence network that would have impressed his old masters. He relied primarily on the human touch, recruiting a team of ten officers who were called 'traders', charged with obtaining information and also useful items. Most of them could speak German but also possessed the necessary patience, tact and powers of persuasion to exploit their contacts with the German and Polish guards and local workers who came to the camp every day to cook, clean and carry out building work and repairs. 'The "trader" gained a "contact" by chatting with him in a quiet corner and offering him a cigarette or piece of chocolate,' the camp history reported. 'Once the contact proved to be helpfully disposed, the trader would ask him for some innocuous item such as glue, ostensibly for making a bedside cupboard or shelf, for which he would pay handsomely in cigarettes, chocolate or any other commodity.' After a while they would ask for less innocent seeming goods. By then the contact was compromised and open to blackmail. The traders found, though, that 'this rarely was necessary'.[2]

Crawley could not resist using the system to disseminate some black propaganda among the camp staff. He sifted BBC bulletins and German newspapers for items likely to undermine morale. By the end of 1942 it was becoming difficult for the Germans to disguise the extent of their setback at Stalingrad. Crawley briefed the traders, who shared the bad news with their contacts. It rippled satisfyingly through the enemy ranks and was often amplified and repeated back to the traders as original information. Prisoners thought they detected a slump in the guards' morale. It certainly had the effect of making some of their contacts even more inclined to cooperate.

By subtle human manipulation the escape-organization officers were thus able to acquire an extraordinary range of useful kit. Their contacts supplied them with clothing, badges and military insignia. They got their hands on specimen documents from which to produce forgeries, train timetables and maps. The traders also gleaned information about the layouts of Schubin and nearby Bromberg and details of railways, airfields and barracks. Prisoners leaving the camp to pick up deliveries of mail from the station were briefed by Crawley on what to look out for, and interrogated on their return. Those who were sufficiently sick to merit treatment in Bromberg hospital were quizzed about what they had seen.

All this material was of immense help to the latrine-tunnel team as they considered their onward strategy once they had emerged from the tunnel. In Stalag Luft III two schools of thought had emerged about the best way of travelling. One favoured moving in the open, making maximum use of public transport, and staying in cheap hotels. The second, the 'hard-arses', believed in footslogging, lying up by day and walking at night, making every effort to avoid human contact.

The first method was less risky than it sounded. In Germany, the trains were packed with shabby, submissive men who spoke neither Polish nor German, part of the army of 9 or 10 million foreign workers drafted in to run the war economy. The important thing was to not stand out. For that the escaper needed certain essential knowledge about the way things were done. For example, Crawley's intelligence service learned that railway passengers were allowed to sleep in station waiting rooms, but if they didn't have a ticket they would be arrested.

Schubin was well placed for rail connections. Bromberg was only a three-hour train journey to Danzig. In the minds of many kriegies, Danzig was the gateway to freedom. Most of the air force prison camps were closer to the Baltic than to any of Germany's other frontiers, and the ports were full of craft sailing to and from neutral Sweden. From Danzig there was a ferry service to Stockholm and the quays were lined with cargo ships flying the Swedish flag.

Thanks to the efforts of Crawley's traders, the escape-intelligence organization had obtained maps from German and Polish sources. They covered the surrounding area and also big centres like Warsaw and Danzig. The original maps were copied and duplicated using ink from boiled-down indelible pencils, and paper from the exercise books which were on sale in the camp canteen.[3]

Danzig was an outpost of Germany. It had been separated from the Fatherland by the provisions of the Treaty of Versailles, and Hitler had used the alleged mistreatment of the German population as one of his pretexts for going to war with Poland. In early 1943 it was back in the German fold, but among the population were many enemies of the Reich, including members of the Polish underground and French workers and prisoners of war.

Several weeks before the latrine-tunnel breakout, those who would be taking part were given an initial intelligence briefing by Crawley on the general situation and the options that were open to them. The men, wrote Crowley, 'many of them wearing beards and most of them showing signs of fatigue and strain, would crowd into one of the small lecture rooms of a wooden hut.'

> In front of them was a blackboard and on the wall a map...
> On one side of the blackboard was a plan of the camp and
> its surroundings and on the other some sketches of clouds or
> a genealogical tree, so that if a German came into the hut
> the 'brief' could turn at once into a lecture on navigation or
> ancient history.[4]

Crawley's intelligence was supplemented from some details provided by Harry Day. He had acquired it in tragic circumstances. Crawley had deputed a young pilot, Flying Officer Peter Lovegrove, who had been the only survivor when his Manchester bomber was shot down over Hamburg in April 1942, to help draw up maps of the local area.[5] One day Lovegrove received some bad news from home. He climbed to the top of the White House where Harry Day had his office and shortly afterwards his body was found on the ground below. The Germans allowed him to be buried with full military honours in a nearby church and Day was in attendance. During the excursion he was able to reconnoitre many of the details that Lovegrove had been trying to map. An RAF document lists his death as due to 'fall from window'.[6] There was an obvious explanation. Even someone as resilient as Bill admitted that 'there were few of us who did not at least think about suicide at some point in our captivity.'[7]

As spring approached, though, spirits among the latrine-tunnel team were high. By the end of February the newly aligned tunnel was almost under the wire and the preparations for their onward flight were intensifying. The camp tailors were busy running up civilian clothing. Most of the escapers would be passing themselves off as foreign workers so would require only low-quality garments. The work of providing them was done by the Escape Clothing Department, which had been set up in September 1942. It was now under the control of Flight Lieutenant J. W. G. Paget, who oversaw a team of nine amateur tailors.

The material they had to work with was not promising. The British government sent out uniforms via the Red Cross. Surplus items were kept in the Red Cross store in the camp, along with blankets, towels and sheets. Prisoners also received pullovers and suchlike in personal parcels from family and friends. Back in November, Day had asked Paget and his men to use the material to provide civilian escape clothing for forty prisoners.[8] Tunics were modified to make jackets. The top pockets and lower pocket flaps were removed and the fabric shaved with a razor blade to make it look worn. They were then rubbed with chalk to make them a lighter blue or dyed a different colour.

The Czech airman Josef Bryks was the most successful of the traders and had managed to persuade Polish contacts to supply large quantities of fabric dye. The clothing was boiled up in dixies borrowed from the kitchens in the camp washhouse. The same process was applied to trousers and service great-coats. Civilian buttons obtained from Polish workers were used whenever possible.

Each blanket could be turned into ten flat caps, with peaks stiffened by cardboard from Red Cross boxes. Kitbags were easily converted into haversacks. The pressing was done with an iron made from a Red Cross cake tin filled with hot sand.

The finished clothing was stored in empty beer barrels from the camp canteen, which the carpenters fitted with false bottoms. Elaborate precautions were taken to give the team enough warning, when ferrets were on the prowl, to hide drying garments and remove all traces of the dye. Despite all the intense activity, the Germans discovered nothing.

Even the most authentic clothing was no protection against German bureaucracy. Everywhere they conquered, the Nazis instituted an elaborate system of passes and identity cards to control their new subjects. Any escaper – and particularly those travelling by rail – needed a full set of the appropriate papers if he was to stand any chance of surviving the frequent checks. A ten-man forgery department had been set up in October 1942, under the control of Squadron Leader Dudley Craig. He decided that, rather than deal with the needs of each escape bid as it came up, he would build up a stockpile of standard documentation, based on originals obtained from sympathetic Poles or borrowed from compromised guards. He divided his department into three sections. One dealt with passes. They forged *Ausweis* identity cards covering a variety of different categories from originals obtained from Polish and German sources, and faked travel permits to go with them. All the documents were left blank for names and dates to be inserted just before departure.

A second section produced headed notepaper for letters purporting to be from firms on whose behalf the holder was ostensibly travelling. The contents would match the cover story the escaper was intending to use on his travels. The paper was embossed and varnished and carried telephone numbers and the names of directors gleaned from advertisements in the German newspapers.

The tools of forgery came from a variety of sources. The forgers persuaded – or blackmailed – a tame German to fill in the entries on some of the passes on a typewriter in the *Kommandantur*. Otherwise the writing was faked with a fine brush and paint, a long and laborious task. The paper, card, inks, pens and brushes for the tasks were acquired from 'contacts' or from the camp education section. Stamps were fashioned from boot-heel rubber and seals from painted paper, elaborately cut out with a razor.

Without photographs, the passes were useless. What pictures the prisoners had of themselves tended to show them in service uniform, and if cropped too closely would arouse suspicion. The problem of how to produce new ones seemed likely to defeat even the kriegies' boundless ingenuity. Once again the Poles came to the rescue. A Polish prisoner who had been flying with the RAF when shot down knew a girl who lived near Schubin. Through one of the local workers he managed to get a message to her explaining the situation. She provided the contact with a camera and films which were smuggled into the camp. Photographs were taken of each member of the escape team dressed in his getaway clothes. The camera and films were then returned to the girl. She developed and printed the film overnight, sending the photographs back to the camp next morning. This unknown heroine did all this in the knowledge that discovery would mean death.

The effort, skill and risk involved in producing the paperwork was enormous, and great care was taken to safeguard the results. Some were placed in tightly sealed tins and buried in the gardens. Others were sewn in to medicine balls supplied by the Red Cross or the YMCA.

For the 'hard-arses' who chose to walk to freedom, one piece of kit was essential. Two prisoners were charged with manufacturing compasses and managed to produce quite serviceable ones from unlikely materials. The cases were made from washbasin plugs, the tops from broken glass and the needles from razor blades which had been rubbed on magnets.

Everyone would take at least a few days supply of food. The 'mixture' of chocolate, sugar, oatmeal and other high-energy fare devised by David Lubbock in Stalag Luft III had become the standard escapers' food. Lubbock had moved to Schubin in the autumn of 1942 and was once again put in charge of nutrition. Amassing the ingredients was made easier by a system called 'food-acco', which operated in the camp from November 1942. This enabled prisoners to exchange unwanted food from their Red Cross parcel for something they preferred. The profit in kind that resulted from these transactions was handed over to the escape food department.

The breakout was set for early March. As the date approached, some alarming intelligence arrived from London. The prisoners stayed in contact with the authorities at home via letters carrying coded messages, sent back and forth between the camp and an organization called IS9. Intelligence School 9 was set up in January 1942 under the control of the War Office. Its purpose was to help British and Commonwealth soldiers and airmen caught behind enemy lines to evade capture. It was also tasked with providing escape materials to prisoners of war and gathering and imparting intelligence. IS9 was hampered by a lack of resources and was resented by MI6 and the Special Operations Executive, who felt it was poaching on their territory. It nonetheless managed to communicate with the camps via an efficient system of coded letters. Designated prisoners would write to their families, passing on in code whatever information the camp intelligence service had gathered. IS9 operatives would then insert messages into the families' replies. In 1943 nearly a thousand coded letters were sent from London to camps in Europe. More than 3,500 messages were received by IS9 during the same period.[9]

The organization also sent escape material hidden in welfare packages. They decided against using Red Cross parcels, which would have breached the Geneva Convention and invited reprisals. Instead they invented fictitious charities, such as the 'Lancashire Penny Fund', which despatched comforts, board games and the like, some of which contained compasses, maps, forged passes and local currency. The organization's operatives revelled in devising ingenious hiding places. A consignment of Christmas crackers contained maps, and a batch of shaving soap contained compasses. Some of the contraband was useful, some less so. What was particularly welcome was money, and in 1943 the organization would smuggle 147,200 Reichsmarks to the camps.

As the countdown began for the escape, Day received a message via coded letter from IS9, warning him that the Germans were planning to move all the inhabitants of Schubin back to Stalag Luft III. If true, this was very bad news. Unless they acted quickly, all the effort expended on the latrine project would be in vain.

There was no time to lose. The tunnel was due to be finished on 3 March. They decided to make the break two days later, when there would be virtually no moon. Once the date had been set, the air of unreality that invariably hung over tunnelling projects evaporated. The enterprise project had buoyed the spirits of all who took part in it throughout the long, hard winter, offering the prospect of deliverance. But to some, the digging and the shoring and the endless subterfuges to outwit the ferrets were more of a therapy than a practical exercise. 'It seemed impossible that it would ever lead to an escape,' wrote Robert Kee. 'No one really thought about that very much. It was all just a daily routine to be worked through.'[10]

Now the moment had arrived. On the eve of the big day the air was charged with excitement tinged with apprehension. Tommy Calnan, who arrived back at his barrack after two weeks in hospital recovering from appendicitis, just in time to take his place, recognized the atmosphere immediately: 'It reminded me of the briefing room before a big operation,' he wrote. 'Part fear, part excitement, with the inevitable reaction on stomach and temper.'[11]

The escapers had had plenty of time to think about what they were going to do once they left the tunnel. Calnan suspected that some had not really devoted much attention to the realities of life on the run. Too many were 'suffering from wire psychosis. They had a compelling impulse to get outside the fence. At that point, however, their thinking stopped. From then on it was a matter of luck and providence. They had no plans.'[12]

Almost everyone felt the need to travel with someone else. Bill was one of many who had experienced the loneliness of wandering enemy territory alone, without a companion to buttress morale and fight off despair. Over the last weeks and days, by the mysterious processes of human chemistry, most people were now paired off.

Bill and Eddie Asselin had spent months side by side clawing at the Polish subsoil. It seemed right that they should continue together. As the spearhead of the tunnel team it also seemed just that they should be first in the queue of escapers. The rest would have to draw lots. The number of those going had expanded. Day had decided that for services rendered to kriegiedom, another eight, nominated by the escape committee, were to be included. This provoked some initial grumbling from Calnan and others but was eventually accepted with reasonably good grace. One way or another the late additions had earned their place. They included Jimmy Buckley, the chairman of the escape committee, who devoted all his waking hours to the job, Johnny Dodge, the veteran kriegie who had jumped off the train on the way to Schubin, and Day himself, who was bringing along Dudley Craig, the genius behind the forgery department, as his escape partner.

Calnan conceded that Day's presence brought moral authority to the enterprise. 'Daily and relentlessly he fought the Germans with the few weapons he could use,' he wrote. 'Escape was the most telling weapon he had. Coming out of the tunnel with us was both a gesture of defiance and a declaration of war.'[13]

Apart from the main organizers, who were guaranteed a place at the front, the order in which people lined up in the tunnel would be decided by drawing names from a hat. The nearer the front the better, for it increased your chances of getting away before the alarm was raised and reduced the time spent in suffocating darkness awaiting your turn to creep forward.

As the hours ticked away the escapers tried on their civilian outfits and checked their identity passes and paperwork. As well as the forged documentation they would also be carrying their identity discs, well hidden but ready to be produced if they fell into the hands of the Gestapo. The slim wafer could mean the difference between life and death. Without it they would have no proof that they were combatants protected by the Geneva Convention, and would be liable to be shot as spies. There was time still to run over plans. It did not do to reflect too hard on their defects, for it was too late to change them now.

Bill and Eddie had decided to head for Warsaw, where they hoped to make contact with the Polish underground. They would travel by foot, trusting that if they were detected by the local people they would not be given away. Bill already had good reason to trust in the kindness of strangers from his experiences in France. He also knew very well the risks those who helped him had run. The Germans had even fewer scruples about how to deal with Poles who helped their enemies than they did towards the French. It was a sobering thought amid all the bubbling excitement.

Paddy Barthropp was another 'hard-arse'. He would be travelling with an old comrade, Wilf Wise. Like Ash and Asselin they were heading to Warsaw. Their plan was certainly ambitious. 'We had learned, via the grapevine, a Heinkel III had force-landed in Yugoslavia and was in the hands of General Draža Mihailović, leader of the Chetniks, a patriotic partisan group,' he wrote. 'The plan was for six of us, moving in pairs, to make our way to Warsaw to be handed down through the underground movement and to fly the aircraft to the Middle East.'[14]

Aidan Crawley had opted for the train. He believed that self-assurance was the best protection and had adopted the role of a travelling engineer working for the giant German steel company Krupp, an imposture given substance by a beautifully forged letter. His companion for the first part of the escape was Flying Officer Stevens. That was not his real name. He had been born a Jew in Germany and had joined the RAF after his family fled to Britain.

Tommy Calnan's first choice had been Tony Barber, a fellow photo-reconnaissance pilot from RAF Benson, who had been shot down over France the year before and who he regarded as being exceptionally resourceful and determined. Barber, though, had set his mind on heading for Denmark, where he had close relatives. Calnan was equally bent on going west to

Switzerland or France, in the hope of finding his way eventually to Spain. Neither would budge and Calnan fell back on Robert Kee, who had 'all the qualities and talents which a successful escaper needed. Nothing took him by surprise and he was never at a loss for an answer… with his fluent German I had no doubt at all that he would be able to dominate any conversation, even with a suspicious German policemen.'[15] Calnan was henceforth Tomasso Calabresi, an Italian technician also employed by Krupp. The burns he had sustained to his face after being shot down would explain why he was not in uniform and doing his bit for the Axis. The cover story was that had been invalided out of the Italian army after his tank was hit by British artillery in North Africa. Kee would be his French sidekick.

There were bursts of nervous hilarity as they checked out each other's escape gear. The tailoring department had done a superb job. Out of tunics, trousers, blankets and sheets they had fashioned a range of outfits to cover the roles that the escapers were playing, from engineer to itinerant labourer. They were a little threadbare, perhaps, but that in itself gave them a patina of authenticity. It was wartime and most people not in uniform looked shabby.

At lunchtime on 5 March the draw was made for the line-up in the tunnel. Like Bill Ash and Eddie Asselin, Bill Palmer and Charles Marshall were exempted, and would be third and fourth in line. When it was over and everybody had their number, Marshall stepped forward to detail the arrangements. The final *Appell* was at five o'clock, when the inmates would have to line up outside their barracks to be counted. Lights out, when everyone had to be back inside, was not until 7 p.m., however. That gave the escapers time to drift down to the *Abort* in groups of four at ten-minute intervals so as not to arouse attention.

Marshall's authoritative voice laid out the orders. Knapsacks and attaché cases were to be delivered to the *Abort* before the final *Appell* for storage in the entrance chamber to the tunnel. They were to wear their escape clothes hidden beneath a greatcoat, which was to be discarded on arrival at the *Abort* and carried back by one of those who were staying behind. Cases were to be pushed in front when crawling along the tunnel. Marshall asked Asselin if he had anything to add to the instructions. Asselin had. Some of the escapers had been engaged in other duties and had yet to experience the tunnel. It was not going to be easy inching along it fully dressed and pushing a bag. The technique was to fight your way along with your toes, knees and elbows. What they emphatically were not to do was to grab at the shoring planks for leverage. A dislodged strut could bring the whole tunnel down killing everyone. He signed off with a cheery 'See you in Shepherds!' – a reference to a London club popular with aircrew.

Soon after the afternoon *Appell*, Bill and Eddie strolled from their barrack down to the *Abort*. As dusk descended, the camp seemed its normal self. On the sports field a rugby game was in progress, a kriegie international, England vs. Australia. The shouts and grunts faded and the muddied players made their way back to their blocks, passing the small, innocuous knots of men wandering through the dusk. Inside the *Abort*, Bill went through the familiar routine for the last time. Up came the lid of the lavatory bench. He ducked through the hole, inhaling once again the stench rising from the morass below, disengaged the brick hatch and pushed it inside. He reached for the handles under the bench, lowered himself down and jack-knifed through the hole and into the chamber.

NINE

S oon the chamber was crowded with bodies as the first batch of escapers clambered in. The margarine lamps gave off an orange light, casting gigantic shadows over the walls. Many of the escapers were wearing dyed black combinations to protect their civilian clothing. It looked to Tommy Calnan like a 'scene from Dante's inferno'. He made his way over to Eddie Asselin, who was preparing to squeeze his broad ice-hockey player's shoulders into the entrance of the shaft. 'Good luck, Eddie,' he told him. 'I hope you make it home. I'll buy you dinner at Prunier's in a week's time.'[1] Asselin managed a smile. He seemed nervous. 'That'll be the day,' he replied. Then, after urging Calnan to see that he 'got plenty of air', he disappeared into the black maw of the tunnel, followed closely by Bill and the first escapers in the queue.

In the chamber Calnan and Kee were working the air pump, pushing it back and forth like demented oarsmen. Then more feet were swinging through the chamber entrance and it was their turn to go. Up at the front, Bill and Eddie wriggled towards the tunnel's distant end, pushing their luggage before them. Although strict silence had been ordered they could hear the grunts and curses of the human chain crawling nose to toe behind them. By about 7.30 the tunnel was full up, with twenty-six men stretched along its length. Another half a dozen waited in the chamber. The last part of the operation was the most risky. Bill knew very well that potential catastrophe was awaiting them. Tunnel collapses were an occupational hazard, but in normal circumstances if the shoring was sound there was no great cause of alarm, for it was a relatively easy matter for one or two men to dig themselves out. This was different. 'With the men lying head to toe all the way back behind us, even a slight tunnel collapse would mean the end,' he wrote. 'It would take hours for each man to wriggle backwards, allowing the one ahead to do the same.' In that case only those nearest the entrance stood any chance of getting out alive. The rest would face a slow death by asphyxiation.[2]

Tommy Calnan was also feeling a mounting sense of alarm. It was pitch black and a boot in the face told him he had caught up with the man in front. His shoulders were scraping the walls on either side and if he raised his head an inch it hit the roof. He felt the first stirrings of claustrophobia.

I tried not to think of the tons of sand above me, supported only by flimsy pieces of wood. But the closed-in feeling was growing. The absolute darkness, the physical impossibility of making any but the slightest movement, and worst of all, the knowledge that any retreat was completely blocked by the long line of men lying behind me, all these sensations were beginning to strain my self-control to the limit.[3]

Robert Kee, lying behind him, had a different anxiety.

I found myself listening in the darkness to my heart beating against the packed earth of the floor, clutching an attaché case filled with escape food and fingering a pocketful of false papers, but still not really believing that I should escape... Somehow I was sure that the alarm would be given before anyone had got away and we should all be hauled ignominiously out again.[4]

Either that or they would be spotted when they emerged from the tunnel. 'There would be a shot, a thumping of heavy boots down the path over our heads and then, provided that the guards did not start more shooting, fourteen days solitary in the "cooler".'

The minutes crawled past and turned into hours. Calnan's incipient panic had subsided now. 'The familiar touch of the wooden shoring frames and of the damp sand on which I was lying again became ordinary and reassuring sensations. My exaggerated fears dissolved and, after a while I was able to doze with my head resting on my forearms.'[5]

At the front, Bill and Eddie worked carefully, driving the tunnel upwards at a shallow angle. It was essential that they broke through the topsoil at exactly the right point, so they would emerge in the slight fold in the ground fifteen yards from the wire. Lying in the dip were some clamps, mounds of earth used to store potatoes over the winter. They scraped away, piling the sandy soil in a pit they had dug in the tunnel floor, as there was no possibility of passing it back down the line. Excavating upwards was more difficult than burrowing horizontally, and progress was slow. They also had to fit boards to the side of the exit shaft to prevent it collapsing as the escapers kicked and levered their way out.

None of these preparations was appreciated by those behind them. The orders were for strict silence, but complaints and queries began to ripple up and down the line. 'From behind me whispered messages were being passed from man to man,' wrote Tommy Calnan.

'What the hell's gone wrong?'

'When are we going to break?'

'For Christ's sake, hurry it up or the last ones won't be out before daylight.'

Only one message came back from the face and it was rudely unhelpful. '—— well shut up and keep pumping.'[6]

The air was piped straight to the men doing the digging at the front, who needed it most. It was hardly the sweetest, being sucked from the chamber next to the pit. It was better, though, than the deoxygenated fug which was all that the men in the tunnel had to breathe. Anxiety about a collapse alternated with fear of suffocation. How much more of this could they endure?

By now Ash and Asselin were close enough to the surface to hear the tread of the guards' boots as they passed overhead. The sound was alarming yet inspiring, a harbinger of the world outside the wire. There were only inches to go. Eddie raised his arm and with a triumphant shove of his homemade trowel broke through to the surface. It was a great moment for both of them. 'The scent of living plants joined the wonderful rush of fresh cold air which will forever be linked in my mind to the smell of freedom,' Bill remembered. 'Men further back along the tunnel gasped and gulped in great lungfuls of it. We had reached the outside world.'[7]

To those inside the tunnel the draught of pure, clean oxygen was as intoxicating as a tankard of cold champagne. 'As I crawled forward I smelled the fresh air,' wrote Calnan. 'It was now coming back from the face in a strong current. I filled my lungs breathing deeply.' There was no need to pass any progress reports back down the line now, for 'everybody could smell the cold air of freedom'.[8]

But they were not out yet. Cautiously, Eddie cut away the roots and shoots around the hole, handing them back to Bill who trampled them into the dirt. Then, slowly, he pushed his head out into the night. They were exactly where they were supposed to be, bang in the middle of the dip and next to a potato clamp. Footsteps sounded near the wire. Eddie froze as a guard came into view. The German strolled complacently past, silhouetted against the wire which was lit up by lights which, mercifully, all pointed inwards on the camp. As the guard's footsteps faded, Eddie scrambled through the hole. Then it was Bill's turn. He had just poked his head through when the guard turned back on the return leg of his patrol. Bill waited, afraid to make any sudden movement, feeling that his head must seem as big and obvious as a pumpkin. But the guard strolled past oblivious and then Bill was scrabbling through the hole and crawling commando-style into the cover provided by the hump of a potato clamp. Beyond it lay a field that sloped downward away from the camp, and two hundred yards or so further on stood a wood. 'The silence held and I waited for the right moment to make a last terrifying dash into the trees,' he remembered. 'I scurried forward, half-crouching, half-running.' It seemed that 'every footstep sounded like someone dropping an entire set of crockery, and every twig snap sounded like a rifle being cocked to finish me off.'[9] But then he was inside the welcome darkness of the wood, where Eddie was waiting for him, still panting with exertion. There was no time to see how the others were faring. Once they caught their breath they were off.

Back in the tunnel the exhilaration the others had felt at the breakthrough was beginning to fade. Forward progress was spasmodic, and after each man exited there was an agonizing wait for those behind as the next one struggled to haul himself out. They were desperate to leave and the flurry of each departure sent more earth tumbling back in, so that by the time Robert Kee got there the exit 'drew elegantly narrower' like 'a bottle of hock lying on its side'.[10]

He was number fourteen in the queue. When he poked his head out, the guard was still oblivious of the drama taking place a few yards from his jackboots. Kee waited as he ambled past, humming to himself and stamping his feet. When he made his move, his shoulders got wedged in the hole. He tried again, this time poking his arms through first, but his waist would not go through. It did not help that he was wearing a thick, cut-down overcoat, and the pockets were stuffed with escape rations.

He now realized that he had left his attaché case behind him. He dropped back into the tunnel, retrieved it and started the whole process again. The entrance was too narrow, even for a skinny man like himself. As he wriggled and kicked the guard came into view again. Kee became frantic. Finally he dragged himself clear just as the guard came level with him. He lay dead still, pressed to the ground, and the guard strolled harmlessly by. He was whistling now. Kee waited a minute or two then set off, half-crawling, half-scurrying through the potato clamps and into a ditch. He dared to turn back for a last glance. The camp looked smaller now, and 'seemed to hang in the darkness on the chain of lights which shone at regular intervals all around it'.

He picked himself up and set off again in a crouching run across the two hundred yards of open ground to the wood. In the feeble moonlight he could see others doing the same. They reminded him of 'soldiers of the '14–'18 war, going over the top'.

When he reached the wood he could hear voices calling out, trying to locate their partners. There was no sign of Tommy Calnan. Just as he was despairing of ever finding him, Calnan emerged out of the field and collapsed in an exhausted heap. Only a few days before he had been in a hospital bed recovering from appendicitis. Kee, though, was anxious to press on. In his account of the episode he fictionalized Calnan as 'Sammy' and described the incident thus:

'Let's go,' I said to Sammy.
   'When I've got my breath back.'

'The sooner we put some distance between us and the camp the better.'

'I quite agree, but I can't do that without any breath, can I?'[11]

At that moment Kee 'realized the strain that was going to be placed on our partnership. Our fate and actions were now linked together as closely as those of Siamese twins and every decision contained a potential quarrel.' It was the same for all of them. Most preferred not to travel alone. The solace of companionship, though, could easily sour and old friendships would be tested to the limit in the times ahead.

By half past midnight all thirty-two escapers were clear of the tunnel. The last man out was Harry Day. The night was cold and silent, undisturbed by shouts, gunshots or blaring klaxons. It looked as if it would take until morning *Appell* before the alarm was raised. They had eight hours to put as much distance as they could between them and the camp.

They would be heading to all points of the compass. Bill and Eddie's plan had been worked out over many hours and was based on what intelligence they could glean from Crawley's briefings and their own analysis of the geomilitary situation. They both discounted the Baltic route. Once the breakout was discovered the first thing the Germans would do would be to redouble the already formidable security at the ports. They planned to move southwards, hoping that the enemy would be less alert to escapers travelling in an unexpected direction. They were heading to Warsaw in the hope of making contact with the Polish underground in the city. Like Paddy Barthropp they hoped that the Poles would help to pass them to Yugoslavia, where they would join up with Mihailović and the Chetniks. 'We intended then either to remain with him or if possible be evacuated through the Adriatic,' Asselin told his intelligence debriefer after the war.[12]

Calnan and Kee set off north for Bromberg, intending to take trains westward, with the ultimate aim of getting to France and from there across the Pyrenees. Calnan had made a study of train times with information gleaned from German newspapers, and had drawn up a schedule which he believed would get them out of Germany in the shortest possible time. Aidan Crawley had decided to travel solo, by train west to Berlin then south to Cologne and Innsbruck, from where he would attempt to cross the border into Switzerland. Tony Barber was heading to the Baltic with the intention of finding a passage to the Danish island of Bornholm, where his mother's family lived.

By morning Bill and Eddie had covered more than fourteen miles. They would have got further were it not for the marshy terrain, and the fact that they had to stay clear of roads and houses, knowing that there was a 9 p.m. curfew in place and any movement would raise suspicion. Before dawn they took shelter in a wood and fell into an exhausted sleep.

It was 5 March, almost a year since Bill had been shot down. Sleeping on a bed of leaf mulch was nothing new to him. It was how he had spent his nights on the first days after the crash. He was better prepared now. He and Eddie had a map and compass, a few days supply of food and some cash. Their clothes were rough and ready, made from cut-down uniforms and dyed blankets, but that did not matter too much in a land where many of the men were dressed like scarecrows. They had come to accept, though, that if they relied on their own resources alone they were bound to fail. If they were to make it to Warsaw, sooner or later they would have to seek the help of the local population.

Calnan and Kee planned to cover the sixteen miles to Bromberg in time to catch the 6 a.m. train heading west to the town of Schneidemühl (Piła to the Poles). That was a reasonable ambition, providing there were no setbacks or diversions. Taking their course from their compass, they would head north-east until they hit the railway line, then follow it to Bromberg station. Calnan noted warily that Kee was 'eager and energetic'. He knew he would have trouble keeping up. Walking on a moonless night across unknown territory proved much more difficult than it had seemed when they were drawing up their plan. They 'fell into ditches, walked into fences, tripped over logs and startled a number of animals out of their wits. Frequently we frightened ourselves.'[13] At one point Kee plunged chest-deep into a pond. The mishap only spurred him on, but Calnan had the compass and he was forced to wait for him to catch up, teeth chattering in the cold.

They reached the railway two hours after setting out, and their spirits rose. It was now simply a matter of walking in a straight line along the permanent way to their destination. But as other escapees had found before them, following a railway track was more difficult than it seemed. The space between the sleepers was just short of a normal stride, so they could never hit a regular marching rhythm. Calnan was feeling the effects of his illness and after a few hours he was exhausted.

They tried resting for five minutes in each hour but he fell further and further behind. They finally arrived in Bromberg at 7.30 a.m. The train to Schneidemühl had long gone. The town was wide awake. It was the first time on their journey that they had come across other people, and it seemed to them that every eye was upon them and everyone must know immediately who they were.

Aidan Crawley had a definite destination when he emerged from the tunnel. He was friendly with a Polish officer called Alexis Kowalski, who gave him the address of some relations living near Bromberg who, he believed, would harbour him for a day or two. He was well kitted-out in an overcoat, cardigan, plus fours made from blankets, and a felt trilby obtained from one of the guards. He had 200 Reichsmarks, which was a good supply of cash, and plenty of escape 'mixture' in his suitcase. He walked all night without encountering anyone except a boisterous Alsatian dog. He caught a few hours sleep before dawn then went on his way, passing through a small village. A man eyed him knowingly then spoke to him in French. 'The next time you spend a night in the forest you must clean the sand off your back,' he told him, and proceeded to do it for him. It seemed like a good omen. He thanked him and carried on walking.[14]

Tony Barber was eighteenth out of the tunnel. He was well turned out in an air-force raincoat that could easily pass for a civilian one and had forged papers identifying him as a Danish *Freiwilliger* – a volunteer worker – a role he was able to carry off since he had learned the language from his mother. He had managed to get a swastika lapel badge from one of the guards, an adornment that would come in very useful. He also had a good supply of Reichsmarks, which had been sent into Schubin in a phoney relief parcel by IS9. His plan was to catch a train from Bromberg back to Schneidemühl, then get a connection to take him to the Baltic port of Kolberg. From there he could catch a ferry to the Danish island of Bornholm to shelter with his relatives. He was sure they would be able to arrange for a fishing boat to take him to Sweden. Back in the camp he had made friends with a prisoner known to the Germans as John Thompson but in reality Jørgen Thalbitzer, a 22-year-old Dane who had escaped from Denmark in December 1940 and made his way via South Africa to Britain, where he joined the RAF. He was shot down during a cross-Channel operation in July 1942. They had discussed travelling together but in the end Barber had decided to go it alone and Thalbitzer teamed up with Jimmy Buckley.

By the morning Barber was sure he had made the right decision. He arrived in Bromberg after walking along the railway line. To play his part he needed to keep neat and tidy, a good Danish Nazi who took a proper pride in his appearance. After tidying up his clothes and giving his muddy shoes a polish with the brush and cloth he had brought with him for the purpose, he looked convincing enough as walked into the station. He had enough money to ask for a return ticket, which he believed would look less suspicious than buying a single. Nevertheless, 'it was with some trepidation that I went up to the ticket office and said: "*Schneidemühl, hin und zurück, bitte*" [a round-trip ticket to Schneidemühl, please].'[15] The clerk took the note and pushed the tickets under the glass. Barber thanked him and strolled out onto the platform. Everything was going very well.

Paddy Barthropp and Wilf Wise intended to cover twenty miles before dawn broke, a march that would take them over the river Oder. They managed it quite comfortably. With dawn streaking the sky they looked around for somewhere to shelter and sleep. The only possibility was a stone quarry, which seemed to have been abandoned. It was hardly ideal but it would have to do. They dug themselves a burrow out of the loose shale and fell asleep immediately.

Back at Schubin, the morning began as any other. At 8 a.m. the prisoners filed out of the barrack blocks and lined up in files of five for morning *Appell*. There was no possibility of disguising the huge holes in the kriegies' ranks. The number of escapers had increased overnight. Three more officers had decided earlier that morning to take advantage of the tunnel before it was filled in. Josef Bryks had also put his plan to exit the camp via the honeywagon into practice. Dressed in protective overalls and wearing gauze masks soaked in disinfectant, he and Squadron Leader B. G. Morris had climbed into the cleaned-out sewage tank and been driven through the gates by the Polish contractor and taken to a local farmhouse, where they were given shelter.

At first Simms thought that the prisoners must be playing a practical joke and the missing men were hidden somewhere in the camp. When it became clear that they had gone the klaxons sounded and the compound echoed to angry shouts and barking dogs. It took the Germans a while to find the tunnel exit. The next thing was to discover the entrance. A Russian prisoner was ordered to tie a rope round his body then crawl back down the tunnel. When he finally scrambled into the chamber he alerted the guards by banging on the concrete underside of the latrine.

Shortly afterwards pickaxes crashed through the ceiling and the ingenious beauty of the latrine tunnel was exposed.

The large number involved in the escape made the Germans suspect that something more than a mere bid for freedom was involved. The idea began to gain ground that the breakout had been engineered from London. The authorities believed the prisoners planned to form a fighting cadre who would stay in place to direct an uprising by the Polish underground. The prisoners were long gone but it was nonetheless decided to reinforce the camp. At 11 a.m., busloads of SS troops arrived. After inspecting the tunnel exit they formed up and marched into the camp, to be greeted by derisive cheers from a crowd of delighted kriegies. The SS men turned them out of their barracks and began a search. The prisoners left them to it and went off to play football. The SS troops were new to the business of camp security. They made a half-hearted trawl through the barracks then moved on. They left undisturbed the rival tunnel started by Dickie Edge back in December, which had caused the escapers such concern. It now stretched forty feet from its starting point under a night latrine. Later that day the troops departed. German pride was hurting. The escape had made them look stupid and inefficient. Every effort was now directed at finding the escapers and returning them to captivity.

TEN

By noon thousands of soldiers, German militiamen and Hitler Youth were combing the countryside around the camp, prodding haystacks and searching barns in the hope of flushing out an Allied flier. All bridges and crossroads were guarded and motor and foot patrols roamed the roads. Police swarmed over the railway stations and train passengers were subjected to multiple identity checks. Frontier guards as far away as Belgium and Switzerland were warned to be extra vigilant and the Baltic ports were put on high alert. The wires hummed as images of the fugitives were transmitted to police stations and border posts.

Those who had chosen to escape on foot were finding that geography was against them. Warsaw, where most of the 'hard-arses' were heading, lay 180 miles to the south-east. The most direct road was on the far side of the Vistula, the bridges across which were heavily guarded. The alternative route meant zig-zagging along country lanes and trekking across fields. They had already learned how difficult it was to make progress that way. The chances of getting lost were high, and of detection even higher.

Bill and Eddie spent most of their first day of freedom hiding in a wood. As night fell they became aware of the hue and cry that had been raised by their departure. Beyond the cover of the trees, the area was crawling with Germans. The pair were forced to 'sit perfectly still as what seemed like half of Germany passed within a few feet of us, shouting and beating bushes, waving flashlights. When they had passed by we moved quietly on.'[1]

Despite the dangers the taste of liberty was intoxicating. 'The feeling you get from being free after so many months when the barbed wire at the edge of the camp represents the limits of your horizons is like no other freedom,' he wrote. 'Never before have I felt so alive.' There was also some satisfaction to be had from the sheer scale of the German effort to recapture them. Every soldier who was employed looking for fugitive airmen had been diverted from more useful war work, and there were thousands – perhaps tens of thousands – now engaged in the hunt. It made men who had been languishing impotently behind barbed wire feel that they were once again engaged in the battle against Hitler. Nonetheless the going was tough. Spring came late this far east and their improvised civilian clothing was little protection against the rain, wind and cold. That night they took shelter in a large barn, hoping that if they were discovered the owners would not turn them in. They did not have to worry. Over the next days they had several encounters with farmers and their families, who shared what food they had with men who they regarded as their allies in humanity. Bill and Eddie never knew the names of their saviours. They did not want to know. Bill understood what it was to undergo a Gestapo interrogation. If you knew nothing, there was nothing to give up if the blows and threats became too much. The truth was that the risk the escapers were taking did not compare with that embraced by any Polish civilian who took the decision to help them. Unless a POW was shot while making a run for it, he was unlikely at this stage to face anything worse than a spell in the cooler. For the Poles it meant interrogation, torture and the firing squad.

One night trek brought them to a wide river, a tributary of the Vistula. To get to Warsaw they would have to cross it. They followed the bank until they came to a road leading to a bridge that spanned the river. They knew the bridge would be guarded and for a while considered continuing along the bank on the chance of finding a quieter place to cross. It was a vain hope.

Neither of them could bear the thought of swimming across. They would have to take their chances on the bridge. There was one sentry posted at each end but they seemed to prefer the shelter of their sentry boxes, only occasionally emerging to march up and down in the cold.

They waited until both were back inside their boxes then scuttled to the parapet of the bridge, dropped to the ground and started to crawl. The night was silent. It seemed to them as they inched their way forward that their laboured breathing and the scrape of toecaps on tarmac must surely alert the sentries. But all remained quiet. As they approached the guard post on the far side, a bulky figure emerged. He walked over to the parapet and leant over. They both froze, struggling to control their breathing. He was no more than twenty feet away. It seemed impossible that he would not see them. The guard, though, seemed sunk in his own thoughts. After several minutes staring into the dark waters he turned away and disappeared back into his shelter. Bill and Eddie wriggled past and were swallowed up in the shadows on the far bank.

Since setting off, Paddy and Wilf had been having their own share of dramas. After an uncomfortable night in the quarry they stretched their stiff limbs and started out once again. They had given up on travelling in darkness and by the end of the day had abandoned the idea of walking altogether. On the afternoon of 7 March, after two clear days of travel, they reached the town which the Germans called Hohensalza and the Poles Inowrocław. It was only twenty-five miles south-east of Schubin. At this rate they would never make it to Warsaw. They began to think again. A main railway line ran through the town, going east to Warsaw and west to Posen (Poznań). They crept into the sidings and hid, looking for a goods train that was going in the direction of Warsaw. A locomotive was shunting a line of wagons with 'Kutno' chalked on the side. Their map told them that Kutno was about sixty miles to the south-east and well on the way to Warsaw. The train stopped and started, going back and forth as additional wagons were coupled up. They darted closer, waiting for the engine to stop long enough for them to climb aboard. The train kept moving off just as they approached, forcing them to dive back into cover. Eventually they were able to wrench open the doors of a wagon and scramble in. They sat back to enjoy the journey to Kutno.

Tommy Calnan and Robert Kee had bickered all the way to Bromberg. When they arrived at the station they were bickering still. Calnan had urged Kee to make sure he was wearing decent footwear when they made their escape. Kee had neglected the advice and as they entered the town, the sole of his boot had come unstuck and the pair attracted many curious looks as he flapped along. When they reached the station the booking hall was crowded. They felt less conspicuous now. Many of the passengers were as badly dressed as themselves. Calnan went to buy two tickets to Schneidemühl, seventy-five miles to the west, where, according to his study of the timetables, they could get an onward connection. The transaction went off easily.

There were several hours to wait before the train was due. They had no idea whether or not the alarm had yet been raised in Schubin, but it was best to be on the safe side. They decided to hide in the lavatories. They locked themselves into adjoining cubicles. A few minutes later Kee was startled to see a sheet of lavatory paper appear under the partition wall with a biscuit and a slice of cheese and a scrawled note: 'For the morale'. He accepted it gratefully and pushed a note back: 'Thanks'. Then he ate the biscuit and stared at the pornographic drawings on the wall. He was dog tired and fatigue made him gloomy. A phrase his grandmother was fond of kept echoing through his head: 'Where will it all end, my dear, where will it all end?'[2]

He 'began to be frightened in a new way, a way that was no longer either amusing or exciting… Perhaps it was because we were quite trapped if anything should go wrong… now I began to understand the full strength of our enemy. It was no longer just a matter of a few guards to be outwitted. A whole society was against us and for practical purposes that meant all society, the whole world.'

The main door of the lavatory swung open. They both heard the swish of a mop. Calnan was still munching his escape rations when the door of his cubicle rattled violently. Then it flew open. He 'stared aghast at a fat, dirty woman who stood there with a bucket and mop. She gave me a contemptuous look and slammed the door shut again.'[3] He felt more embarrassed being caught with his trousers up than down. It seemed a highly suspicious way to be occupying a public lavatory. Next it was Kee's turn. As the charlady shook the door he rustled the lavatory paper, hoping she would leave him alone, but the cleaner was having none of it. She stopped rattling the door and began kicking it. Kee and Calnan exited with as much dignity as they could muster and headed for the relative safety of the platform.

They sat down on a bench, willing the hands on the station clock to move faster. Kee read a newspaper. Calnan covertly observed the other passengers. One in particular caught his eye. He was 'wearing a neat blue-grey raincoat, carrying an attaché case and had a folded newspaper tucked under his arm. He looked like a superior bank clerk.' Calnan felt that there was 'something vaguely familiar about him'. It was only when he passed right by that he recognized him. It was Tony Barber.

Barber recognized him too but rapidly turned away. Some irrational impulse took hold of Calnan. 'I could not resist getting up to greet him. His look of panic when he saw me coming should have discouraged me, but I was enjoying the moment too much. I gave him a nicely casual Nazi salute and greeted him.

'"Heil Hitler," I said.'

Barber was forced to snap a salute in response. Calnan then shook his hand and told him how delighted he was to see him. He got a brusque response. "'Go to hell," said Tony. He was shaking with anger. "And stay away from me. You look like a tramp.'" Then, smiling and bowing, he retreated down the platform to make sure he was as far away as possible from Calnan and Kee. The Schneidemühl train arrived and they all got aboard.

Aidan Crawley's good luck was holding. He was still confident that he had taken the right decision in going it alone. On the afternoon of his first day of freedom he arrived at the house of the Polish family who he had been told were prepared to give him sanctuary. There were three of them. Pete Kowalski was a former cavalry officer who was active in the resistance. His wife Tanja was 'a loyal and delightful woman', who kept the farm going during his frequent absences. The couple had an 18-year-old daughter, Kate.[4] His hosts seemed unperturbed by the fact that German soldiers were billeted less than a mile away. They were heart-warmingly hospitable, feeding him and taking away his clothes to dry them. He spent the night in their barn and the next morning was directed to a bus stop from where he could get a bus to the town of Nakel (in Polish Nakło nad Notecią) sixteen miles from Bromberg. He spent the morning in the park while waiting for a train to take him to Schneidemühl. His papers identified him as a Sudeten German schoolteacher who was being transferred to Berlin. They were checked twice on the journey but the quality of the forgery and Crawley's excellent German were enough to satisfy the guard. It was clear that the alarm had been raised. As the train rocked along placidly he could see lines of soldiers moving methodically through fields at the side of the track like beaters at a pheasant shoot, scouring the land for escaped prisoners.

There was another wait at Schneidemühl for the next train westwards. Again he went off to the local park to kill time. It was full of people taking the air, including some German officers and their wives. He was wearing his RAF officer's greatcoat, suitably civilianized by the camp's tailors. 'My word that *is* a smart overcoat,' he heard one women say to her husband as they passed.[5] It was a light moment in an experience that was getting steadily darker for all the fugitives.

After four days living rough, Bill Ash and Eddie Asselin were exhausted, dirty and starving. Their escape rations had long gone. Occasionally they managed to beg food from farmhouses. They learned to avoid the more prosperous looking ones, knowing that the likelihood was that they were occupied by ethnic German families who had been settled in the area for centuries and would be delighted to turn them in. They were making very slow progress. They had stuck to the routine of lying up by day and walking by night, relying on their compass and maps to point them in the right direction. They followed deserted country roads when they could, taking to the fields to skirt villages. On the evening of Tuesday, 9 March they set off as usual and had been walking for five hours when they came to a railway crossing. It was very dark and quiet and there seemed to be no one around. They were about to follow the track when they heard footsteps behind them. They swung round to see a man pointing a rifle at them. He commanded them in German to stop. There was no chance of making a run for it. They raised their hands and prepared to trot out their rehearsed story. The man was a member of the local home guard. He had been posted at the railway crossing with specific orders

'If any spur had been needed to induce prisoners to escape… the bleakness of the surroundings would have provided it.' Stalag Luft III, Sagan, *c.* 1944.

Goon box.

Left: Robert Kee, 1951. Like several escapologists he went on to a brilliant post-war career.

Below: Wing Commander Harry Day provided the prisoners with outstanding leadership as they faced life behind the wire. Here, post-war, he briefs Kenneth Moore for his role as Douglas Bader in *Reach for the Sky* (1955).

Prisoners laying the foundations for a hut in Stalag Luft III.

Making themselves at home. Kriegies in a hut at Sagan in 1943.

The Germans were keen to advertise their correct behaviour. Cheerful co-operation between prisoners and camp staff is pointedly on display in this picture of the Red Cross parcel store.

Prisoners prepare a news sheet. Information about the progress of the war had a crucial effect on morale.

Gardening helped the days pass – and supplemented rations.

Prisoners attend an outdoor church service.

The veneer of correctness: an American airman who died in captivity is buried with military honours.

The road to freedom: the avenue leading away from Stalag Luft III where the long march began.

Halbau today.

Liberation day at Marlag und Milag Nord.

Left: American prisoners celebrate their release by British troops.

Below: Steve McQueen as Virgil Hilts, 'The Cooler King', in *The Great Escape* (1963).

to look out for escaped prisoners. Bill and Eddie explained in their best camp German that they were French workmen employed in the railway yards at Kraków. Somehow they had lost their way. They produced their forged papers identifying them as foreign workers. The story sounded lame even as they recited it. Kraków was about 250 miles to the south. The guard was apologetic but firm. He had orders to hand over anyone who seemed remotely suspicious to the Gestapo. The nearest headquarters was Hohensalza. The guard summoned reinforcements and they set off. By now the ethnic German population was in a ferment of excitement over the manhunt. At one stage on the journey they were confronted by a crowd of farm workers brandishing pitchforks. A woman among them seemed keen for the guards to shoot the captives on the spot, and when they refused tried to wrestle a rifle off one of them to carry out the execution herself.

Before they reached Hohensalza they managed to get rid of compass, maps and forged identity papers, anything that would reveal to the Germans the sophistication of the escape organization. Their time with the Gestapo was mercifully short. Once they had established who their captives were, they passed them over to the police, who locked them up in the local jail. It was already full up with pimps, thieves and black-marketeers as well as deserters from the Germany army. It was an ignominious end to the great adventure. Eddie felt the failure acutely. The latrine tunnel had been his life for the past few months. With Bill he had planned the project, promoted it and done much of the digging. All this effort had ended in bathos, and he was a prisoner once again, locked up in a cell only twenty-seven miles from where he had broken out. As he lay on his bunk bed he told Bill that the experience had turned him against further attempts. He would not be joining the ranks of obsessive 'escapologists' like Bill and the Dodger. When they returned to camp he would use his considerable energies in other ways – ones that made it more likely that he would live to see the end of the war. 'I did not press him,' wrote Bill. 'Each man had to decide for himself what was right in terms of the balance between suffering and defiance, between risk and foolhardiness.'[6]

For Bill their recapture was merely a setback. It would do nothing to deter him from trying again and again. 'For me the issue was simple,' he declared. 'I had joined the war to resist and I would keep resisting with every breath until I escaped or until the enemy helped me to get away on a more permanent basis, six feet underground.' It was not really a matter of choice, he explained, for 'my escaping gene was just as much a part of me as my instinct to keep breathing.' They went back to Schubin by way of several other prisons. On their return they were subjected to repeated interrogations before being sentenced to a fortnight each in the cooler.

Paddy and Wilf's adventure had also come to an end in Hohensalza. Their joy at having apparently hitched a ride on a goods train was short-lived. A few minutes after apparently setting off down the track towards Warsaw it stopped without even leaving the goods yard. They passed the night in the wagon, hoping that their luck would change. But next morning they heard the sound of barking dogs and peered out to see a line of soldiers searching the train. They jumped down onto the tracks without being seen and made it out of the yard, only to be spotted by a local official who summoned a patrol, and they were hauled off to the police station. Before being transferred to Gestapo headquarters they managed to get rid of their false ID cards, but not the rest of the escape kit. Paddy's carefully maintained insouciance crumbled on arrival, as they underwent 'an extremely frightening and unpleasant experience'.

'Here were two filthy, smelly, unshaven individuals with no identification documents claiming to be British,' he wrote. 'From time to time I could hear screams coming from the other inmates and I really thought my luck had finally run out.'[7]

The pair were subjected to a thorough body-search but the expected beating never came. Instead they were taken out and paraded in front of a gathering of troops and Hitler Youth. By now the RAF night-bombing campaign in Germany was taking a terrible toll on German cities. What would become known as the Battle of the Ruhr had just begun and in the days since the break-out, Bomber Command had mounted mass raids on Essen and Nuremburg. In Essen nearly five hundred people had been killed, matching or perhaps exceeding the number who died in the 'thousand-bomber raid' against Cologne ten months before. The Nazi propaganda minister, Josef Goebbels, had branded the bomber crews *Terrorfliegen*. The opportunity to put two captured terror-fliers on show was too good to miss. As the Germans stood and stared, one of the Hitler Youth said in English: 'Hitler is a good man and Churchill is a very bad man.' Paddy could not hold his tongue. 'My answer was somewhat unflattering to the Führer whereupon the boy spat at me. This gave his friends a good excuse to follow suit and I ended up looking like a slimy creature out of a Hammer horror movie.'[8]

They were taken back to their cells and spent a fearful few days before deliverance came in the form of a Luftwaffe major, who prised them from the Gestapo. After another night in Hohensalza they were sent back to Schubin, arriving on 13 March. They were sentenced to ten days in the cooler. It was only what they expected and seemed much preferable to captivity Gestapo-style.

Since boarding the train at Bromberg, Tommy Calnan and Robert Kee had made good progress. While waiting at Schneidemühl for the train to take them further west to Küstrin (Polish, Kostrzyn nad Odrą) they had been stopped by two plainclothes policemen. Calnan had feared that their forged letters supporting their claims to be Krupp technicians would not bear close scrutiny. Thanks to Kee's excellent German and impressive self-assurance, however, they had been sent on their way, with the policemen's best wishes and a telephone number to call should they need any assistance en route.

From Küstrin they caught a train to Berlin, arriving at the Schlesischer Bahnhof in the east of the city. They spent the day walking the streets, to avoid the feeling of anxiety that overwhelmed them if they remained stationary for too long. Initially they had been excited by the idea of penetrating the enemy citadel, but they were so exhausted by now that they barely noticed their surroundings. Early that evening they took a local train from the Zoo station to Stendal, eighty miles west, where they were to change for Hanover. It was packed with civilians taking refuge in the suburbs for fear of further raids on the city, which had been bombed heavily just over a week previously. At Hanover they took the midnight express for Cologne, which was due to arrive at five in the morning. Calnan's research had told him that there was a workman's train that left for the border town of Aachen shortly afterwards. From there it was only a short tram ride to Eupen in Belgium, where they could begin to try and make contact with the underground.

They were travelling second class and as soon as he settled onto the upholstered seat Calnan fell into a deep sleep. He was shaken awake by Kee. A policeman was standing over them and wanted to see their identity cards. They produced them and the policeman and his colleagues glanced at them and departed, apparently satisfied. The train stopped for a long time after passing through Hamm, whose railway junction was a favourite target of Bomber Command. By the time they crossed the long bridge over the Rhine on the approach to Cologne the sun was already above the horizon. It was then that the police returned. Kee began to repeat their story but they were in no mood to listen. They demanded to see their papers again and then left the compartment, taking the identity cards with them. It was obvious the game was almost up. They made a quick decision. They would jump out and make a run for it, but when they got to the door a soldier was standing guard.

At Cologne they were led away to a police station. They trotted out their story once more but by now the police seemed to be enjoying themselves, confident that they had their men. A search produced a quantity of 'mixture' food bars, a collection of maps and a supply of Player's cigarettes. 'We know all about you,' declared the sergeant in charge. 'You've caused a lot of trouble. Every policeman in the country has been looking for you. We did not expect you to come so far.'[9] The following day they were taken to Gestapo headquarters. Their interrogator spoke good English and pressed them for information about how the escape was engineered. For a while they baited him, giving ridiculous answers until he lost patience with their impertinence. Calnan recalled how his 'voice dropped to a whisper' as he told them that he could 'shoot you where you stand and never have to answer for it. Do you think the Geneva Convention means anything to us?' It was a good question. In the world the prisoners had escaped from, rules had some meaning. The Gestapo operated under no restraints. For the first time, Calnan was scared. 'There was a menace in that whispering voice which I recognized as real,' he recalled. 'That man had immense power and could have carried out his threat with complete impunity.'

It was, Kee realized, the other side of Germany, the one that until now they had seen remarkably little of. There was 'the Wehrmacht Germany which saluted when it passed you in the camp and allowed you to write home three times a month', and the other, 'which beat you in the stomach with lengths of hosepipe and shot you in the early morning'.[10] When later that evening he and Kee were put on a train at Wuppertal bound for the east and Schubin, they were careful to humour their Gestapo escorts, accepting their beer and sharing their cigarettes with them.

Aidan Crawley had made excellent progress since leaving Schneidemühl. He arrived in Berlin via Posen at the same time as Calnan and Kee. He was heading to Switzerland via Munich so took the underground to the Südbahnhof, where the southbound trains left from. Departures were disrupted because of air raids and he learned he might have to wait several days for a service. He knew that civilians could stay for up to three nights in a hotel without questions being asked, so he checked in to a small place in the centre. For the next two days of waiting he wandered unmolested around the city, eating in restaurants and visiting the cinema. So far the raids on Berlin had done little to alter the look of the city. It sprawled over eighty square miles and the townscape was interspersed with parks and lakes. The RAF was still acquiring the technologies and perfecting the techniques of concentrated bombing. But they were learning fast and the 'Big City', as the bomber crews called it, would be the main focus for their efforts later in the year.

On the second day he learned a train was due to leave for Munich the next morning. He slept on the floor of the station waiting room and arrived at his destination late in the evening. An air raid was in progress and the passengers were hustled to an underground shelter. Crawley had never been in one before, but the atmosphere was how he imagined it would be in Britain. People talked constantly and handed around food and wine. One woman had been in Cologne, subject of a thousand-bomber raid. She teased the more frightened inhabitants, telling them: 'You don't know what air raids are like. When we were in Cologne we had buildings crashing all around us.'[11]

Next morning, 8 March, only two days after breaking out, he took a train to Innsbruck, intending to carry on westwards to Landeck in the Austrian Tyrol, where he planned to leave the train and continue on foot to the Swiss border, only twelve miles to the south. Not long after leaving Munich, border guards who were aboard the train asked for his papers. Crawley handed them over with confidence. By now they had passed inspection with ease on about twenty occasions. When the guards left the carriage telling him they would return his papers he failed to smell danger, missing the chance to jump from the train, which was moving slowly at the time. When they returned he was led off to a police officer on the train. The policeman who had checked his papers had spotted a defect on the stamp on his *Ausweise*. He was arrested and put off the train at Kufstein in the Austrian Alps, where he was taken to Gestapo headquarters for questioning. 'I maintained my story of being a French worker for a time, but I realized that to continue to do so would be useless,' he told an intelligence debriefer after the war.[12] After a roundabout journey, including a day in Berlin accompanied by an SS officer who took him on a sightseeing tour, he was back in Schubin on 12 March.

By then almost all the other escapers had been rounded up. Tony Barber got as far as Belgard (in Polish, Białogard), only about seventeen miles from Kolberg, where he planned to take a boat to Denmark. He was strolling around town killing time before his train when he was stopped by two elderly storm troopers who asked him what he was doing. He said he was going to visit his sick brother, picking out an address at random in the street on which they were standing. They insisted on going with him. The woman who came to the door denied all knowledge of him and he was carted off to the Gestapo.

After two days Harry Day and Dudley Craig were starving. They made the mistake of asking a boy who they thought was Polish for food. He turned out to be a member of the Hitler Youth, who summoned help. They were captured after a short chase.

The countryside was full of trigger-happy troops, eager to play a role in the manhunt. When a senior officer in the Posen police failed to respond to a sentry's challenge at a roadblock he himself had thrown up, he was promptly shot dead.

Charles Marshall and Flight Lieutenant Webster, travelling on foot, were caught after forty-eight hours, trying to bluff their way across a bridge over the Vistula. Bill Palmer and Flight Lieutenant J. W. Wood hopped a series of goods trains, which took them to Falkenburg (Polish, Złocieniec). Unfortunately it was in the opposite direction to Danzig, their intended destination. They too were nabbed by a member of the home guard.

In the end everyone who took part in the tunnel escape was recaptured. Most were caught within a few days. It was months, though, before the Germans caught up with Josef Bryks. The Polish contractor who smuggled Squadron Leader Morris and Ricks out in the honeywagon hid them in his house on the outskirts of Schubin, then took them to a German state farm where the workforce was all Polish, who fed and looked after them. They were joined by Flight Lieutenant Otakar Černý, another Czech serving with the RAF, who had arranged to meet with Bryks after escaping through the tunnel. After five days hiding in a barn they split up. Morris set off under cover of darkness for Danzig but was soon captured trying to cross a bridge. Bryks and Černý walked for three weeks, moving on by night and hiding by day, until they reached Warsaw, where they made contact with the Polish underground. They were arrested on 2 June when the house they were staying in was raided. The Gestapo accused them of being Russian spies and threatened to have them shot. They were saved when they produced their prisoner-of-war identity discs.[13]

The exercise confirmed the truth that getting out of the camp was the easy part. The German apparatus of repression was remarkably effective. It was honed to new levels of efficiency due to the belief that an RAF fifth column was abroad, seeking to open up a new front behind the German lines. The scale of the manhunt made it clear that this was more than simply a matter of rounding up absconding prisoners of war. The captives were subjected to exhaustive questioning, with particular attention focused on what aid they had received from the local population. Day's Gestapo interrogators seemed convinced that he was working with the Polish underground.[14]

Two of the escapees would never be coming back. Jimmy Buckley, the cheerful, dauntless overseer of the operation, had been travelling with the young Dane Jørgen Thalbitzer, posing as Danish sailors. They made it all the way to Thalbitzer's home in Copenhagen for a joyful reunion with his family. The local underground provided them with a two-man canoe for the short voyage to Sweden. They departed on a calm sea late on the evening of 28 March. Thalbitzer's body was washed ashore some months later. Buckley was never found.

ELEVEN

The escapers consoled themselves with the thought that though they were back in captivity they had at least created a great deal of trouble for the Germans. They had also succeeded in revealing the fundamental incompetence of the camp authorities. In the process they lived an adventure; arduous, uncomfortable and nerve-wracking, but also exhilarating. The consequences of their defiance were surprisingly slight. Everyone got a spell in the cooler, with Day as the most senior culprit drawing the longest sentence of fourteen days. Once the cell door clanged behind them, though, there was plenty of time for longer reflection. Bill Ash was not the only one to weigh the effort against the results. He 'stared at the concrete walls and bars and wondered if it was all worth it'.[1]

When they emerged from solitary they learned there had been big changes at Schubin. Simms and his team had gone, sacked and court-martialled for their failure to control their charges. Some of the old guard remained, but control was now in the hands of the Gestapo. The prisoners' satisfaction at their old adversary's humiliation was tempered by the fact that the devil they knew had been replaced with a much more venomous and unpredictable regime.

Dickie Edge and his team had been preparing their own tunnel when the breakout happened. They were determined to continue, despite the change in regime. The intense searching that followed the escape had left the tunnel undisturbed. From its starting point in the barrack night latrine on the western side of the camp it now stretched for 110 feet, which put it sixty feet beyond the perimeter fence. Undaunted by the failure of any of the earlier escapers to score a 'home run', Edge was now proposing to send an even larger number under the wire. On 26 March the last section of tunnel was dug out, leaving only a few feet to go. The night latrine was a urinal only, so there was no pit in which to dump the spoil. Dispersal was tricky and the team had to scatter it where they could, protected by a network of lookouts. On this day the system failed. A guard saw someone pouring sand out of a barrack window onto the slope behind and raised the alarm. Russian prisoners were set to work with shovels and picks and eventually discovered the entrance. Before they did, two prisoners managed to get into the tunnel, wriggle down it and break out. They were picked up a few hours later.

It was one of the last dramas in the Schubin story. The krie-gies had known for some time, via the warning from IS9 in London, that they might soon be on the move. In April the rumour was confirmed. The expansion work at Sagan was now completed. They were leaving the escapers' paradise of Oflag XXIB and returning to their old abode – Stalag Luft III.

As they trudged through the gates once more they saw that the camp had been transformed. There was a whole new compound on the northern side and another was being built for US air-force prisoners in the south. Centre Compound was already full of American airmen. 'It was good to glimpse so many Americans, if only through two layers of barbed wire,' Bill Ash remembered.[2] The camp now had many of the facilities of a small town. There was a flourishing theatre and the public rooms were booked solid by clubs and societies. Much of the ground was under cultivation by newly enthusiastic gardeners supplementing their rations with fresh vegetables. The food situation had improved considerably. The Red Cross parcels were arriving regularly now and there were frequent surpluses of some items, so that a flourishing commodities market had grown up, operated by camp entrepreneurs who to Bill's honest eyes seemed little more than spivs. Nor did he approve of the long-running poker schools in which wily operators fleeced the gullible of years of back-pay.

The camp had an air of permanence. It was not just the size of the place, which had doubled in the intervening months. It was noticeable in the attitudes of the inhabitants. There were now about 8,000 of them, and most seemed content to sit out the war, spending their days as best they could.

As the months passed and the seasons turned, it became easier to accept and harder to rebel. Time no longer hung quite so heavily on the prisoners' hands. There were plenty of uses to which it could be put. By the middle of 1943 a regime had evolved in which a kriegie could exercise his brain studying Shakespeare and his body playing football or doing gymnastics. The camp was full of experts, eager to impart their skills. He could learn a musical instrument, study a language, play chess, bridge or poker, or take part in the increasingly sophisticated productions being staged in the camp theatre. The mail functioned efficiently enough for kriegies to be able to take correspondence courses in the law, accountancy or some other subject that would help set them off on a career after the war was over.

The signs were that the end was not so far away. Try as they might, the Germans could not keep the progress of the war a secret. Each compound had its clandestine radio, built and maintained by the bomber wireless operators whose numbers had increased as the Allied bombing campaign rolled over Germany. The details were taken down in shorthand and disseminated by word of mouth. The Germans offered their own version of events through bulletins broadcast over the camp loudspeakers. By now, though, even the guards seemed to doubt their veracity.

In June 1943 it was clear the war was not going Hitler's way. The catastrophe at Stalingrad had ended the great surge forward. It was Germany's turn to be on the defensive. A landing in Western Europe was inevitable. The only question was when and where it would fall. Bill detected a new attitude among the camp staff. While no longer sure of victory, they were by no means convinced that the war was lost. The most likely scenario the Germans now believed was a truce in the west followed by a joint campaign against the Communist menace in the east.

This view was not entirely unrealistic. Since the summit meeting in Casablanca in January that year, the Allies were supposedly committed to accepting no terms short of unconditional surrender from Germany. The policy had been insisted on by President Roosevelt, but there were some highly placed figures in Britain and America who believed that it would be abandoned if Hitler was overthrown. Bill was convinced that turning on the Soviet Union was unthinkable for another reason. The ordinary people who had gone to war against Hitler regarded the Russians as friends and allies. An attack on their partners would receive no support.

Despite the petty persecutions, the camp authorities often strove to treat the kriegies with something approaching respect. Their motives were mixed. They regarded the British as equals, worthy opponents who should be handled in as civilized a manner as the circumstances allowed. At the same time, as the war progressed and the outcome became increasingly uncertain, the prisoners became an appreciating asset. An individual guard might decide that if Germany lost, a good report from the prisoners might be helpful in allowing him to adjust to the new conditions. A more sinister calculation was that the kriegies might come in very useful as hostages, whose lives could be used as bargaining chips by officials seeking to escape punishment for their crimes.

The Germans were therefore anxious to convey their essential decency. At times, the prisoners were prepared to accept that their enemies were not so different to themselves in their values and their outlook. 'Towards us the Germans behaved themselves with a disciplined formality and correctness,' wrote Tommy Calnan. 'They liked us to think they were gentlemen and we were often stupid enough to think this way.'[3] There was much evidence in and around the camp to undermine that assessment. It was there in the shape of the forty or so Russian prisoners who lived on starvation rations in the *Vorlager* and were used, as long as their diminishing strength lasted, as slave labour.

Calnan looked on them and felt a shudder of pity. 'These men were being deliberately destroyed by a long drawn-out and carefully phased programme of cruelty,' he wrote. 'To our comfortable British consciences, they were a nasty embarrassment. It was easier to pretend they were not there, rather as one crossed the street to avoid a passing beggar.'

The growing evidence of a programme of mass extermination of the Jews and other enemies of the Third Reich had not reached the kriegies. But beyond the wire there were occasional glimpses of the nightmarish world the Germans were building in the conquered lands. Calnan glimpsed 'one single horrifying sight of reality' from the window of a truck which was taking him from the camp to Sagan for a trip to the dentist. 'At a level crossing I saw ten or a dozen figures, herded in a group and surrounded by SS guards. They were not human figures, just angular skeletal forms clad in pyjamas with yellow and grey vertical stripes. There was no substance to them and no personality.' They disappeared from sight as the truck turned a corner. He was 'left with a strong sensation of evil and an unexpectedly powerful fear of something unknown'. Some instinct prevented him from asking questions of the guards.[4]

Bill had already seen a similar sight from the window of the Schubin cooler when he witnessed the party of women being herded along the road. His theoretical hatred of the Germans had hardened into a practical one. He was also driven by convictions and sentiments that few of the other kriegies shared. When he looked at the starving Russians he felt not just pity but comradely solidarity. He and they were more than temporary allies. They were profoundly and ideologically on the same side.

Ever since childhood he had been angered by injustice. He had seen how white Americans treated black Americans and it sickened him. An episode he witnessed while at a boys' summer camp in Texas stayed with him all his life. A black youth was employed to do the cooking. While returning to the camp at night-time after an excursion into town, the young man was confronted by two of the camp counsellors dressed in sheets daubed with luminous paint. 'Not unnaturally the youth took off across the fields with the two figures in close pursuit emitting eerie wails,' he wrote. 'There was a loosely strung barbed-wire fence at the edge of the ploughed area and he ran into it full tilt, becoming enmeshed in the strands whose vicious barbs punctured him in a dozen places.' Bill remembered 'looking at him, trussed up on the ground, eyes rolling, and I recall the anger I felt – not just because they had hurt him but more because they had made their humiliating little contribution to the racist myth that black people are ignorant and superstitious.'[5] He felt a profound hatred for 'those who degrade other human beings to make them into menials and then despise them for their degradation'. His experiences of Nazi Germany would provide plenty of material for the hatred to feed on.

His upbringing had also given him first-hand exposure to the inequities of raw capitalism. He had watched the indignities suffered by his father as he struggled to make a living. Bill himself had slaved to put himself through university only to find when he got his degree that there was no proper job waiting. He had been forced to hop freight trains, live rough and go hungry in his search of work that barely kept him alive.

There were millions like him in 1930s America, but most survived the experience with their faith in capitalism undented. Bill was different. From the outset he was drawn to socialism, a creed with few followers in 1930s Texas. He watched the struggle of the Spanish Republicans against the Nationalist rebels and their Nazi and Fascist backers and boiled with frustration that he was too young to join the fight. When the next war came he went eagerly. He would not be fighting for Canada or Britain or America but in the great cause of anti-Fascism. The pathetic Russian starvelings being worked to death by the Germans were as much his brothers-in-arms as his comrades in the RCAF and RAF.

These convictions fed his determination to keep on trying to escape. There were enough like him to ensure that, once back in Stalag Luft III, the business began anew.

All the returnees from Schubin were put into East Compound, their old stamping ground. Meanwhile a large proportion of the camp's population was occupying the new North Compound, which was half a mile away and out of sight. Between the two lay the Centre Compound and the *Kommandantur* administrative area and German quarters. The Schubin escape committee reconvened, but with Jimmy Buckley's disappearance Harry Day took over as chairman. They gave the go-ahead for several new tunnels, but as they soon discovered the ferrets had grown more cunning during their absence. Inspection tunnels had been dug beneath each barrack to check for signs of excavated soil. If a tunnel was discovered, the German security team was inclined to let it be, leaving the would-be escapers to toil away for weeks or months until they neared the wire before moving in to shut it down and cart the diggers off to the cooler.

Those involved in the Schubin latrine tunnel found their ability to participate constrained. As notorious escapologists they were under closer surveillance than the other kriegies and, despite their expertise, their assistance on an escape project actively increased the chances of detection. Bill had time on his hands. He read voraciously and for a time he kept up a correspondence with a girl who worked in the Red Cross department in Geneva, which despatched books to the prisoners. It ended when she took to regaling him with steamy details of amorous weekends spent with her boyfriend, in the mistaken belief that it would be good for Bill's morale.

He consoled himself in other ways. Since first hearing classical music drifting from a church hall one night in Texas he had been enchanted by it. In London he had attended lunchtime concerts, laid on by the authorities, which brought beauty to the drabness. There were fewer opportunities in the messes and anterooms of the fighter stations where the squadron was based. When they were at Digby someone had made the mistake of giving Bill some mess funds to go into York and buy some records. To the disgust of his colleagues he returned bearing not the latest discs by Glenn Miller and the Andrews Sisters but the works of Bach and Beethoven. As far as his fellow pilots were concerned he was welcome to them and he whiled away many hours listening in solitary rapture.

There was no such possibility in Stalag Luft III. The few gramophones were monopolized by the non-classically minded majority and the radio was far too precious to risk it being discovered while broadcasting a symphony. Kriegie life taught you that there was always a way round a problem, and Bill found one.

'In every camp there was only one place where classical music was sure to be played,' he wrote, 'and that was on the gramophone or radio in the German officers' quarters.' He was prepared to risk 'a long spell in the cooler, or even being shot, by slipping out of my hut after curfew and crawling and running between the huts until I reached an internal fence that separated us from a hut full of off-duty German officers.' He 'crouched by the wire, spellbound as the music drifted across, an unwitting gift from my captors'.[6] That a culture that could produce and love such music was capable of such gigantic cruelty was an enduring mystery.

Bill's reading had led him to the conclusion that the Allied treatment of Germany after the First World War had created the conditions that encouraged the rise of Hitler. He also believed that Western capitalism had at first regarded Hitler with favour, as a bulwark against the Bolshevik menace in the east. None of this reduced his hostility to the Nazis. Now, it seemed, the battle against the Fascists had reached a turning point. He itched to be a part of it. His obsessive urge to break out was practical not symbolic. This was not merely a pastime or a gesture of defiance to embarrass his captors and expose their inadequacies. It was a warlike exercise, designed to get him back in action at the controls of his Spitfire as soon as possible.

The chances of making it out of Stalag Luft III seemed severely limited. What he needed was a change of circumstances that would allow his skills and experience to be put to their best use. One day the camp rumour-mill produced an interesting item. The sergeant pilots in Centre Compound were being moved. They were to be shipped out in batches of two hundred to Stalag Luft VI, a new camp built amid flat, swampy terrain near the small town of Heydekrug, nearly two hundred miles away to the north-east, in the wilds of Lithuania. The first party was due to leave in June.

Bill immediately saw an opportunity. 'If I could get to a different camp, I could use the period of chaos [that exists] at the founding of any camp as a happy hunting ground for future escapes with untrained guards and fresh routes for new tunnels.'[7] The problem was that he was not an NCO.

That difficulty was soon resolved. Bill had made friends with a young New Zealander in Centre Compound called Donald Fair. He managed to persuade him that the two should swap identities. Fair would avoid being sent off to the wastes of Lithuania, and he became a Flight Lieutenant (Bill had been promoted *in absentia*). The main problem was how to change places. East Compound and Centre Compound were separated by a ten-foot-high double fence, which was within sight of the perimeter fence watchtowers.

To get across would require speed, agility and a major diversion to distract the guards. Bill enlisted the services of Paddy Barthropp and other friends. At the agreed time, Bill took up his position on his side of the divide while Don Fair loitered innocently on the other. Paddy and his accomplices began to play a noisy game of football. The guards' eyes wandered towards the group of shouting, jostling kriegies, scuffling in the summer dust. Their interest mounted as the game became more boisterous, then degenerated into a minor brawl. Bill and Don took their chance. They skipped over the warning wire on their respective sides of the fence – beyond which they were liable to be shot –and scrambled over the wire, dropping into the gap between the two fences. There they crouched down, shook hands and swapped their identity papers and discs.

Then they were off again for another heart-stopping assault on the wire to the other compound. Behind them the shouts of the fight subsided. The guards' gaze turned away. If they glanced towards the boundary between East and Centre compounds all they saw were two insignificant figures strolling harmlessly back towards the huts.

Bill never saw Don Fair again. In order to maintain their false identity they had to keep up the imposture in their letters home, which were read by the camp censors.

TWELVE

As Bill Ash prepared to set off for Heydekrug an unexpected difficulty arose. Commandant von Lindeiner-Wildau decided to bid a personal farewell to the departing NCOs. He was in paternal mood, making a short speech in which he urged them to behave themselves in their new camp. In retrospect it sounded like a veiled but well-meant warning: the days of gentlemanly correctness were coming to an end and henceforth it was the methods of the Gestapo that would prevail. Bill tried to make himself as inconspicuous as possible at the back of the parade. He was well known to Lindeiner from the numerous dressings-down that preceded his despatch to the cooler. After the risks he had taken it would be a bitter anticlimax if Lindeiner spotted him and demanded to know what an officer was doing among the ranks of the NCOs.

The speech ended. They marched out of the camp like soldiers and the Luftwaffe officers watching held their salutes until the last man passed. At Sagan station they climbed into special carriages, with a wired-off section in the middle where armed guards kept watch, for a meandering and eventful journey to Heydekrug.

Bill soon learned that the NCOs had their own way of doing things. In contrast to the system prevailing in the officer compounds they organized themselves along democratic lines, electing a leader, a 'man of confidence' who liaised with the German authorities. The leader of Centre Compound was a figure who commanded the respect and admiration of all who came in contact with him. Warrant Officer James Deans was a 29-year-old Glaswegian who joined the RAF before the war. On 10 September 1940 his Whitley bomber was shot down over Holland after a raid on Bremen. He and the rest of the crew survived and spent the war in a succession of camps. 'Dixie' Deans was a man of quiet natural authority. He had mastered German which helped him develop a grasp of his captor's psychology. He was correct, and courteous, always neatly turned-out in uniform and tie, and highly adept at manipulating camp life to the kriegies' advantage. His diplomatic skills wrung many concessions from the staff. Through bribery and charm he extracted escape materials, vital components for the clandestine radio, and information which he sent back to IS9 by way of coded letters. At the same time he exercised subtle control over the men who had chosen him, settling disputes and setting the tone for how camp life was lived.

Bill saw him as 'a brilliant example of someone who could use his head as well as his heart… he tended not to waste words but said what he meant and meant what he said. Jimmy was proof positive that you didn't have to shout to be a commanding presence.'[1]

*

As he sat on the train waiting for it to depart, Bill was about to catch his first sight of another remarkable character. He noticed some of his new comrades staring at a smartly dressed German civilian who was sitting at a table outside the station cafeteria drinking a stein of beer, while the German officer in charge of the prisoners rushed up and down the platform shouting orders. Eventually the civilian rose and approached the harassed officer. In the conversation that followed it seemed clear that the civilian was the one with the authority, and the officer cringed and nodded. 'Gestapo,' said one of the kriegies. 'No it's not,' said another. 'It's bloody Grimson.'

George Grimson was a stocky Londoner with close-cropped blond hair and a pugnacious manner who, like Deans, had joined the pre-war RAF and was flying in Bomber Command when he was shot down in 1940. He was a dedicated and daring escapologist. His preferred method was impersonation and he had managed to bluff his way out of camps twice disguised as a German. As the move to Heydekrug approached he decided to try again.

The scheme succeeded brilliantly. It was, in Aidan Crawley's view, 'one of the cleverest escapes of the whole war'.[2] Grimson's plan required great assurance, considerable acting ability and icy self-control. He intended to disguise himself as a German electrician tasked with carrying out tests on the telephone wires which ran from the *Kommandantur* offices over the top of the perimeter fence. His aim was to get into the German area, where the main gate was situated, and walk out. Assiduous bartering by the compound's escape organization provided him with all the props he needed for his imposture. Grimson dressed up in a dark-blue boiler suit, Luftwaffe cap and leather belt, and carried a dummy electrician's meter for testing wiring. He was also armed with forged documents and some bars of escape 'mixture'.

Carrying a ladder borrowed from the camp theatre and a bag stuffed with electrical cables he walked casually over to the warning fence, waving a salute to the guard in the watchtower. The guard beckoned him on. He propped his ladder against the fence, climbed up and began a lengthy pantomime, pretending to check the telephone lines. Gradually he worked his way round to a part of the fence which separated the compound from the *Kommandantur*. There, according to Crawley, he 'deliberately dropped his test meter among the barbed-wire entanglements but close to the German side of the fence'.[3] He cursed his clumsiness and turned in appeal to the guard. Was it all right if he climbed over to retrieve them? The guard nodded. Grimson scrambled over and ambled off to await a suitable moment to brave the main gates. Eventually he made his move. The sentries glanced at his forged identity card and waved him through. Once safely out of sight he removed his workman's overalls. Underneath he was dressed in a sober suit of the sort worn by the Gestapo, with a swastika lapel badge.

Now, at Schubin railway station, he seemed to have decided to join the prisoners on their journey to the Baltic. He had little difficulty boarding. It emerged later that he had told the officer in charge that he was a security official who would be coming some of the way. He left the train near Stettin, but was picked up four days later while trying to find a neutral ship, and packed off to Heydekrug where he would play a central role in escape activities.

The journey was slow and erratic. The train followed branch lines, apparently to avoid the risk of being bombed if they took main routes. This took them hundreds of miles out of their way, heading westwards towards Berlin before moving north and east. Outside Berlin they were shunted into a marshalling yard and the train stopped. 'Soon we heard the heavy throb of aircraft engines as Allied bombers rolled over the city,' wrote Bill. The sky was illuminated by swivelling searchlights and anti-aircraft fire. Many of the men in the carriages had served in Bomber Command and 'clapped and cheered from this unexpected ringside seat as the German capital took a pasting'.[4] It was a small raid by a handful of Mosquitoes but the kriegies revelled in the thump of descending bombs, jeering at the guards who sat in the partition dividing the carriage. Fingers flicked at triggers. One guard cocked his weapon. Just as it seemed the prisoners might have goaded the Germans beyond endurance, the quiet voice of Dixie Deans ordered them to pipe down. The tension subsided, the din faded and the train moved on again.

Stalag Luft VI lay on a flat, sandy peninsula that jutted into the Baltic two miles from Heydekrug, not far from the old Teutonic city of Memel. It was surrounded by swamps and woodland and often covered by mists that rolled in from the sea. A strong northerly wind blew all year round, carrying fine sand that worked its way into every crevice and stung the eyes. It was in the middle of nowhere. The roads around it were mostly cart tracks and its principal link to the outside world was a single-track railway that ran from Memel to Tilsit, today Sovetsk in Russia.

The camp was divided into three compounds, 'A', 'E' and 'K'. The new arrivals from Sagan were put into 'A'. The layout was drearily familiar, with its fences, guard rails and watchtowers. Heydekrug had been in operation since 1939 and held successively Polish, French and Russian POWs. It was now reserved for air-force prisoners and over the next eight months would fill up with 6,000 Allied and American airmen. They were housed in long, single-storey brick buildings, whitewashed on the inside and divided into nine rooms each holding fifty men. One wooden barrack was set aside to accommodate a group of thirteen prisoners who were regarded with particular disfavour by the Germans, for persistent attempts to escape or pronounced anti-German attitudes.

In his new guise as Don Fair, Bill was not identified as one of the bad boys. His decision to swap identities, ranks and places caused puzzlement among some of the NCOs. His record as a determined, if so far unsuccessful, escaper went in his favour, though, and he was soon being consulted for expert advice by the cadre of escape-minded prisoners. The escape committee was known as the Tally-Ho Club, a name that Bill found amusingly redolent of upper-class England. It was headed by Warrant Officer R. J. 'Jock' Alexander, who had held the same position at Sagan, and overseen by Dixie Deans. The democratic spirit which prevailed among the NCOs brought its problems. Most of the prisoners were sergeants and did not take easily to being given orders by men of equal rank. There was another problem. The camp history written after the war admitted that the majority of prisoners were 'generally apathetic to escape matters'.[5] Unless the committee could rely on the at least tacit support of a majority of the kriegies, their chances of success were limited.

Before getting down to serious planning they decided to make a direct appeal to the compound. Committee members went around the barracks 'outlining the ideals of the Escape Organization' and suggesting ways in which every prisoner could help. They included donating clothing and bed boards, 'adopting an attitude of wariness towards the Germans and to give a warning if a German was in or near a barrack room' and to 'avoid holding conversation or [engaging in] trading activities with Germans as this was to be done on an organised basis with selected individuals.'

The last was particularly important. Unbridled trading between inmates and staff seems to have got underway almost immediately. Heydekrug was run by the Luftwaffe. In all there were about five hundred administrators, ferrets and guards, most of whom had no previous experience of dealing with British and American prisoners. The exception was Major Peschel, the kriegies' old adversary from Sagan, who had been brought in to command the *Abwehr* anti-escape department.

The dispiriting news seeping from the Eastern Front had persuaded some guards that there was no harm in cultivating friendly relations with their captives. Others were simply seduced by the merchandise that the kriegies had to barter. In this outpost of the German empire, chocolate and cigarettes were luxuries. When the Red Cross parcels were flowing, the prisoners had plenty of both. But there were also anti-Nazi guards at Heydekrug who saw their charges as kindred spirits. At least two of the 'contacts', as the escapers called camp staff who could be useful to them, were acting out of ideological motives. They would eventually pay a high price for cooperating with the prisoners.

The committee wanted to control the camp's black market in order to lay their hands on the items they most needed for escapes. They authorized about two dozen 'traders', all of whom spoke some German, to forge links with guards and camp staff. They sounded them out with friendly approaches, asking for help improving their language skills, then rewarding them with small gifts. Once a degree of trust had been established they made small requests in return, which gradually increased in significance. In this way they were able to amass a wealth of valuable material, including German uniforms, cameras and photographic equipment.

Some of the entrepreneurs who were trading for personal profit resisted the appeal to their better natures. One recent arrival complained to Deans that his rights were being trampled on. Bill recalled that Dixie's normally placid demeanour dissolved and he 'turned himself up to full volume', yelling at the grumbler, 'Good men are out there getting killed in the air every night and other good men are in here risking their lives trying to escape and you talk about rights? Get out of my sight!'[6]

The camp history recorded that most of the prisoners came to 'realize that the ideal of escape was a worthwhile object' and that 'bitter complaints and active opposition were expressed by only a few individuals.'[7] However unauthorized trading remained a problem, and in the end Deans was forced to issue an order forbidding it.

The committee also had to take the prisoners' opinion into account when it considered its escape strategy. Initially, most attention was focused on tunnelling. It was decided early on to concentrate on one tunnel at a time rather than multiple projects. The reasons were interesting. The committee cited the usual practical difficulty of disposing of excavated soil. But there was also the social cohesion of the camp to be considered. The camp history noted: 'It was felt that the discovery by the Germans of one tunnel after another would have hampered the plans of the escape committee regarding other methods of escape by placing the escape organization in a position where its activities could be ridiculed by the majority of [prisoners] who were not interested in escape, but whose cooperation, or at least inactive resistance, was essential to the success of the organization.'

By pressing forward with an escape bid in the face of general apathy the committee was taking a risk. Failure would wipe away what prestige they enjoyed and undermine the structures of authority controlling a robustly independent-minded community. They knew that when they decided on which tunnel they were going to go for, it had better be a good one.

Bill's experiences in Schubin had earned him the status of tunnelling expert. After surveying the possibilities within 'A' Compound, Bill believed that he had found a location which offered a good chance of success. Once again, latrines were involved.

On the west side of the compound was a washhouse which combined toilets, showers and a room equipped with giant copper boilers where the prisoners could do their laundry. An initial exploration revealed that the structure of the latrine was much as it had been at Schubin, the toilet seats suspended over a sewage pit bounded by brick retaining walls. Using the same methods as at Schubin it was surely possible to breach the brick wall, excavate a chamber and begin burrowing.

Together with a sergeant called Paddy Flynn, Bill led an exploratory team to begin work. It was just like old times. They lowered themselves through a hatch made in the toilet seats and inched along a ledge set in the wall to the chamber entrance. Very soon though they made an unpleasant discovery. The water table was only five feet below the surface, much higher than at Schubin. As they shovelled dirt from the tunnel, the water level rose, filling it with diluted sewage. There was no way around the difficulty. Digging was abandoned.

Then a prisoner called Jack Catley came up with a solution, involving the washhouse copper boilers. These sat over metal fireboxes which held the burning coal that heated the water, and were held in place by wooden frames. Here, it seemed, was the perfect cover for a tunnel entrance. It was a simple matter to lift the boilers from their frames. Then they could cut a hole in the bottom of the firebox, break through the concrete floor and sink a vertical shaft to a level just above the water table. From there a chamber could be excavated from where horizontal digging could begin. Disguising the entrance was simple. All that was needed was a concrete lid to fit the hole and a removable piece of metal for the bottom of the firebox. Getting in and out was quick and convenient. It took only a few minutes to remove the boiler, lift the metal and concrete covers and slip into the shaft. Lookouts could warn of approaching Germans and the tunnellers could be out long before they arrived, with time to slip under the showers to wash off any telltale sand. Meanwhile, helpers in the laundry room would transfer a few shovelfuls of coal from one of the other fireboxes to the empty tray and pour water from another boiler into the copper. A quick sluicing of the floor to wash away any traces completed the cover-up.

Initially ventilation was provided by a standard kitbag bellows. Then someone had a better idea. If the boiler was actually lit, it would act as a flue. As the tunnel progressed they poked unobtrusive holes to the surface, so the outside oxygen was sucked back along the shaft, creating what Bill described as 'the first air-conditioned escape tunnel in the Third Reich'.[8]

Work began early in July. The labour was hard. The high sand-content in the soil made it treacherous, and cave-ins and floods were frequent. Elaborate shoring was required to prevent collapse, with a box frame made of bed boards every two and a half feet and a complete wooden roof overhead. Because of the high water table they could not burrow too deep. The geography of the camp created extra difficulties. The tunnellers used wooden sledges to haul back the earth from the face. Because there were underground drain pipes between the washhouse and the perimeter fence, the tunnel could not be dug straight. Men had to be stationed at the bends to make sure that the sledges and haulage ropes did not erode the tunnel walls.

The sand itself was piled in the entrance chamber and

shovelled into kitbags which were hauled up after the after-noon *Appell*. The bags were then carried into the latrine area. The floor was made of wooden planks which were easy to lever up. The spoil was poured evenly over a wide area to disappear into the sea of sewage.

While the diggers burrowed, the committee was busy acquir-ing the material the escapers would need once they broke out. Fifty men were scheduled to take part, all of whom would need identity cards, maps, clothing and food. Keeping a judicious eye on the enterprise was the calm, efficient Deans.

His coolness was extraordinary, as was demonstrated when a display of sangfroid averted a certain tragedy. One day a pris-oner received a 'mespot' from a woman at home telling him their relationship was over. Just as Flight Lieutenant Edwards had done at Schubin, he ran towards the warning wire, stepped over and began to climb the fence.

The drama was witnessed by Dixie Deans, who was enjoy-ing a stroll around the compound with his deputy and friend Ron Mogg. Deans shouted at the guards not to shoot. Then he stepped over the wire himself, trusting they would recognize him and hold their fire. 'Arms raised, he walked slowly across to the man, who was now sobbing, clinging to the barbed wire and waiting for the bullet that would put him out of his misery,' wrote Bill. 'Instead he heard the quiet, calm Scottish voice of Dixie Deans, who gently disentangled him from the wire and led him back to safety.'[9]

They had been lucky. For every guard who was willing to chat and trade with the kriegies there were others who would happily shoot them, given the opportunity. A prisoner was fired at for throwing washing-up water from a basin over the guard rail, and hit in the arm. A guard in a watchtower opened up with a machine gun at a kriegie who threw some cigarettes to a Russian POW working nearby, in defiance of German orders. A British sergeant who tried to break out of E Compound was shot dead after he surrendered. An American prisoner making an early trip to the washhouse before the permitted hour was also killed by a guard. As the prisoners had to remind themselves, the Germans might sometimes show a civilized side, but you had to remember that they were capable of anything.[10]

Though new to the business, the camp authorities were soon alert to any sign of suspicious activity. The ferrets carried out regular searches. They wisely assumed that the fact that they had not discovered any evidence of tunnelling did not mean that there was none going on. Their suspicions were shared by the local Gestapo, who one day turned up at the camp and joined the *Abwehr* staff in a whirlwind search, rampaging through the huts, ripping up floorboards and turning out cupboards.

By now the Gestapo was playing an increasing role in the running of the camps. 'During 1943 the Gestapo… interfered more and more in the affairs of the armed forces, including prisoner of war camps,' wrote Aidan Crawley, 'interfering not only with the activities of the prisoners but of the Germans who guarded them.'[11]

The raid was a partial success. A quantity of documents was seized along with escape clothing, maps and compasses. The main objective of the operation was a failure, however. The tunnel entrance under the laundry coppers was undisturbed and once the Gestapo left normal business resumed.

Early one morning Bill was on his way to work in the tunnel when he heard a long, low rumbling, and the earth trembled beneath his feet. For a joyful moment he thought it was the thunder of Soviet artillery, but then the rumble turned into a roar. 'Out from behind some buildings came one of the most eager ferrets, looking pleased with himself, and mounted on a huge steamroller that belched smoke as it trundled around the perimeter,' he wrote.[12] The driver was a corporal called Heinz, an enthusiastic Nazi who was as unpopular with his comrades as he was with the kriegies.

Heinz steered the five-ton machine back and forth, up and down the length of the compound, with the obvious intention of collapsing any tunnel in his path. But, as Aidan Crawley told the story, 'after the roller had travelled some distance it became stuck in a patch of soft sand and the smile on Heinz's face faded. The more he tried to extricate the roller by accelerating the engine, the more deeply it became embedded.' A crowd soon formed to enjoy his misfortune. 'The prisoners began to jeer and Heinz, who understood English perfectly, became angry.' After 'each fresh effort had been greeted with roars of laughter from hundreds of throats he stalked off in a towering rage and returned with a small army of Germans carrying planks.'[13] Eventually the steamroller was freed, but the manoeuvre had failed. When Bill reached the boiler room he found the diggers, who had sat out the ordeal underground, unharmed and the tunnel intact.

The episode made everyone wonder how much longer their luck could last. By now it was late August and the tunnel was 140 feet long and already about 40 feet beyond the perimeter fence.

The ground above did not offer much cover and the escape committee's view was that it should continue for another thirty feet so that the escapers would emerge just inside a patch of woodland, out of sight of the watchtowers and the perimeter sentry patrol. The question of whether to break the tunnel now, even though the chances of detection by the guards was increased, or carry on and risk it being discovered was hotly debated.

A group of escapers was determined to go early, and seemed willing to defy the committee and go ahead without its approval. To calm things down it was decided to hold a meeting to determine the matter. The tunnel was long enough to accommodate fifty men. On the morning of 29 August, those selected to go gathered to weigh the arguments. The committee chairman, Jock Alexander, told the meeting that their intelligence sources suggested there would be no further large-scale searches for some time, and highlighted the dangers of an early exit, where the risk of being spotted – and shot – by the guards was high. He asked them to wait another week until the last section could be dug. Others countered that the tunnel was already far enough from the wire for the escapers to leave it under cover of darkness in reasonable safety.

Bill favoured an early break, not least because something told him that the psychic energy crackling around the project heightened the risk of discovery. 'It is hard to quantify,' he wrote, 'but somehow the tension prior to a jailbreak is like an invisible wave of static electricity that spreads through a camp, and somehow the ferrets often seemed to sense it, just as some people or animals can sense a storm coming long before the first cloud has appeared on the horizon.'[14]

Though normally reluctant to take the floor he decided to speak out. The official history related how 'Ash then addressed the meeting and stated his point of view which was that the tunnel should be used at once.' He 'contended that as the tunnel was now well beyond the fence, the risk of its discovery before it could be used should not be increased by further delay'.[15]

There was strong support for both points of view. Alexander decided to put it to the vote. When the count was taken there was a majority of one in favour of an immediate departure. There were no further interventions from the committee. All that remained was to sort out the order in which the escapers would leave the tunnel. Priority would be given to those who had put in the most work. That meant Bill was at the front.

There were about nine hours for final preparations. The former divisions were forgotten. 'Immediately the decision was made, everyone, no matter how they had argued earlier, threw themselves completely into making the escape a success,' wrote Bill. 'The NCO camp, from its election of a sergeant as leader to its determination to have a vote, even on escaping, was one of the most democratic structures I have been in.'[16]

The committee had argued that there was little chance of a major search in the near future. But what if the guards decided, as they sometimes did, to mount a snap check of the barracks after lights out and discovered fifty empty beds? That eventuality had already been covered. A team of helpers had used their art classes to make papier mâché dummies, with real hair collected from the barber shop. To add to the potential confusion, holes were cut into partition walls so that prisoners could be counted in one room then slip through to an empty bed to be counted again.

At about 7 p.m. the escape team drifted over to the laundry room. The copper boiler was removed and one by one they followed Bill through the hatch and began to crawl along the tunnel. When the last man had disappeared, the hatch door and firebox were replaced and half-burned coals scattered over the latter. The boiler was not used at night, so the escapers would have to wriggle forward without the benefit of a cool draught.

Crawling for fifty yards along a passage two feet square, pushing your luggage before you, was an exhausting and frightening experience. The air got fouler the further you went down the tunnel, and the escapers soon felt they were suffocating. The sensation heightened the mounting claustrophobia. There were two hours of this to endure before the topsoil was breached and the column began to move. It was the end of August, and darkness did not descend until 10 p.m. It was then that Bill broke through the last crust of earth. It was a beautiful moment. He felt a 'great first icy blast of air' which 'rushed and whistled along the tunnel'. From the kriegies packed in behind him he 'could hear the gasps of delight as the... taste of potential freedom allowed them to breathe once again.'[17]

Before they set off the weather had been gusty and there was rain on the wind. If that pattern persisted they would be emerging into a wet, cloudy night. In the intervening hours, though, things had changed. When Bill cautiously poked his head through the hole, all was bright and still. He could hear the footsteps of the guard as he plodded the perimeter circuit. When

Bill was sure he had passed, he scrambled out of the hole and began to commando-crawl to the cover of the trees. They were only ten yards away but the journey seemed to take an eternity. Once in the wood he looked back. The guard was nowhere in sight and the next man was wriggling free. He waited until he was safely in cover then set off, jogging through the woods towards the east, where he hoped his salvation lay. He had not got far when he heard gunfire coming from the direction of the tunnel. Searchlights were flickering through the branches and a siren wailed. There was nothing he could do. He kept on running.

Only eight men had made it out. The ninth mistimed his departure from the hole and emerged in sight of the sentry, who fired warning shots that stopped the escaper in his tracks. The guard soon found the exit and fired a few more shots to deter anyone thinking of making a break. Down below, the prisoners began to drag themselves in reverse back along the tunnel. Inside the camp, the hunt had begun for the tunnel entrance. A search of the laundry had produced nothing until the guards heard noises coming from the base of one of the boilers. The man at the rear of the column was trying to push back the concrete slab over the entrance.

As the escapers were led away to the cooler they managed to pass on the information that eight of the team had got away. One escapee, though, had been caught. The kriegies hoped that if they removed all but seven of the dummies placed in the escapees' beds, the authorities would go on thinking that only a single prisoner had escaped. The tactic worked and the Germans retired for the night, satisfied that they had thwarted a major breakout. The following morning the prisoners were paraded and the numbers checked again. This time seven men manoeuvred themselves down the line so they were counted twice, creating an apparently full compartment of prisoners.

Later that day, one of the escapers was recaptured, revealing the deception. At 8 p.m. Major Peschel ordered another recount. The prisoners were lined up and marched in single file through a gate, while four or five officials counted them off. The kriegies were enjoying themselves. 'The Escape Committee incited the mass of the POWs to upset the count and to treat the whole thing as a huge joke,' the official history recorded. They lit bonfires of waste paper 'and were dancing round them behaving like dervishes'. They bleated like sheep, jeered and catcalled. This went on until 11 p.m., when 'the Germans gave it up in disgust with a count of seventeen men too many.'[18]

Next morning another special parade was ordered. This time the cards the Germans kept of every prisoner, with his photograph and fingerprints, were brought into the compound and placed on tables. Each man was called forward and checked against his record. Order soon broke down. The prisoners edged closer to the tables until they were milling around them. One of the trays holding hundreds of the cards was stolen from under the guards' noses. By the time the theft was discovered the documents had been tipped into a hut stove. The antics continued for several more days before the Gestapo arrived. All the prisoners were transferred to another compound, then fed back in to A Compound, checked against their cards and fingerprinted. Those without a document were issued with a new one. Only then did the authorities learn the number and identities of the missing men.

The prisoners had enjoyed themselves and the Germans had suffered another humiliation. The satisfaction this gave the krie-gies could not disguise the fact that the decision to break the tunnel early had been the wrong one.

THIRTEEN

Bill ran on. The shooting had stopped but in the distance he could hear guards shouting and the excited barking of dogs. He stumbled through the darkness, tripping on roots and crashing into overhanging branches. The noises seemed to be getting closer. Then the ground fell away and he was slithering down the bank of a small river. He plunged into the water and waded across. The dogs would not be able to follow him now. He was safe, at least until the next inevitable hazard appeared.

He felt a great burst of happiness. 'There can be no sense of freedom like the first few minutes of a prison break,' he wrote. This far north, at this time of year, the nights were short and strangely luminous, more twilight than darkness. He was running through a landscape of wood and water. The silver bark and pale leaves of the birch trees 'seemed to glow in the grey dusk as though lit from within. The countryside seemed haunted, like something out of a sinister fairytale.'[1] He could not maintain the cracking pace and his legs began to weaken. It was hardly surprising. Eighteen months of bad food interspersed with numerous spells in the cooler, together with the exertions of digging the tunnel, had left him in poor shape.

Later, when he tried to recall those days on the run, they felt more like a dream than a reality. He walked eastwards as steadily as his legs allowed, crossing the Lithuanian border, skirting villages and fields where he might encounter workers. The escape rations were soon used up but, hungry though he was, he resisted the temptation to beg food from farmhouses. The Lithuanians were not the Poles. He was unsure of what kind of reception he would get and was not inclined to take the risk.

His condition got steadily worse. He found himself dizzy and short of breath. The going was treacherous in this land of bogs and marshy meadows. Stepping on what appeared to be grass-covered solid ground you might plunge up to your waist in a swamp. He learned to follow goat paths and stick to fields where livestock were grazing. He was hungry and felt desperately tired but when he tried to sleep he was soon jerked awake by the strange noises of the countryside.

One night he settled down on the shore of a lake. It seemed unusually deep and the water shone like a black mirror. He fell into a fitful, feverish sleep. When he woke it was still night. All around the lake he could see pinpoints of light, which he assumed at first came from the torches of a party of soldiers who were out hunting for him. Then he noticed that 'the torches were different colours, blue, green and orangey red and... the soldiers kept throwing them up in the air so that they twisted and turned and gyrated above the reflecting surface of the motionless water, all without the slightest sound.' He realized that he was seeing not flashlights but ignis fatuus, the phosphorescent light that flickers over bogland, caused by the spontaneous combustion of gases. The rational explanation did not help his nerves. He grabbed his bag and hurried on.

Another night, under a full moon and in the middle of nowhere, he came across an old manor house. It seemed deserted, so rather than making a detour round the walls he risked entering the grounds. He was in 'the most beautifully kept Italianate gardens' with hedges clipped into bird and animal shapes, stone-flagged paths and immaculate lawns. 'I seemed to be walking through those gardens for a long time,' he wrote. 'I cannot say whether there was anything in that part of the world to give rise to such a vision, or whether the whole thing was simply in my mind.'[2]

The details of Bill's strange journey are hard to establish. The accounts he left behind vary significantly. By far the fullest version is contained in two memoirs, published decades after the events he described. In one narrative he says he set off with 'some half-baked notion of heading east rather than west as expected, in order to hook up with the advancing Russians or maybe a group of partisans.'[3] He says he had decided to travel alone this time – but does not explain why.

The idea of meeting up with the Red Army was optimistic. The nearest frontline was three hundred miles away. The plan anyway came to nothing, for he was soon too tired and hungry to carry on. What happened next is unclear. One recollection was that he took the risk of knocking on a farmhouse door to ask for food. In another, he bedded down in one of the farm's outbuildings and was prodded awake by a pitchfork. Either way, he fell into the hands of a Lithuanian farmer and his family. With no common language it took a while to convince them that he was neither a Russian nor German deserter but an escaped Texan airman.

Once persuaded, the farmer softened. He made it clear to Bill that if he wanted to stay on and work the fields in return for food and shelter he was welcome. Exhausted and half-starved, Bill thought it was a good idea. 'That is how I found myself starting a new life as a Lithuanian peasant,' he wrote. 'If a German patrol went by I would stop and gawp with the rest of the farm workers, then turn back to shovelling whatever was on the end of my pitchfork.'[4]

It was harvest time and the work was gruelling. He was getting fed and evading capture but he could not stay a farmhand forever. After a while it was time to move on. The question was where? Through talking to his fellow workers he learned that the farm was only a few days walk from the sea. If he could get to the coast and find a boat, he might just make it to Sweden.

The peasants seemed quite sorry to see him go and sent him on his way with some food for the road. After a few days hiking, mostly by night, he arrived at dawn at the coast, just as the mist was rising. His spirits rose. The beach was lined with boathouses. He crept up to one of them and peered through the window. Inside was a sailing dinghy which appeared to have been laid up for the duration of the war. He broke the lock on the door and stepped inside. He knew next to nothing about sailing and had no idea how he would navigate across the Baltic to Sweden. There was no other means of getting there, though, and he decided to give it a try.

The first thing to do was get the boat into the water. He pulled and pushed for a while, before accepting that he would need help. He walked outside. In the distance were several men in overalls, digging in a field. His experiences on the farm had inclined him to feel trusting towards Lithuanian peasants. He walked over to them and explained by words and mime that he was an escaped American pilot who needed their help in getting to Sweden. 'The diggers exchanged glances,' he wrote later. 'Then one wearily stopped digging and rested his hands on the top of his spade, eyeing me with something approaching pity.' To his great surprise he then answered in good if heavily accented English. 'Yes, we would love to help you,' he said. 'But we are soldiers of the German army, and you are standing on our cabbages.'[5]

Soon afterwards a large black car arrived to take him away. When it arrived in Heydekrug he thought at first he was going back to the camp. Instead he was taken to a building in the town, over which a large swastika flag was flying. He was back in the hands of the Gestapo. When the questioning began he gave his name, rank and serial number, using the identity of Don Fair, and produced the identity disc to prove it. The Germans were not satisfied. They took his fingerprints and put him in the cells, where he stayed for 'a few days'. Then he was taken out and marched to the railway station with an escort of six armed guards. No one told him where he was going, but he assumed that this time, in the interests of bureaucratic tidiness, he was being returned to Fair's camp, Stalag Luft III.

The journey was long and the guards told him nothing. He 'looked out of the windows at the devastation caused by war

– a world of refugees from the east and bomber raids from the west. Ragged children watched the train roll by from shells of burned buildings.' Eventually the train pulled into a big city 'heavily pockmarked with bomb-damaged buildings. As it hissed to a stop in the station and I saw the station nameplate, my blood froze. I was in Berlin.'[6] This was the end of the journey. The station was decorated with gigantic pictures of Hitler and Himmler. He was driven to a building that looked like a prison or a courthouse and locked in a cell in the basement. The following day a long series of interrogations began.

In the earlier version of his memoirs Bill wrote that his true identity had been discovered while he was at Heydekrug. In the second, he was unmasked in Berlin. One way or another, the Gestapo now knew they had a hardened escaper on their hands. They were not inclined, though, to believe that he was an ordinary prisoner of war. Instead they accused him of being 'a professionally trained escapologist'. According to his interrogator, 'I had been parachuted in with a cover story about crashing in the Pas-de-Calais before I was picked up in civilian clothes in Paris. Then I fomented more than half a dozen escapes in Germany, Poland and Lithuania... I had moved from country to country training other eager POWs in the black arts of escapology.'[7]

He learned that he was to be charged with espionage and put on trial. The Gestapo man pointed out that if the charges against him were proved, he would no longer have the protection of the Geneva Convention. He asked Bill if he knew what that would mean for him. He knew the answer to that one. It was all familiar from his encounter with the Gestapo in Paris.

Once again he was in line to be taken out and shot. The trial would start immediately. Bill would get regular updates on its progress delivered in person by his interrogator, who, disconcertingly, would also be acting as his defending officer.

As he sat in his windowless cell he reflected on a characteristic feature of the Nazi mentality. 'The strange thing [was] that as they obliterated innocent lives over an entire continent they always liked to do so under the rule of law,' he wrote. 'If they did not have a law that said they could torture or execute you, they would rustle one up and put it on the statute books, so they could kill you in a tidy manner.'[8]

By now Berlin itself was firmly in the firing line. Bill had arrived there just as Bomber Command was preparing its great assault on the 'Big City'. Its commander-in-chief, Sir Arthur 'Bomber' Harris, had persuaded Churchill that his men could hasten the end of the war by battering Berlin to rubble. Over the coming winter, huge raids were mounted and huge losses sustained among the bomber crews. The Battle of Berlin did not bring victory for the Allies. It did, though, teach Berliners the price of supporting the Nazis.

One casualty of the campaign was Bill's court case. The visits from his defending officer grew fewer and fewer. One day he turned up and explained apologetically that 'a minor case like yours couldn't have much priority under the present circumstances'. The case was being postponed. Bill joked later that he 'assured him that I harboured no resentment at all that my crimes against the Third Reich should be treated as insignificant'.[9] A few days later he was put on a train and sent back to Stalag Luft III.

The first account Bill gave of his wanderings told a different story. It was given to an IS9 intelligence officer a few months after he got back to Britain. All returning prisoners of war were questioned about their escape experiences, and the interview with Flight Lieutenant William Frank Ash took place on 20 August 1945. Whereas some, like Eddie Asselin, went into considerable detail, Bill confined himself to the bare outlines. In the report he described how, once out of the tunnel, dressed in civilian clothes and with an *Ausweise* identifying him as a Polish worker, he set off with map and compass, 'walking towards Libau and received a few lifts, but when I got there, could find no ship, so started back towards Kovno on a goods train and was picked up on the way by station guards, as the alarm had been raised. I was taken back to Heydekrug and was given five weeks solitary confinement. My true identity having been discovered I was sent back to Stalag Luft III.'[10] Libau is modern-day Liepāja, a port on the Baltic coast of Latvia, about eighty miles north of Heydekrug. Kovno is Kaunas, a major Lithuanian city more than a hundred miles south-east of the camp. There is no mention of his time on the farm or the journey to Berlin. But nor, in the same interview, did he give any details of his adventures in France following his crash. My researches in the Pas-de-Calais confirmed the account given in the memoirs. The lack of hard information in the passages dealing with Lithuania make it difficult to check. But as Bill pointed out with disarming candour in the introduction to his first book, *A Red Square*, 'I am writing these memoirs off the top of my head.'

During his absence Stalag Luft III had grown enormously. It now housed about 10,000 prisoners and was the size of a small town. Two new areas had been added, North Compound, where a large number of British and Commonwealth aircrew were rehoused in the spring of 1943, and South Compound, built to accommodate the increasing number of American fliers shot down since the US Army Air Force's bombing campaign accelerated.

Bill was put back in the familiar surroundings of East Compound. It was a homecoming of sorts. Some of his old friends were there to greet him, but others, including Paddy Barthropp, had been moved to North Compound, so were half a mile away on the other side of the camp.

After his recent experiences he was inclined to take it easy for a while. In his absence, escape-minded kriegies had continued their battle of wits with the authorities and brought off one spectacular escape. It resulted, very unusually, in the three men who conceived it reaching Sweden, then home. The officers who had been transferred to Schubin while the expansion work was carried out at Sagan found on their return in the summer of 1943 that the new security measures made escaping much tougher. The inspection pits, dug beneath all the huts, meant that unless someone could find new ways of hiding a tunnel entrance and disposing of the spoil, digging was no longer an option.

Once again, kriegie ingenuity cracked what appeared an insoluble problem. Flight Lieutenant Eric Williams and Lieutenant Michael Codner had already made one unsuccessful escape attempt when in Schubin. Undeterred by the tougher conditions at Sagan, Williams came up with an idea that carried a touch of genius. Remembering the vaulting horses that he had hopped over at school he proposed having a modified one built which could carry one or two men inside it. If a routine was established whereby the horse was placed in the same position each day, as close to the wire as possible, the hidden men could start digging, covering the hole with a wooden trap and loose earth at the end of each session. The proposal attracted much scepticism, but the escape committee decided it was worth a try and gave the go-ahead. Work began on 8 July 1943. Nearly four months later, on 29 October, the pair, joined by Flight Lieutenant Oliver Philpot, a Canadian who had helped with the operation, crawled through the tight, shallow shaft and broke out to freedom. Several weeks and many adventures later they were back in Britain after finding ships in Stettin and Danzig which smuggled them to Sweden.

When Bill arrived back, another major tunnelling project was just about to reach fruition. A team led by Squadron Leader Roger Bushell was engaged in the most ambitious construction programme ever undertaken in a prisoner-of-war camp. It began after prisoners were moved into the new quarters in North Compound in the spring of 1943. Bushell's idea was to dig three tunnels simultaneously, codenamed Tom, Dick and Harry. He intended to pass two hundred prisoners through them to freedom, the largest mass escape of the war. Even if one tunnel was discovered it did not mean the end of the enterprise, for the Germans were unlikely to imagine there were any others in progress.

The Wooden Horse escape, as it became known, had faded into legend by the time Bill returned to Sagan at the beginning of 1944. If he had been placed in North Compound, and not back in East Compound, he would have undoubtedly joined

Roger Bushell and the Tom, Dick and Harry team, alongside Paddy Barthropp. Soon after his arrival in East Compound he was placed at another remove from the action.

Since his departure from Stalag Luft III he had racked up a number of offences for which he had not been punished, including impersonating another prisoner in Schubin and breaking out of Heydekrug. The fact that these offences had taken place elsewhere made no difference. Once again Bill found himself in the cooler – and for a protracted stretch.

Bill was not dismayed to find himself back in solitary. 'Despite the isolation it was good to be back,' he wrote. 'The Luft III regime, even in the cooler, was still more civilized than those I had experienced elsewhere, and considerably better than waiting to be shot in Berlin or flattened as collateral damage in the bombing raids there.'[11] He had become the real-life Cooler King. The prospect of passing your days alone confined in a narrow cement cell would strike fear into most. Bill was able to regard it with something like equanimity. He might only have his thoughts for company, but he liked thinking and he had plenty of experiences to ponder on.

He treated it as might a mediaeval hermit – an opportunity to retreat from the world and consider its follies and greatness and to form a philosophy with which to deal with both. 'Never before or since have I had such a sustained period to think about myself, the world and the actions of those around me,' he wrote. 'I had seen heroism and treachery, selfless generosity and animal selfishness.'

Bill had always had a leftwing outlook. Growing up in fiercely patriotic Texas, steeped in a tradition of red-blooded capitalism, such views were considered at best eccentric, at worst akin to treason. In a modern, forward-looking service like the RAF there were plenty of young men of progressive views. Bill was unusual in the depth and sincerity of his commitment, not just to socialism but to something more radical. That was to set him apart from some of his fellow kriegies, especially those whose trading activities he considered little more than racketeering.

His travels around occupied Europe had given him plenty of exposure to the realities of fascist rule. When at Schubin, like Tommy Calnan, he had been moved by the sight of the Russian prisoners who were used as slave labour around the camp, fed a quarter of the rations that were given to the other prisoners and literally worked to death. He learned that when one of them died, the others would hide the body for as long as possible in order to keep getting his bread ration.

The Russians at Schubin were comparatively fortunate. In the first, successful phase of Operation Barbarossa, the vast number of captives who fell into German hands were corralled in the open to die of exposure and starvation. In the winter of 1941–2, more than two million perished. To the Germans, Russian lives were valueless. In Heydekrug, Bill met British soldiers who had been put to work in a mine alongside Russian slave labourers. They had witnessed an incident when a roof collapsed trapping many Russians. For the Germans there was no question of going to the trouble of attempting to rescue them. They were simply left buried alive.

Bill's preference for a quieter life persisted after his release. Before going into the cells he had resumed contact with the book department of the Red Cross in Geneva. He returned to

East Compound to find a stack of the material he had requested waiting for him: Pascal's *Pensées*, works by Descartes, Leibnitz and Spinoza. After living on bread and water, he was too weak to do much more than read. After a time he felt strong enough to return to writing. He bought some notebooks, which were sometimes on sale in the canteen, and began work on a novel. He had whiled away many hours lying on his bunk, scribbling away at stories. This time the results were more satisfying. He called it *Happy in Ulubrae*. The title was taken from one of Horace's epistles, which claimed that if you had the right frame of mind, you could be happy anywhere, even in Ulubrae, an insignificant village near Rome and a metaphor for the back of beyond. The project might have suggested that Bill had settled into passive acceptance of his lot and would be causing no further trouble to the authorities.

In one way escaping was a displacement activity, under-taken with only a notional expectation of success. It was a very effective way of speeding up time, hastening the arrival of that unknown point in the future when the war was over and the gates would open.

But there was more to it than that. Some prisoners had one go at escaping and, having failed, gave up. But men like Bushell, Barthropp, Crawley and Ash discovered that once they had started they couldn't stop. They found it hard to analyse what drove them. Bill, who had had much time to reflect on the question, struggled to answer it as much as anyone.

Occasionally he would wonder whether he would not have been better off settling down to learn a language or study for a diploma that might get him a job when the war was over.

He soon concluded 'I am simply not like that. The Houdini syndrome of getting myself into situations just to see if I can get out of them again is too much part of my nature.'[12]

By the end of winter the manuscript of the novel was finished, inscribed in a pile of notebooks which he kept in a locker by his bunk. He now had time on his hands and it was not long before he was feeling the old itch again. One day he was walking in the compound when he noticed, close to the main gates, a parked lorry being loaded up with what looked like bits of broken-down machinery. He stood back and watched a guard poke through the junk on the lorry then walk away. For a moment he hesitated. He had enjoyed writing the novel. Why didn't he accept that he had done his bit, enjoy the peace and stability of the camp; in short, heed the words of Horace and be 'happy in Ullabrae'? The urge was too strong. Once the driver was in the cab and the engine was running, he jumped over the tailgate and flattened himself on the floor of the truck. It was, as he recalled ruefully later, 'possibly my shortest and most badly planned escape of them all'.[13] When the lorry stopped at the next gate, it took only a few moments for the guards to spot him and haul him out.

He was escorted back to his barrack to pick up his washing kit before being parked in the cooler. The eye of the officer escorting him was caught by something as Bill opened his bedside locker door. 'What's that?' he asked, pointing at the pile of notebooks,' Bill recounted later. He assured him that it was 'a novel set a long time ago and in another land and contained no reference whatsoever to the present war, to any characteristics of the detaining power or to anything else that need trouble a security officer with so much to worry about already'. The officer appeared not to have heard him. He 'took the notebooks out of the locker and very methodically, one by one, tore them into little pieces which he ordered a guard to sweep up and take away'. Of all his literary endeavours, he decided later, 'it was perhaps the most definitive rejection I have ever received'.[14]

During his time in solitary he was woken early one very cold morning by the blare of the camp's sirens. He learned later that the alarm had been raised when a guard spotted a prisoner emerging from a tunnel just outside the North Compound fence. After eleven months of hard labour and intricate organization, the mass breakout that would be celebrated as the Great Escape had finally happened. It was a cheering thought to sustain him during the rest of his sentence.

On the first day after his release from the cooler he learned the price that the escapers had paid for their audacity. He took his place in the rows of kriegies for the ritual of morning *Appell*. This was one that no one would ever forget. Instead of count-ing the prisoners, a Luftwaffe officer began to read out a list of names. There were fifty of them and they were all very familiar. It sounded to Bill like 'a roll call of my old friends and comrades'. There was Roger Bushell, 'one of the greatest natural leaders I ever met', Ian Cross, one of the Schubin escape fraternity, and Tom Kirby-Green, 'a tall, suave and very well-educated young man who shared my love of books and also my allergy to bul-lies'. The officer announced that all fifty had been recaptured but subsequently 'shot while resisting arrest'.[15]

'A great gasp went up from all the men on *Appell*,' Bill wrote. 'Even by the standards of this dirty and vicious war, this was a brutal deed.' No one believed the claim that they had been shot while trying to escape. Otherwise why were there no wounded? The assumption that they had been murdered after capture by the Gestapo turned out to be all too accurate.

When Hitler heard of the breakout he gave an order that all recaptured airmen were to be shot. He also demanded that Commandant von Lindeiner and other camp personnel be arrested and put to death. After an approach by the Luftwaffe and Army chiefs Hermann Göring and Wilhelm Keitel, who warned of possible reprisals against German prisoners in Allied hands, he modified his demands. He now wanted at least half of recaptured escapers killed. Of the seventy-six men who made it out of the tunnel, all but three were captured within a few days. In the end fifty would be murdered, shortly after their arrest. The prisoners were killed singly and in pairs. They were put in cars and driven off, as if they were being taken back to the camp. Their Gestapo escorts would stop the car in an isolated spot and invite them to relieve themselves. Then they would shoot them in the head. Of the remaining twenty-three some were returned to Sagan and a few to Colditz. Harry Day and Johnny Dodge, who were among them, were sent to the Sachsenhausen concentration camp. The list of the dead might have included Paddy Barthropp. He was part of the 'Great Escape' but was still in the tunnel when the alarm was raised.

The murders were a signal, if any were needed, that as far as the treatment of prisoners was concerned, respect for the Geneva Convention and for military formalities was over, and it was the methods of the Gestapo rather than the Luftwaffe that were in the ascendant. The lesson would soon be learned at Heydekrug. Undeterred by the failure of the August 1943 breakout, the escape organization began work on a new scheme which, in its way, was just as impressive and ambitious as Roger Bushell's project. They decided to smuggle a man out of the camp tasked with forging strong links with the local underground and establishing an infrastructure of safe houses and contacts to speed escapees to Danzig and on to Sweden. The man chosen was George Grimson.[16]

On 21 January 1944, in another brilliantly executed operation, he walked out of the compound dressed as a 'ferret' and then through the camp gates. He was followed a few weeks later by Sergeant Cyril Flockhart, who like Grimson spoke fluent German. They met up and after many difficulties Grimson helped Flockhart to board a cargo ship in Danzig and escape to Sweden. He stayed behind, giving assistance to two other escapers, one of whom made it back to Britain. In the months that he was at large, Grimson worked indefatigably, travelling up and down the Baltic coast, successfully navigating hundreds of security checks, making contacts and building the escape network and returning frequently to Heydekrug to pass on reports of his activities.

The operation would not have been possible without the help of members of the camp staff. One was a young German interpreter, an idealist who hated the Nazi regime. Others were Poles connected to the underground. The operation collapsed in mid April when Sergeant Ned Leaman, who was next on the list to escape, was caught as he tried to walk out of the camp disguised as a member of the *Abwehr*. His friendship with the interpreter, who was one of the escape organization's most important contacts, had been noted by the authorities. The interpreter was arrested and later shot. A Polish guard who had provided shelter for Grimson was also believed to have been executed. A young Pole who worked as a Luftwaffe photographer and supplied the prisoners with film and other materials killed himself while awaiting interrogation by the Gestapo. Following Leaman's arrest a message was sent to Grimson to get out of the country. It was too late. He was arrested at the end of April. 'Little more is known about Grimson,' the camp history recorded. 'It is believed that he was executed by the Germans.'[17]

Looking back on these episodes years later, Bill was struck by an overwhelming sense of waste. Persistent escapers tended to be exceptional men. They were unusually determined and undaunted by risk. He had also noted something else among his fellow escapologists. Many seemed to share a desire to build a better world after the war. Before it, Roger Bushell had lived a privileged life and seemed to share the assumptions and prejudices of the upper-class circles he moved in. The war changed him. By the time of his death he had developed a radical streak. At one of the camp's mock parliamentary debates he had taken the role of a Labour Party leader and announced the nationalization of all the country's major industries. Tom Kirby-Green, who had grown up as the son of a colonial civil servant, wanted to dismantle the British Empire. These were men who could have made a great contribution to a new Britain built on fairness. Instead they had literally been reduced to ashes, cremated by the Germans and their remains returned to Stalag Luft III.

For days after the announcement of the killing of the Great Escapers, a pall of anger and sadness hung over the camp. It had become a different place. Lindeiner was gone, marched off to prison for his failure to prevent the outbreak. He survived the war and was to meet his former charges in happier circumstances. The Gestapo and the SS were now in charge. Whatever differences the kriegies might have had with the Luftwaffe staff, they had often shown a human face. The Gestapo seemed to belong to a different race. 'They were peculiarly alike, as if poured from the same loathsome mould,' remembered Richard Passmore, a long-time Sagan inmate. 'They wore identical dark-green soft hats, pulled well down over the eyes, long drab overcoats reaching down to overlap the high military boots... The faces of these men were oddly blank, brutal, inhuman...We hated the Gestapo as we hated nobody else... we would have killed any of them, given the opportunity.'[18]

The change at the top made little difference to the appearance of the camp, as the guards remained largely the same. Everyone knew, though, that escaping had become a far more dangerous activity. Enthusiasm for further attempts fell away. In East Compound, the number of those willing to get involved shrivelled to a small core of diehards. Inevitably Bill was one of them. So too were Aidan Crawley and Joe Kayll, a Battle of Britain veteran who had been one of the organizers of the Wooden Horse scheme. Together with a few others, they made up the escape committee. As it was, events in the outside world intervened, further reducing the chances of any major undertaking.

On 6 June the prisoners monitoring the secret radio ran around East Compound to announce the news that everyone had been dreaming of. The Allies were ashore in Normandy.

The end of the war was finally in sight. That night they got drunk on hooch distilled from raisins and potato peelings. Henceforth the preoccupations of the kriegies shifted dramatically and irrevocably. Now even hard line escapologists were wondering if there was any point in carrying on.

The new mood was demonstrated when two men who had spent weeks digging a blitz tunnel from East Compound announced to the escape committee that they had decided not to use it. It seemed to Bill a great waste of effort and opportunity. Aidan Crawley, who had been selected as a future Labour parliamentary candidate and was anxious to get home to start his political career, felt the same way. Bill and Crawley were joined by a 'spectacularly mad but very brave New Zealander'.[19]

When word got around the compound that an escape bid was imminent, wrote Bill, 'some of the more timid prisoners became very indignant. They did not much mind us risking our own lives, but they were convinced that there would be reprisals on those still in the camp.' He asked them to consider that 'if the brave ordinary French people who had risked their lives to help me and so many others had thought that way, they would all have collaborated meekly in return for a quiet life.' What they were doing was, he admitted, 'less a tactic and more a simple statement of defiance – an unwillingness to crawl in the face of oppression'. The other prisoners were unconvinced. They 'took their worries to the commanding officer and he gently but firmly ordered us not to go'.

Bill felt a certain relief. He could now fall in with the new mood of the camp. The scent of real life was in the air again. Men began to talk – albeit not too confidently, in order to shield themselves from devastating disappointment – of when liberation might come. This year, perhaps. Next year, surely. Lectures and study courses were crammed with kriegies preparing themselves for civilian life, and the debates and mock parliaments ceased to be theoretical and became noisy forums in which the future of post-war Britain was thrashed out by men who wanted fervently to be there to help shape it. And in between times they waited: for the Russians to arrive from the east or the British and Americans from the west. Or for the Gestapo to decide to shoot them all if their efforts to use them as hostages in bargaining with the victors came to nothing.

FOURTEEN

The New Year of 1945 opened on a dispiriting note. The defeat of Germany was taking far longer than the prisoners had hoped. In the West the German counter-offensive in the Ardennes showed there was still plenty of fight left in Hitler's forces. In the East, the Red Army appeared to be pausing until the Spring thaw before resuming its attack. The news – or lack of it – made what was the coldest winter of the war even harder to endure. The camp was blanketed in snow and at nights the temperature plunged to twenty degrees below zero. To compound the prisoners' misery Red Cross deliveries were drying up and each man now received only half the contents of a parcel each week.

Then, suddenly, came a surge of good tidings. Red Cross parcels began to arrive in torrents. More importantly, the Red Army was on the march again and soon the rumble of artillery could be heard in the distance. After resuming their attacks, Soviet forces advanced a hundred miles in five days. On Sunday, 21 January Russian tanks crossed the River Oder at Steinau, just forty-five miles from Sagan. The details from each BBC news bulletin rippled through compounds and the prisoners rushed to maps in the libraries to see how far they were from liberation.

The great question was how would the Germans react? Would they stand and fight? Would they flee, abandoning their prisoners? Or would they take the kriegies with them? Though the prisoners did not know it, their captors had longstanding orders concerning their fate in the event of enemy encroachment. On 19 July the previous year Adolf Hitler had ordered 'preparations for moving prisoners to the rear' if their camps looked like being overrun by the Russians. This directive meant that the last act of the war would hold much more suffering and peril for the prisoners than anything they had endured so far, as the Germans herded them on a series of desperate treks through a chaotic landscape.[1]

For the moment the kriegies had only rumour to go on and the compound commanders gave orders to prepare for all contingencies. There was no point in hoarding the Red Cross parcels and everyone got their allocation. They would need all their strength for whatever lay ahead. Even the most lethargic were caught up in the excitement of events and joined those striving to get fit in preparation for the next – undoubtedly challenging – phase of the story. 'The circuits of the compounds were crowded…with prisoners walking in the snow to harden their feet,' Aidan Crawley remembered. 'The thought that men who had been spectators for so long might once again begin to take part in events was wonderfully stimulating.'[2] In anticipation of a move, some of the more prudent began nailing together Red Cross packing cases and bed boards, to make sledges to transport their supplies over frozen ground, and to fashion knapsacks out of kitbags.

Work parties were formed which would go into action if the camp turned into a battle zone. There were trench-digging teams, first-aiders and firefighters. 'Commando' units were charged with taking over local power stations and waterworks when the time came. In East Compound, Bill Ash and members of the escape committee decided that if the SS contingent in the camp decided to wipe them all out, they would storm the *Kommandantur*, grab weapons and at least take a few of the enemy with them.

The German front was collapsing. Outside the camp gates a flood of civilian refugees coursed westwards, the lucky ones on carts, the rest walking, laden down with whatever they could carry. The prisoners heard of a train of open trucks which had arrived from Breslau filled with children who had been separated from their parents. After a night in the open some of them had frozen to death.

The camp guards waited their turn to be swallowed up in the chaos of the endgame. They were on two hours' notice to move, but whether to march east to confront the Russians or retreat westwards they did not know. A handful of the camp's officers and NCOs volunteered to join an airborne unit and disappeared. The rest, all hope of victory extinguished, wanted only for the war to be over with quickly. Their power was ebbing away and it was impossible not to relish the sight. 'Pleasantest of all', wrote Aidan Crawley, 'was the feeling that control was slipping from German hands… it was still necessary to obey them, but moral authority lay within and not without the wire.

It was the Germans who were harassed and worried. It was the Germans who were uncertain of their future.'³

When the Russians were only thirty miles away, some of the camp's senior staff went to the commandant and asked if they should move their families. They were told to stay put and get on with their jobs. As no orders had come from the German high command concerning the prisoners, the commandant was as much in the dark as anyone.

It was not until Saturday, 27 January that a signal arrived from Berlin. At 2 p.m., the senior British officer in East Compound was told confidentially by the German major in charge that the prisoners would be staying put. Six hours later, the order from Berlin was revised. The camp was being evacuated, after all, and there was no time to lose. The cultural life in the camp was flourishing now, and even the climactic events of the previous few days had not disrupted it. The North Compound theatre was packed with kriegies watching a dress rehearsal of *The Wind and the Rain,* a London stage hit from the 1930s, when the adjutant announced that everyone was to pack up and be ready to move in an hour's time. The same announcement was echoing all around the camp. Robert Kee returned to his barrack to find 'the chaos was terrifying. Food, clothes, books and cigarettes were scattered thickly over the floor, the table and the beds.' Those who had not had the foresight to make a knapsack or sledge were desperately trying to knock one together with whatever came to hand. 'Carefully built shelves, bookcases and lockers, the pride of their owners for years and guarded with strict jealousy, had been torn off the walls... Hammond was almost in tears trying to make himself a rucksack at the last moment. Michael was building a sledge out of a bookcase and part of the table, hammering nails in with a flat piece of iron...'[4]

Stalag Luft III now housed more than 10,000 prisoners. Moving them westwards was going to be an enormous job. In order to create a manageable column, departure times were staggered, with the Americans in South Compound slated to leave first, at nine that night. In the haste and confusion it was ten o'clock before the first contingent marched through the gates.

The East Compound prisoners would be the last to leave. The calculations that had obsessed them all for years suddenly became meaningless. Food – the presence and absence of it – had dominated their lives, shaping their moods and their attitudes to those around them. Friendships had shattered over a spoonful of jam or a slice of spam. Now there was an absurd abundance of it. 'Every stove in the camp was going full blast,' Bill remembered. 'We could only take what we could carry and every scrap of food, carefully hoarded for weeks or even years, was now being wolfed down.'[5]

The camp kitchens had just been issued with a rare ration of fresh meat. 'All this was distributed and the smell of roast joints, a delicacy which prisoners experienced once every two months, pervaded every barrack,' Crawley remembered.[6] The kriegies gorged until their shrunken stomachs could take no more. Tables in the huts were stacked with a cornucopia of canned food and cigarette boxes, free for anyone who wished to take them. The tragedy was that they would have to leave most of it behind.

The prisoners would also have to abandon things that had meant much to them. In the years of captivity they had built up

small hoards of possessions that had enormous personal significance. There were sketches, paintings and carvings, manuscripts
of novels, plays and poems. There were favourite books and
photographs of loved ones. They were the heart of the home
that every kriegie had made for himself in his corner of the
barracks and now he had to make painful choices about what
to take and what to leave.

Survival might depend on what you had loaded onto your
sledge or crammed into your knapsack or pockets – forty
pounds was the recommended maximum weight. If the prisoners had left quickly, the choice would have been swift and there
would be no opportunity for regrets. As it was, the initial panic
subsided and the departure times had kept slipping, giving the
men time to reflect. The loads on the sledges climbed higher
and higher.

Rumour had it that a Wehrmacht armoured unit was due to
take over and the prisoners were determined that they would
destroy what they could not carry. 'The incinerators were soon
alight and piles of old clothes, furniture and anything else that
might add to the comfort of the incoming Germans were burned
steadily through the night,' wrote Crawley.[7] A barrack in North
Compound was set on fire just as the last men departed. The
sense of waste was enormous. For bookish prisoners like Bill it
was painful to think of the million or so volumes left behind, gifts
from his friends in Geneva and the YMCA. The smokers had
to say goodbye to 2.5 million cigarettes stored in East and North
compounds. The knowledge that they were abandoning some
23,000 Red Cross parcels afflicted everyone. Each prisoner was
given one to bring with him, and encouraged to rifle through

others to take what he fancied. They discarded the tins of milk, cheese, butter and meat, in search of the chocolate, coffee and cigarettes which had the highest barter value.

The parcel store was next to the area where the sixty or so Russian prisoners were penned. Bill had befriended one of them, an airman called Artum, whose dignity in the face of the Germans' cruelty had touched him. When, at about six in the morning they finally got the order to move out, he saw Artum waiting with the other Russians at the wire to wish them goodbye and good luck. Bill 'grabbed a tin of Klim milk and lobbed it into their compound'. The rest of the kriegies joined him and 'soon it was raining food on the delighted Russians. Cheese, butter and bully beef poured from the sky as the over-laden guards tried to shove us along.'8 Even before the prisoners were clear of the camp the German women who worked in the censorship office checking parcels and letters, as well as local civilians, had descended to scavenge among the prisoners' leavings.

It was 6 a.m. and still dark when the East Compound prisoners, muffled in layer upon layer of clothes and masked in balaclava helmets, set off at the back of the 10,000-strong column. The skies were clear and the temperature had sunk to twelve below zero. The fields around were thick with snow and it seemed unlikely that in their desperate situation the German authorities would have been able, even if they wished it, to make any proper provision for them along the route to wherever it was they were going. At the beginning, according to Crawley, 'nobody cared very much.' They were 'outside the wire and the mere prospect of moving each day to some unknown destination gave a new purpose to life.'9

The prisoners were in five columns with the South Compound prisoners at the head. In order to make room for those who followed, the Americans were forced to march nearly thirty miles before they bedded down for the night. By that time, the last man in the last British column was twenty miles behind. They headed south from Sagan then west. They had set off in good order, which soon broke down as, despite the efforts of the guards, the marchers settled into groups that moved at a pace dictated by the speed of their sledges or the weight of their packs. The sledges came in all shapes and sizes. The largest, when fully laden, needed three or more men to haul them. But the packed snow beneath their feet made the walking easy and the sledges skated gaily along. The biggest obstacle to progress was the groups of German refugees fleeing the Soviet advance, whose horse-drawn wagons got caught up in the column, slowing everyone down.

The countryside looked wonderful as the dawn came up. Rime glittered like diamonds on the twigs of the trees and the blazing white fields contrasted beautifully with the deep, clean blue of the sky. It seemed to Robert Kee 'as if we were walking through some pantomime set on an enormous stage. The sledge flowed smoothly behind us. The cold air nipped our cheeks and noses, and yet we were snug inside our balaclavas. I was suddenly completely happy.'[10]

Before long the landscape began to lose its allure. The lack of cloud cover kept the temperature well below freezing. There were frequent blizzards, whipped up by bitter winds. After an hour or two every kriegie looked like a walking snowman. Whenever they stopped, boots and clothing froze solid and fingers, toes and every exposed inch of flesh were vulnerable to frostbite. Bread was transformed into crystalline, inedible blocks. When Bill extracted a canteen from inside his jacket and poured a cup of water it turned to ice before he could drink it.

They were supposed to stop for the night at a village called Halbau (Polish, Iłowa), south-west of Sagan on the main Berlin–Warsaw road. When they arrived, the Germans changed their mind and said they would now be billeted at Freiwaldau (Gozdnica), five miles further down the road. But the two halls available were too small to accommodate everyone. They waited in the numbing cold for an hour while the Germans tried to find larger premises. Some of the prisoners sought shelter in the village houses. Then shouts sounded down the main street. SS men and the local police were going door to door, ordering the kriegies out. Impending nemesis from the East had done nothing to dampen the zeal of the local Burgomeister, a Nazi diehard who had sought the help of the local security forces to prevent the prisoners from 'contaminating' his village. The prisoners were told they were moving on to the next village, Lieppa (Lipna), four or five miles away, where there was a large barn where they could spend the night.

The next few hours were the worst of the day. When on the move, the warmth of the prisoners' exertions kept their clothes and packs from freezing. When they stopped for any length of time, everything turned to ice. They marched now, wrote Crawley, 'with bent backs, taking it in turns to haul on the sledge ropes, or, if they were carrying packs, stopping every now and then to jerk the load higher on to their shoulders or bending double to let the pack lie horizontally and give a rest to their muscles.'[11] The only encouragement came from the sound of the Russian guns booming in the east. Rumours flew up and down the column: the Red Army was only twenty miles to the north – they would overtake the prisoners the following day. Sagan had already been overrun. For once, such predictions were no longer just wishful thinking. They were plausible, even likely.

It was dark when they reached Lieppa. When they found the barn it was only big enough for six hundred men. Bill was among the lucky ones. He found a gap on the dirty, straw-covered floor between the bodies of his comrades and collapsed into a deep sleep. The others huddled outside while the Germans tried to find another refuge. The temperature had plunged to twenty below. Clothes, packs and boots became petrified with ice and some began to notice the first symptoms of frostbite. There was a real danger of them all freezing to death. The German officers seemed to have lost interest in the welfare of their charges. It was left to the kriegies' affectionate adversary Hermann Glemnitz to sort out shelter for all but fifty of the prisoners, who spent the night huddled together against a farmyard wall, covered in straw.

They mustered in the morning at eight o'clock. The column had to wait for an hour while the guards made futile attempts to count the men. It was another bright, bitterly cold day. The road they were taking led to the north-west, deeper into the heart of Germany. The first miles passed easily. Every hour, the guards stopped the column for a short rest. Spirits were rising again. It seemed to Robert Kee that 'we were enjoying something close to freedom and whatever else might happen, it seemed certain that... the old life we had hated so long had been smashed forever.'[12]

The comfort these thoughts provided began to fade as cold and fatigue set in. The feeling of impending liberty affected everyone. The guards were under orders to shoot anyone who tried to escape, but no one, not even Bill, felt tempted to. Why should they, when they were marching towards their countrymen advancing from the west? Even if they did, however, the guards were unlikely to do much to stop them. 'With a biting wind blowing the snow into their faces they usually marched with their heads down and their eyes on the feet of the man in front of them, caring nothing for what went on around them,' wrote Crawley.[13] A number of them were elderly. Their kit was carried on wagons that creaked along at the back of the column, but some found even the weight of their guns too much for them. One asked a kriegie to carry his submachine gun for him. Others put their weapons on the sledges, only to have them thrown into a ditch as soon as their backs were turned.

Tolstoy's *War and Peace* was a popular book with the prisoners. Crawley was one of many who felt he was reliving the retreat from Moscow of the Grande Armée: 'Soldiers, prisoners and civilians were intermingled, all were suffering the same hardships, and all were engaged in the struggle for survival.' Hundreds of thousands of human beings, soldier and civilian, were suffering the same ordeal all along the length of the Soviet advance. The prisoners of Stalag Luft III were just another stream in the vast confluence of refugees flowing westwards. All distinctions were obliterated by the crust of snow that covered them all. They clanked and jangled as they walked, weighed down with kettles and pans. Anyone looking on, wrote Crawley, would find it 'difficult to recognize the bent and bedraggled figures as those of military men'.

The prisoners travelled in ones or twos, hunched over to make a smaller target for the wind, hauling the sledges behind them. Rope had been in short supply and they had to make do with knotted strips cut from sheets and blankets, which were always breaking, forcing them to stop for repairs. This provoked the guards into occasional bouts of aggression. Bill remembered a party who had stopped to repack the Red Cross parcels on their sledge and were sampling some of the contents when 'one of the more vicious guards stormed up with two Alsatian… dogs straining at the leash. He yelled at the prisoners to get going but they continued to take their time, munching and packing, as if they were having a bizarre picnic at the edge of hell.' The guard then set the dogs on the picnickers only to see them trot over to the kriegies 'wagging their tails and begging for some food. They were rewarded for their disloyalty with corned beef and chocolate and settled in for a feast while their handler roared, yelled and hopped up and down to no avail.'[14]

Orderly progress was impossible, despite the efforts of the more zealous guards.

The Germans were now undergoing the ordeal they had inflicted on so many in Poland, Belgium, Holland, France and Russia in the heady early years when they were the masters driving the weak and helpless before them. In the case of the civilians, the prisoners' satisfaction at the thought that it was their turn to suffer was tempered with pity. Crawley watched the lines of wagons moving with agonizing slowness towards a haven that seemed always to melt away before they could reach it, and found it 'a pathetic sight. Old men and women dressed in black and muffled up to the eyes sat motionless on the front seat without speaking; children and pregnant mothers lay among the mattresses and furniture in the back; behind, tied to the wagons with ropes, came the two or three loose horses the family had been able to bring along. The elder boys and girls walked.'[15] Many of them had already travelled more than a thousand miles from the steppes of the Ukraine. They had no connection with the villagers whose lands they were passing through except their ethnicity, and 'wherever they went they were unwelcome'.

The places they sought shelter in were already crammed with refugees from the cities, which had been under regular heavy bombardment by the Allied air forces for nearly four years. When no room was available they were forced to circle their wagons in the market square, where fires were lit and the meagre supplies of food distributed, and in the morning they were on their way again.

There was no hostility between prisoners and refugees. Instead they often felt a sense of shared misfortune that brought them together. Crawley recalled how, 'as each column of wagons passed, prisoners would get up and sit beside the old couple who were driving the horse or clamber into the back and play with the children, enjoying the luxury of being carried for half a mile on a mattress. The refugees were too poor to do barter, but the prisoners gave them chocolate and anything else they could spare.'

With the Germans they encountered along the route it was a different story. They were farming folk whose crops and livestock had helped to insulate them from the hardship suffered in the towns. What they could not get were luxuries: coffee, chocolate, cigarettes, and most of all soap. At this stage the prisoners had plenty of everything. The rates were soon established – though those at the back of the column would complain that those up front had set the price too high: twenty to fifty cigarettes or a tin of coffee for an outsize loaf of bread, five cigarettes for a pound of potatoes, thirty for a litre of beer and ten for a single egg or a pound of onions. Unless there was an officer around, the guards usually did not interfere. Bill was standing at the side of the road negotiating with a farmer over the purchase of a loaf of bread when an officer passed, and a guard who until then had been taking no notice of the transaction now rushed over to shoo the farmer away. Once the officer was gone, though, the guard called the farmer back and the deal was concluded. He then 'accepted a hunk of bread for his role as middleman – a tiny gesture proving that the world we had all known was crumbling around us'.[16]

Sometimes the locals resisted these interventions. One couple was handing out cups of watery soup to the passing kriegies. They would take no payment except for some bars of soap. An officer noticed what was happening and came over to order them to stop. The husband cowered but the woman replied sharply that her son was a prisoner of war in England. In his letters home he said that the English were treating him well and she was going to do the same in return. The officer contented himself with kicking over the soup pot, now all but empty. Not long before, such defiance might have cost the woman her life.

It took courage to fraternize. The places they passed through had their own Nazis whose fanaticism was undimmed, and SS troops sometimes appeared along the route. On several occasions the columns were harangued by Hitler loyalists who denounced them as child murderers who had destroyed German cities, but the civilians seemed to take little notice and were indifferent or hostile to what was said to the prisoners.

As the day progressed the number of frostbite cases climbed, afflicting prisoners and guards alike. The worst cases were left behind to await help in whatever shelter was available. There was another danger lurking. At the frequent halts there was a great temptation to settle into the snow and doze off. To give in to it could be fatal. From time to time, prisoners noticed that someone was missing and search parties were sent to find the dropout and rouse him from a sleep that might otherwise have ended in death.

They stopped that night at Muskau, after a twenty-mile march. It was a handsome spa town, built around a domed palace that was the home of the Arnim family. The master of the house, General Hans-Jürgen von Arnim had replaced Rommel as army commander in North Africa and was now a prisoner of the British. His brother was in residence when the kriegies arrived and was hospitable and friendly.

The town was still run along feudal lines and Nazi influence was limited. The column from the East Compound was met by the mayor who arranged for billets so that everyone was housed within a couple of hours. Many were put up in the well-appointed stables of the big house. The others settled into a laundry, a pottery and a French prisoner-of-war camp a few miles outside the town. For some, the trek had been an ordeal too many. Prisoners collapsed in the snow and had to be carried inside. One guard had a frostbitten leg that had turned gangrenous. An Australian prisoner called Digby Young, a medical student before the war, carried out an emergency operation with the only instruments and anaesthetic available – some kitchen knives and a bottle of alcohol – and saved the man's life.

Muskau was awash with prisoners. Waiting to be housed was no hardship. The people of the town, from the lord of the manor down, were remarkably friendly. The bakeries worked overtime producing bread for everyone. Some prisoners were able to take a hot bath. Fear of the future dissolved all differences and the hosts sought reassurance from their guests. 'The Germans as a whole were longing for the end of the war,' wrote Crawley. They 'were terrified of the Russians, and the British prisoners were asked anxiously how the Russians were likely to behave and whether the civilians should join the flood of refugees or stay where they were.'[17] Arnim was under no illusions about the catastrophe awaiting him. The house was full of fine furniture and paintings which he was sure would be seized or destroyed by the conquerors. So it turned out, when the Russians eventually rolled in, ten weeks later.

Bill Ash and the East Compound party arrived in Muskau on the afternoon of Wednesday 31 January and were billeted in a large glass-factory in the town. The brick halls of the works were dominated by large furnaces which had to be kept white hot to produce the molten glass. On arrival the prisoners lay gratefully along the padded sides of the furnaces luxuriating in the heat.

There were still better things to come. The factory was manned by French prisoners of war who rustled up hot soup.

Over the next hours they enjoyed their good fortune, breaking out the remains of their Red Cross parcels and items obtained by barter en route and cooking them on the steel doors of the kilns. They took the chance to dry out their clothes and every hot surface was covered with steaming garments.

The camp radio experts had brought at least one of the clandestine sets with them. In a corner of the factory they set up their equipment and rigged an aerial to listen in to the BBC news. There was disappointingly little new information about their sector of the front. Bill fell off to sleep to the familiar sound of kriegies speculating about what would happen next.

When he woke the factory was transformed. Prisoners were snatching up their possessions and getting ready to leave. They were saying goodbye to their snug haven and moving on. Bill went to the place by the kiln where he had left his boots to dry. When he pulled them on, the extreme heat had caused the soles to start coming away from the uppers. He bound them together as best he could with strips of torn-up cloth. Then, as so often, the sudden urgency evaporated. The mass of prisoners was to be broken up and sent off in different directions. Everyone would have to stay put until the plans were finalized.

Overnight the weather had changed. A fine drizzle was falling and the snow that only the previous evening had seemed a permanent feature of the landscape was disappearing before their eyes. The thaw had not been expected for another month. Like the Russians, it had come early. That afternoon the division was announced. All the prisoners from North Compound and half of East Compound were to march that evening for Spremburg, a sizeable town seventeen miles away, where trains would take them to Bremen the following day. The rest of East Compound, together with prisoners from the Stalag Luft III satellite camp of Belaria, would follow later and then be put on trains for Nuremburg. While they waited to depart, discussion raged about which was the better option. Bremen was nearer the Allied Front, but with the Russians advancing so rapidly, the Nuremberg contingent might stand a better chance of early liberation. Some men agitated to transfer from their allotted group and were allowed to do so. Then came the time for farewells. Men who for years had shared the same confinement, endured equal hardships and despaired and laughed together were parting, perhaps for ever.

Bill was in the first column to leave. It was dark when they set off out of town, once more heading north and east. The snow in the streets had turned to black slush. The sledges that had been their salvation now became a liability, bumping over the cobbles, then the mud and stones of the open road. One after another, sledges were abandoned. A few groups pulling larger sledges struggled on for some hours, unwilling to jettison their extra food parcels, before giving up.

The column arrived at a village called Grunstein at 6 a.m. on the morning of 2 February. They grabbed some sleep in barns for a few hours before setting off again. Bill remembered seeing German troops heading for the front and a column of Russian prisoners whose appearance made him realize again how comparatively fortunate he and his comrades were. 'They were all skeleton thin, their brave, sunken eyes burning out of skull-like faces covered in full, ragged beards,' he wrote. Their SS guards herded them as if they were wild animals, urging them along with whips and rifle blows. One of the kriegies threw a tin of cigarettes into their midst, another some chocolate, and soon the Russians were deluged with Red Cross goodies. One packet of cigarettes fell short and when a prisoner darted out to get it an SS guard began smashing him with his rifle. 'A collective roar went up from our side of the road and several hundred Allied prisoners stopped and moved a few dangerous inches towards the Russian column,' he remembered.[18] SS fingers tightened on triggers. Then the realization struck them that though they had the guns, they did not have the numbers, and if they opened fire they stood to be torn to pieces. The guard was pulled away by his colleagues. The Russian picked up his cigarettes and got back into line, throwing a blood-stained smile and a look of thanks at the kriegies before the columns moved off in opposite directions.

They reached Spremburg, a sizeable town on the river Spree, in the early afternoon, and marched down to the railway yards. An hour later they were loaded onto cattle trucks. As usual no one told them where they would be taken to next. Throughout the long march, elation at the prospect that they would soon be liberated was tempered with the thought that at any moment they might be shot out of hand. Perhaps it would be the result of a demented order from on high, perhaps simply because they were an inconvenience and were deemed to have no further value. As they clambered into the trucks, the prospect that they were being carried off to a place of execution seemed all too plausible.

The train wheezed out of the sidings. The guards had crammed them in so tightly that it was impossible to stretch out on the dung-encrusted floor and sleep. As they rumbled down the track, the sound of coughing and retching filled the trucks. Bill was suffering too. He was racked with nausea and a feverish heat was starting to grip his body. The only food available was what they had brought with them, and supplies of water soon ran out. At one of the frequent halts they managed to drain some warm, muddy water from one of the steam-engine cisterns.

It was twenty-four hours before they reached their destination. They arrived at a small town called Tarmstedt, about fifteen miles north-east of Bremen, at 5.30 on the afternoon of Sunday, 4 February. By the time Bill staggered down from the truck he was burning with fever and his skin and the whites of his eyes had turned an alarming yellow. He knew what the symptoms meant. He was going down with jaundice, a common condition in the camps.

As the prisoners milled around in the sidings they learned why they had been taken to Tarmstedt. It was close to a prisoner-of-war camp called Marlag und Milag Nord, near the village of Westertimke, which until shortly before had been occupied by men from the Royal Navy and Mercantile Marine. The organization seemed to be better here than at any point along the route. Before they set off, German medical staff moved through the crowd, assessing the condition of the kriegies. Bill recalled how 'a medic took one look at me and ordered me to remain, along with other prisoners who were too sick to travel.'[19]

There was just enough time to say goodbye to Paddy and a few of his other friends. It was a terrible wrench. Ghastly though the journey had been, they had all been in it together, sustaining each other with the same black humour that had got them through the worst times in the camps. They parted with the ritual that had been spoken at the exit to a freshly broken tunnel, wishing each other good luck and God speed and looking forward to a rendezvous at some London watering hole. Before, the prospect of a drink in Blighty had seemed little more than fantasy. Now it was tantalizingly real. All they had to do was stay alive.

FIFTEEN

All over Germany's shrinking territory prisoners were on the move. Since the beginning of the year, more than 80,000 Allied POWs had been evacuated from their camps and sent off on nightmarish odysseys across Poland, Germany and Czechoslovakia. The experience of the Stalag Luft III columns was just one chapter in an epic of suffering. When it was over the names they gave to their ordeals told the story: the Long March, the Black March, the Death March.

Illness had brought Bill Ash's wanderings to a halt. The account he left behind of his last days in captivity is rather sketchy. He described how after he was taken off the train at Tarmstedt he was moved with the other sick prisoners to 'an encampment somewhere outside Bremen' and dumped in tented sick quarters 'with no facilities, teeming with men suffering from dysentery, gangrene, malnutrition, frostbite' or, like him, jaundice.[1] The report of his interview with IS9 on his return to Britain gives his last location as 'Milag Marlag Nord [Westertimke]', the camp for Royal Navy and merchant seamen where the rest of the Stalag Luft III prisoners were taken.[2] The camp hospital was situated between the two main compounds, which were wired off and separate from each other. He makes no mention of seeing his old comrades in the months before liberation, even though they would have been only a few hundred yards away.

The eight-day journey from Sagan had taken the prisoners five hundred miles from the south-east to the north-west of Germany. Looking up, the inmates often saw the feathery condensation trails of high-flying American bombers or stepped-up formations of Lancasters on their way to targets in the east. Occasionally there was the cheering sight of predatory British fighters, scouring the land below for targets of opportunity. Sometimes the bombs fell on Bremen. Five times during the month of February the much-battered city was hit by small raids, designed to further drain the population's all but exhausted morale. Of Allied troops, however, there was still no sign.

As the weeks passed and the weather relented, Bill slowly recovered. For the first time in his war he felt resigned to his situation and all thoughts of escape were extinguished. There was no longer any point. The greatest victory over the Germans would be to survive. But how long would he have to wait?

The advance into north-east Germany was in the hands of the British Army's XXX Corps under the command of Lieutenant General Brian Horrocks. At its spearhead was the Guards Armoured Division, formed in June 1941 by taking elements from elite units of the Foot Guards and putting them into tanks. They had gone into action a few weeks after D-Day and since then had been fighting almost continuously. They took part in the Battle of Caen, then endured the harsh fighting and bitter disappointment of Operation Market Garden, aimed at capturing the bridges of the lower Rhine river system and speeding up the end of the war. They finally crossed the Rhine on 30 March at Rees, near Cleve in North-Rhine Westphalia, about 180 miles as the crow flies from Westertimke. In the fighting that followed they pushed ahead of XXX Corps on a north-eastern trajectory. Their mission was to cut the Bremen–Hamburg autobahn, block the retreat of German troops falling back from Bremen, and secure the 'peninsula' between the Weser and the Elbe.

The march from the Rhine had been a long series of small but bitter clashes against a fanatically determined and skilful enemy. The defenders fell back, only to regroup and launch a succession of hard-fought delaying actions. The Guards advanced along roads that were cratered, mined and blocked by rubble from demolitions. The landscape was watery, criss-crossed with streams and rivers, each one of which presented a challenge to the armour. When they stopped to find a way round obstacles the defenders sprang ambushes which cost lives and sapped resolve. The German resistance was pointless. These actions might hold up the Allied advance and inflict casualties, but the war was lost and fighting on only added to the devastation of towns and villages and increased the toll of German dead and wounded. The nihilistic determination that had gripped the Germans since the start of the Nazi era was slow to die. It was reinforced by orders from the highest level, for the chief of the SS, Heinrich Himmler, had decreed that 'every village and every town will be defended and held by every available means'.[3] Many German soldiers needed no encouragement. The Guards' war diary is full of encounters that left thirty, forty, sometimes a hundred enemy dead. That their own casualties were comparatively light did not lessen the sense of futility and waste. To die at this point in the war seemed a particularly bitter fate.

On 19 April the Guards crossed the Bremen–Hamburg auto-bahn from the south and captured some villages on the far side. Their next objective was the town of Zeven, which dominated the area's communications. They paused for a while for artillery to come up and took the town with relative ease on 24 April. That night, 32 Guards Brigade, made up of one battalion each of the Coldstream, Scots, Welsh and Irish Guards, was ordered to move south-west the following morning to seize the only relatively high ground in the neighbourhood. This lay about eight miles away and dominated the rear defences of Bremen, whose fall it was hoped to hasten. There was also, the divisional history recorded, 'a secondary objective of importance... a camp at Westertimke which lay just to the south of the high ground and was known to contain a large number of British prisoners of war'.[4]

Everyone in Marlag–Milag had been hearing the sounds of battle for days. The camp was bursting with prisoners. Until the end of 1944 it had housed just over 4,000 Royal Navy and Merchant Navy Officers and NCOs. The arrival of the Stalag Luft III contingent boosted the numbers by 2,000. As the news of the British advance reached the camp, the administration began to fall apart. On 2 April the commandant announced he had received orders to evacuate the camp with most of the guards, leaving only a small detachment to hand over to the Allies. But on the same day a hundred members of the SS

Feldgendarmerie (military police) turned up. They rounded up more than 3,000 men and marched them off to the east. The next day the column was shot up by RAF aircraft and several prisoners killed. As they continued there were further air attacks until the Senior British Naval Officer persuaded the SS men to accept the prisoners' parole that they would not try and escape, in return for letting them sleep during the day and walk at night.[5] The prisoners were finally liberated on 1 May after reaching Lübeck.

On 9 April, the guards at Marlag–Milag disappeared, presumably ordered to take part in the rearguard fighting, and were replaced by members of the local Volkssturm, the last-gasp force scraped together from all males, young and old, who had so far been spared military service. They were stiffened by a contingent of SS guards who lived opposite the camp next to the hospital area. The prisoners watched the changes with a mixture of fear and happy anticipation.

They longed for the clank and rattle that would announce the arrival of their liberators. Then one day, Bill heard 'the rumble of mechanized infantry and self-propelled guns'. He hurried towards the gate, determined to be there to welcome the Allies. But instead of friendly British faces he saw 'row upon row of white-clad German soldiers from a crack mountain division' accompanied by caterpillar-tracked self-propelled guns and Tiger tanks.[6] The troops were in fact from the 15th Panzergrenadier Division and their commander, Lieutenant General Roth, seemed intent on turning the camp into a redoubt, positioning his guns and armour around it in the apparent belief that if the advancing Allies knew that their own people were inside they would not open fire. The prisoners began digging slit trenches in anticipation of the coming battle.

The Panzergrenadiers arrival came just as 32 Guards Brigade also arrived in the area. They were preparing to move on to Westertimke when two emissaries from the camp arrived. The commandant and one of his staff were bearing a message from Roth, who had decided after all to try and avoid a head-on clash. Roth was proposing a ten-hour truce during which the prisoners could be moved out of the danger zone and handed over to the Guards.

'At first sight it seemed an altruistic gesture,' the divisional history recorded. The Guards soon decided though that 'General Roth was no fool and it was a transparent attempt on his part to get some extra time for the extraction of his division.'[7] The next morning, 27 April, the Brigade renewed its advance. Between it and the camp lay the village of Kirchtimke, which the Germans held in strength. The weather was appalling. It had rained heavily overnight and the ground was a morass. As they approached the village, they came under intense shell and mortar fire. Mines were a bigger problem. They had been laid on not only the main route but on all the lanes around. The village was eventually taken and three self-propelled guns destroyed but the Guards took casualties in the process, especially from the mines. In the village the cobblestones contained metal traces that made the mine detectors ineffective. The Germans had laid the mines so deep that the leading tanks could go over one without setting it off, but in the process packed down the earth above it so the next vehicle would set it off. The Welsh Guards contingent lost nine tanks that way. The second battalion of the Scots Guards made up part of the force advancing on Westertimke. The official history recorded that, for them, 'the shelling that day was the heaviest experienced... in Germany and was continuous from dawn to dusk.' In the circumstances their casualties were 'amazingly light'. Nineteen were wounded and three killed in the course of the day, among them Guardsman Gilbert McKeand who had survived many similar encounters in North Africa and Italy.[8]

A reserve force of one company supported by tanks was ordered to push on and try and reach the camp before nightfall. The approach to Marlag–Milag was dominated on the right by some thick woods on rising ground. They were occupied by Panzergrenadiers who opened up on the Guards when they came into view.

'The company routed them after a fierce battle in which they killed about twenty and took about the same number prisoner,' the history noted. As they moved on towards the camp gates they saw a self-propelled gun trundling away from its position in the SS quarters next to the hospital area. The history continued: 'We were taking no chances and the tanks soon set most of the huts on fire with their guns.'

The prisoners found themselves caught in the middle of the fight. 'Rockets screamed over our heads, shells burst around us and shrapnel showered down like rain,' Bill wrote.[9] At first he felt no fear. Then his knees were shaking so violently that he had trouble staying on his feet. He was distracted by the noise coming from the hospital area. The patients were screaming in distress and Bill found his legs were working again. He and some other prisoners ran over and began organizing an evacuation.

Those who were unable to walk they carried on their backs and laid down in a sheltered corner. The Germans seemed determined to fight on. Unless the battle was brought to a swift end, it seemed certain that many prisoners would die with them.

Through the din of battle a clear thought formed in Bill's head. 'Here at last was something I could do to make myself useful in the war,' he wrote.[10] He was going to stage his last bid for freedom and make a run for the Allied lines. He glanced around to check the positions of the prisoners and the enemy tanks and guns. Then he was off, running as fast as his diminished strength would allow.

Later he would try and analyse what it was that had driven him on. 'I should not make out that my motives were altogether heroic,' he wrote. 'I wanted to help my fellow prisoners, and as always found myself on the side of the underdog, attempting to protect those who were unable to protect themselves.' But he also had 'simpler, more human motives. One was pride – I had come into the war on my own terms and I was going to leave it that way.' He would 'rather risk a bullet in the back than cower under a hail of shells wondering if the next incoming round would finish [him] off'.

And then there was what he called 'the old ticking clock, deep within me, that simply saw the chance for one last escape… after a wartime of escaping and being recaptured, this time I was going all the way. This time, for better or worse, life or death, would be my last escape: my home run.' The air was thick with hurtling metal as he dodged round shell holes and negotiated gates and fences. Images of flight coursed through his head – back to when he was an 8-year-old in Texas and seeking freedom with nothing more than ten cents in his pocket and a yearning to discover the great wide world.

As he ran on, the sounds of battle diminished. The camp was well behind him and the way ahead blocked by a hedge. He struggled through it and emerged onto a small road. He gathered his remaining strength and set off along it. Then there in front of him loomed a tank. Some soldiers stood beside it and they raised their rifles as he trotted forward. He slowed down but kept on coming until he heard the click of rifle bolts. Someone was shouting 'Don't shoot! He's British.' He heard himself replying: 'Actually I'm American. And Canadian. And British. It's a long story.'[11]

There would be plenty of time to recount his adventures. His job now was to make sure the battle ended quickly. He reported what he knew about the enemy's dispositions and the locations of the prisoners. Soon after, the Germans had withdrawn and when the Scots Guards visited the camp the next day they were mobbed by ecstatic prisoners, who were 'absolutely amazed that we had been able to free them without any "overs" [stray shells] hitting them'.[12]

That morning, 28 April, prisoner-of-war and medical-relief detachments arrived to take over. On 8 May, the war in Europe was officially over. A few days later Bill was back in the air again for the first time in three years, in the back of a transport plane bound for Britain. He had started life as an American and fought as a Canadian. But as the aircraft touched down and he stepped out into an English summer, he knew he was coming home.

EPILOGUE

Many of the things that Bill had dreamed of during the years of captivity now started to come true. He married Patricia Rimbaud, the beautiful Wren whose affections he had nurtured in monthly letters from the camps, and in time they had a daughter, Juliet, and a son, Francis. Having lost his American citizenship on joining up with the Canadian air force, he now became a British subject and won a place at Balliol College Oxford, to study Politics, Philosophy and Economics, rubbing shoulders with the bright new generation of budding politicians, academics and journalists. After graduating he joined the BBC's External Services and before long was sent as BBC representative to India and Pakistan, just as they took their first steps as independent nations. The job perfectly suited his talents and sympathies. Freedom was in the air, and with it the aspiration to build a modern, equitable society. He admired the Indian leader Jawaharlal Nehru as a fellow socialist and the two became friends. He was on good enough terms with him to be able to arrange for his old friend

Aidan Crawley to dine with the prime minister and his friend
Edwina Mountbatten when Crawley visited India to make a
television programme.

As time passed his politics became 'wilder and redder'.[1]
His journey to the far left was hastened by his experiences as
a prisoner of war. Many years later he would remember how
'whenever things got bad for us like on the march, everybody
would become socialists. They helped each other. If anybody
had any food at all they were sharing it with everybody else.'[2]
In times of plenty, though, the reverse happened, and entre-
preneurial kriegies traded Red Cross parcel items to benefit
themselves. Bill knew which system he preferred. He returned
to Britain in the late 1950s and later applied to join the British
Communist Party, but was said to have been rejected for being
'too quirky and individualistic'.[3] Eventually he co-founded a
breakaway Marxist–Leninist organization.

His views did not affect old friendships. Paddy Barthropp was
no socialist. After the war he stayed on in the RAF, ending up
a wing-commander captain. On retirement in 1958 he started a
business with an old comrade from Battle of Britain days, Brian
Kingcome, supplying chauffeur-driven limousines to the rich
and famous. Bill and Paddy remained close, meeting regularly
to reminisce and engage in good-humoured political sparring.
Paddy's widow, Betty, remembered that 'Paddy loved the fact
that Bill lived in a flat in Moscow Road.'[4]

Many of the escapologists of Stalag Luft III seemed driven
by a determination to make up for the time they had lost behind
the wire. Tony Barber became a Conservative Chancellor of the
Exchequer. Robert Kee was one of the best-known broadcasters

of his time and an outstanding popular historian. Aidan Crawley won a seat as a Labour MP in the July 1945 election and went on to become a pioneer of independent TV, ending up chairman of London Weekend Television and a rich man. His leftist views faded with time and he disappointed Bill by defecting to the Conservatives. Eddie Asselin returned to Canada and gained prominence as a lawyer and politician in Quebec.

Whatever they achieved, their experiences as prisoners of war had shaped them and could not be forgotten easily. Bill was drawn back to the period between the crash landing and his arrest two months later in Paris by the Gestapo. What had happened to the French men and women who had helped him? Some paid heavily for their courage. When Bill went on a voyage of discovery to the Pas de Calais in the early 1970s he learned that Pauline Le Cam, the woman who gave him civilian clothes in Vieille-Église,[5] after arrest and imprisonment had spent three years working as a slave labourer in German factories, an experience which undermined her health for the rest of her life. She married a fellow resister and had two children and was made a Chevalier of the Légion d'Honneur in 1975.[6] Marthe Boulanger, the Neuville innkeeper's daughter, carried on her resistance activities and eighteen months after her encounter with Bill was arrested, beaten, starved and sent to the Ravensbruck women's camp in Germany. She survived, but her health was ruined. Bill visited her a few years later. 'She sat up in bed to greet me but she was very weak and was not thought likely to survive for long,' he wrote.[7] She was awarded the Legion d'Honneur and General de Gaulle came to present it in person. She died shortly afterwards.

It was some time before Bill identified his mysterious French underground courier as Jean de la Olla. He too was arrested in 1943, tortured and sent to a series of concentration camps, but miraculously emerged alive. For years Bill lived with the belief that Joseph and Giselle Gillet, the couple whose Paris flat he hid in and who had been arrested with him, had probably been executed. A memoir written by Louis Nouveau, a member of the Pat O'Leary network, gave him hope that there had been a happier outcome. Nouveau mentioned a man known as 'Miquet' – pseudonyms were obligatory in the underground – who with his girlfriend sheltered an Allied airman in Paris in May 1942. There had been no opportunity to move the airman on and he had stayed there for several weeks before they were all arrested.

Miquet ended up in Fresnes prison, south of Paris, along with Nouveau and la Olla. According to la Olla, Miquet was saved from the firing squad when his girlfriend came forward to claim that she alone was guilty of harbouring the flier. Miquet's death sentence was commuted to imprisonment and the woman was sent to Ravensbruck. Both survived the war. 'I have no way of knowing for sure if this was the couple that sheltered me,' wrote Bill, 'but the circumstances, their remarkable courage and their devotion to each other all seem to fit the bill. I owe them my life.'[8]

He was also eager to find out what happened to his alter ego Don Fair, the New Zealander with whom he had swapped identities in order to get himself transferred to Heydekrug. Around the time of the publication of his memoir *Under the Wire* in 2005, Bill did 'a bit of digging' which 'resulted in the news that Don

Fair had settled in London after the war, had lived less than a mile from [Bill's] home in West London, had married and had a family and a very successful career as an economist.'⁹ It was a source of great regret that he only learned this some years after Don had passed away.

Bill's marriage to Patricia did not last. His relationship with the BBC also faltered, as his employers grew increasingly disturbed by his Marxist views. He got married again, to Ranjana Sidhanta, a leftwing academic, and continued to get work at the corporation as a script reader in the drama department. According to his daughter Juliet he 'had a very, very close relationship with his children and particularly his grandchildren' – of whom there were five.¹⁰ His career had taken him off the path he had set for himself in the camps, lying on his bunk filling notebooks with stories. In the early 1960s, his dedication began to pay off. In 1961, his first novel, *The Lotus in the Sky*, appeared. It was followed by *Choice of Arms* (1962) and *The Longest Way Round*, the latter earning praise from Anthony Burgess. There were two more but sales did not match the critical reception. It did not matter too much to him. Money was never important and the income from his BBC earnings and his Canadian war pension kept the wolf from the door of his and Ranjana's flat in Bayswater, west London.

In 1961 the Sagan kriegies saw their experiences dramatized in a film that became one of the most successful war movies in history. *The Great Escape*, produced and directed by James Sturges, was inspired by the mass break-out from North Compound of Stalag Luft III in March 1944, and contained many scenes that echoed actual events. Some of the characters were based on

real individuals, others were composites of several. One of the
most striking was Captain Virgil Hilts of the USAAF, played
by Steve McQueen. Hilts was the 'Cooler King', a dedicated
escapologist who whiled away his frequent spells in solitary by
endlessly bouncing a baseball off his cell wall and catching it in a
leather mitt. Was Hilts really Bill Ash? It was a question Bill was
asked frequently and his reply was typically modest. He pointed
out that he had not taken part in the Great Escape, as he had
been in a different compound and anyway in the cooler at the
time. He had just returned from his post-Heydekrug spell in the
hands of the Gestapo and was serving a deferred sentence for
having impersonated an NCO in order to get out of the camp.
There are other claimants for the title of inspiration for the role
but Bill seems a very plausible candidate as a model. Stalag Luft
III was full of extraordinary men. There was no one quite like
Bill, however, and Hilts's indomitable courage, laconic manner
and dry wit seem to catch his essence perfectly.

For all his eloquence and love of words, Bill never quite
pinned down what it was that fed his determination to escape.
It seemed to consist of several elements. Escaping was a way of
passing the hours that limped by on leaden feet as the kriegies
served a term that had no predictable end. He was also moved
by a strong desire to get back into the fight. Bill believed that
his career as a warrior had never properly started and felt it his
duty to make a real contribution to the great cause of smashing
fascism. Beyond that, though, was something intangible and
universal. It was above all an act of defiance against all that was
bad in the world, 'an unwillingness', as he had once put it, 'to
crawl in the face of oppression.'[11]

Bill Ash never lost the innocence that he carried with him since his earliest days as a wide-eyed boy in Texas, seeking adventures wherever they might pop up.

He died in London on 26 April 2014. He did not believe in God but he believed in the goodness of man, despite all the evidence he had witnessed to the contrary in his ninety-six years of life. His prisoner-of-war experiences convinced him there was a noble side to everyone, which would flourish if only it was allowed to. It was the great paradox of war. Conflict assuredly brought out the worst in mankind. But it brought out the best as well. 'In peacetime we only tend to see the differences,' he wrote, 'not realizing that what united us then is still there now, like a tunneller approaching the surface, waiting to pull down that first handful of earth that is topped with a tuft of grass; waiting for the first breath of cold night air that will bring us to freedom.'[12]

NOTES

CHAPTER I

1. William Ash with Brendan Foley, *Under The Wire*, Bantam, 2006, 147.
2. Private Papers of Wing Commander H.W. Lamond, Imperial War Museum (henceforth IWM) 6293.
3. Aidan Crawley, *Escape from Germany: The Methods of Escape Used by RAF Airmen During the Second World War*, HMSO, 1985, 182.
4. Stalag Luft III Camp History, April 1942–January 1945, The National Archives (henceforth TNA) AIR 40/2645.
5. Arthur A. Durand, *Stalag Luft III:The Secret Story*, Louisiana State University Press, 1999, 108.
6. TNA AIR 40/2645.
7. Ibid.
8. Crawley, 29.
9. T. D. Calnan, *Free as a Running Fox*, Macdonald, 1970, 163.
10. William Ash, *A Red Square: The Autobiography of an Unconventional Revolutionary*, Howard Baker, 1978, 122.
11. Paul Brickhill, *Reach For the Sky: The Story of Douglas Bader DSO, DFC*, Collins, 1954, 325.
12. Ash and Foley, 324.
13. For full details see www.icrc.org.

CHAPTER 2

1. Aidan Crawley, *Escape from Germany: The Methods of Escape Used by RAF Airmen During the Second World War*, HMSO, 1985, 5.
2. William Ash with Brendan Foley, *Under The Wire*, Bantam, 2006, 152.
3. Richard Passmore, *Moving Tent*, Pitman Press, 1982, 48.
4. Ibid. 31.
5. Ash and Foley, 150.
6. Paul Brickhill, *Reach For the Sky: The Story of Douglas Bader DSO, DFC*, Collins, 1954, 324–5.
7. Ibid. 324.
8. Ibid. 324.
9. Ash and Foley, 161.
10. Patrick Barthropp, *Paddy: The Life and Times of Wing Commander Patrick Barthropp, DFC, AFC*, Howard Baker, 1990, 58.
11. Ash and Foley, 158.
12. Ibid. 159.
13. Barthropp, 58.
14. Ibid. 57.
15. Ash and Foley, 161.
16. TNA AIR 40/2645.
17. Crawley, 182.
18. IWM 6293.
19. Ibid.

CHAPTER 3

1. William Ash with Brendan Foley, *Under The Wire*, Bantam, 2006, 153.
2. TNA AIR 40/2645.
3. TNA AIR 40/2449.
4. Ash and Foley, 172.
5. RAF Air Publication 1548.
6. Aidan Crawley, *Escape from Germany: The Methods of Escape Used by RAF Airmen During the Second World War*, HMSO, 1985, 5.
7. Ash and Foley, 161.
8. TNA AIR/40 2645.

9. Ash and Foley, 153.

10. William Ash, *A Red Square: The Autobiography of an Unconventional Revolutionary*, Howard Baker, 1978, 123.

11. TNA WO 208/3338/703.

12. Ash, 115.

13. Ibid. 117.

14. Ibid. 119.

15. Ibid. 121.

16. Ash, 121.

17. TNA WO 208/3338/703, interview dated 20 August 1945.

18. Ash, 117.

CHAPTER 4

1. William Ash, *A Red Square: The Autobiography of an Unconventional Revolutionary*, Howard Baker, 1978, 117.

2. Patrick Barthropp, *Paddy: The Life and Times of Wing Commander Patrick Barthropp, DFC, AFC*, Howard Baker, 1990, In fact his father died on 21 November 1954.

3. Ibid. 53.

4. Ash, 123.

5. Barthropp, 54.

6. Ash, 127.

7. Aidan Crawley, *Escape from Germany: The Methods of Escape Used by RAF Airmen During the Second World War*, HMSO, 1985, 59.

8. Ash, 128.

9. William Ash with Brendan Foley, *Under The Wire*, Bantam, 2006, 152.

10. Ash, 128

11. Ash and Foley, 163.

12. Barthropp, 57.

13. TNA AIR 40/2645.

14. Ash and Foley, 168.

15. Ibid. 169.

CHAPTER 5

1. Quoted in Simon Pearson, *The Great Escaper, The Life and Death of Roger Bushell: Love, Betrayal, Big X and the Great Escape*, Hodder & Stoughton, 2013, 120.
2. William Ash with Brendan Foley, *Under The Wire*, Bantam, 2006, 161.
3. William Ash, *A Red Square: The Autobiography of an Unconventional Revolutionary*, Howard Baker, 1978, 16.
4. Ibid. 21.
5. Ibid. 74.
6. Canada's Clayton Knight Committee, which encouraged volunteers from the US, had processed 6,700 applications to join the RCAF and RAF by the time America entered the war. See: http://en.wikipedia.org/wiki/Eagle_Squadrons.
7. Ash, 76.
8. Ibid. 78.
9. Ibid. 86.
10. TNA AIR 87/1803.
11. Ash, 81.
12. Ash and Foley, 107.
13. Ibid. 108.
14. Ibid. 109.
15. Ibid. 110.

CHAPTER 6

1. Arthur A. Durand, *Stalag Luft* III: *The Secret Story*, Louisiana State University Press, 1999, 105.
2. Jonathan F. Vance, *A Gallant Company: The Men of the Great Escape*, Pacifica Military History, 2000, 9.
3. T. D. Calnan, *Free as a Running Fox*, Macdonald, 1970, 172.
4. William Ash with Brendan Foley, *Under The Wire*, Bantam, 2006, 174.
5. Ibid. 176.
6. Aidan Crawley, *Escape from Germany: The Methods of Escape Used by* RAF *Airmen During the Second World War*, HMSO, 1985, 199.

7. Patrick Barthropp, *Paddy: The Life and Times of Wing Commander Patrick Barthropp, DFC, AFC*, Howard Baker, 1990, 58.

8. Crawley, 200.

9. Calnan, 173.

10. TNA AIR 40/1908.

11. Crawley, 200.

12. Ash and Foley, 180.

13. Crawley, 201.

14. William Ash, *A Red Square: The Autobiography of an Unconventional Revolutionary*, Howard Baker, 1978, 129.

15. *The Gazette*, 17 May 1946.

16. Ash and Foley, 191.

17. Ibid. 194.

18. Ash, 130.

19. Ash and Foley, 195.

20. Calnan, 170.

21. TNA AIR 40/1908.

22. Ash and Foley, 184.

23. TNA AIR 40/1908.

24. Calnan, 191.

25. TNA AIR 40/1908.

26. Aidan Crawley, *Leap Before You Look*, William Collins, 1988, 178.

27. TNA AIR 40/1908.

28. Richard Passmore, *Moving Tent*, Pitman Press, 1982, 163.

29. Private Papers of Sergeant R. C. W. Watchorn, IWM Documents 3553.

30. Ash and Foley, 201.

31. Ibid. 204.

CHAPTER 7

1. T. D. Calnan, *Free as a Running Fox*, Macdonald, 1970, 178.

2. William Ash with Brendan Foley, *Under The Wire*, Bantam, 2006, 209.

3. Calnan, 177.

4. Ash and Foley, 209.

5. Calnan, 194.

6. Aidan Crawley, *Escape from Germany: The Methods of Escape Used by RAF Airmen During the Second World War*, HMSO, 1985, 206.

7. Robert Kee, *A Crowd Is Not Company*, Jonathan Cape, 1982, 11.

8. Calnan, 189.

9. Kee, 123.

10. Crawley, 77.

11. Calnan, 191.

12. Crawley, 75.

13. Ash and Foley, 212.

14. Crawley, 206.

CHAPTER 8

1. Henry Probert, Introduction to Aidan Crawley, *Escape from Germany: The Methods of Escape Used by RAF Airmen During the Second World War*, HMSO, 1985, viii.

2. TNA AIR 40/1908.

3. Ibid.

4. Crawley, 35.

5. http://www.wartimememoriesproject.co.uk/peterlovegrove.

6. TNA AIR 40/266.

7. William Ash with Brendan Foley, *Under The Wire*, Bantam, 2006, 216.

8. TNA AIR 40/1908.

9. Historical Record of IS9, www.arcre.com.

10. Robert Kee, *A Crowd Is Not Company*, Jonathan Cape, 1982, 124.

11. T. D. Calnan, *Free as a Running Fox*, Macdonald, 1970, 200.

12. Ibid. 202.

13. Ibid. 208.

14. Patrick Barthropp, *Paddy: The Life and Times of Wing Commander Patrick Barthropp, DFC, AFC*, Howard Baker, 1990, 59.

15. Calnan, 203.

CHAPTER 9

1. T. D. Calnan, *Free as a Running Fox*, Macdonald, 1970, 214.

2. William Ash with Brendan Foley, *Under The Wire*, Bantam, 2006, 221.

3. Calnan, 215.

4. Robert Kee, *A Crowd Is Not Company*, Jonathan Cape, 1982, 124.

5. Calnan, 214.

6. Ibid.

7. Ash and Foley, 223.

8. Calnan, 215.

9. Ash and Foley, 224.

10. Kee, 127.

11. Ibid. 129.

12. TNA AIR 40/1908.

13. Calnan, 218.

14. Henry Probert, Introduction to Aidan Crawley, *Escape from Germany: The Methods of Escape Used by* RAF *Airmen During the Second World War*, HMSO, 1985, ix.

15. Anthony Barber, *Taking the Tide*, Michael Russell, 1996.

CHAPTER 10

1. William Ash with Brendan Foley, *Under The Wire*, Bantam, 2006, 226.

2. Robert Kee, *A Crowd Is Not Company*, Jonathan Cape, 1982, 147.

3. T. D. Calnan, *Free as a Running Fox*, Macdonald, 1970, 221.

4. Aidan Crawley, *Leap Before You Look*, William Collins, 1988, 181.

5. Henry Probert, Introduction to Aidan Crawley, *Escape from Germany: The Methods of Escape Used by* RAF *Airmen During the Second World War*, HMSO, 1985, ix.

6. Ash and Foley, 229.

7. Patrick Barthropp, *Paddy: The Life and Times of Wing Commander Patrick Barthropp, DFC, AFC*, Howard Baker, 1990, 59.

8. Ibid. 60.

9. Calnan, 230.

10. Kee, 178.

11. Probert, x.

12. TNA AIR 40/1908.

13. Ibid.

14. Ibid.

CHAPTER 11

1. William Ash with Brendan Foley, *Under The Wire*, Bantam, 2006, 244.
2. Ibid. 253.
3. T. D. Calnan, *Free as a Running Fox*, Macdonald, 1970, 236.
4. Ibid. 237.
5. William Ash, *A Red Square: The Autobiography of an Unconventional Revolutionary*, Howard Baker, 1978, 30.
6. Ash and Foley, 256.
7. Ibid. 261–2.

CHAPTER 12

1. William Ash with Brendan Foley, *Under The Wire*, Bantam, 2006, 267.
2. Aidan Crawley, *Escape from Germany: The Methods of Escape Used by RAF Airmen During the Second World War*, HMSO, 1985, 197.
3. Ibid. 198.
4. Ash and Foley, 270.
5. TNA AIR 40/2449.
6. Ash and Foley, 280.
7. TNA AIR 40/2449.
8. Ash and Foley, 279.
9. Ibid. 282.
10. TNA AIR 40/229.
11. Crawley, 90.
12. Ash and Foley, 283.
13. Crawley, 93.
14. Ash and Foley, 285.
15. TNA AIR 40/229.
16. Ash and Foley, 286.
17. Ibid. 287.
18. TNA AIR 40/229.

CHAPTER 13

1. William Ash, *A Red Square: The Autobiography of an Unconventional Revolutionary*, Howard Baker, 1978, 135.

differs in several respects from Bill's recollections. For further details
see www.resistance62.net

6. TNA WO 208/3338/703.
7. William Ash with Brendan Foley, *Under The Wire*, Bantam, 2006, 125.
8. Ibid. 376.
9. Ibid. 377.
10. Conversation with author.
11. Ibid. 331.
12. Ibid. 381.

INDEX

Air Council
  'Responsibilities of a Prisoner
    of War: Instructions and
    Guidance for All Ranks in
    the Event of Capture by the
    Enemy, The' (1936), 43
Air Sea Rescue Services 80
Alexander, Warrant Officer R.J.
    'Jock'
  head of Tally-Ho Club 206,
    215–16
Allied Forces 8, 18–19, 28, 53, 192,
    171, 198, 227, 236, 239–40, 255
von Arnim, General Hans-Jürgen
    257–8
Artnum 249
Ash, Adele 73
Ash, Flying Officer William 18–19,
    21–2, 28, 30, 41–2, 45–9, 57–62,
    64, 66, 75, 79, 94, 104–5,
    109–10, 114, 135, 151, 191,
    194–5, 199, 203, 208–9, 216,
    232–6, 238, 240, 247, 250–1,
    253, 256, 258, 262, 265, 269,
    271–2, 275, 278, 280
  A Red Square 228
  as Don Fair 206, 225, 278
  background of 24, 73–8, 115,
    231–2, 272–3
  capture and interrogation of
    (1942) 49–53, 226–7
  Choice of Arms (1962) 279
  death of (2014) 281
  escape efforts of 63–9, 102–3,
    119, 122, 124, 126, 132, 134–6,
    140, 151–5, 157–8, 160–2, 165,
    172–3, 199–202, 209–10, 214,
    217–19, 221–4, 240–1
  capture during 179–80, 189,
    225–8
  family of 275, 278–9
  Happy in Ulubrae 233
  imprisonment at Dulag Luft
    56–8
  imprisonment at Oflag XXIB 93,
    96–8, 103–4

later life of 275–6
Longest Way Round, The 279
Lotus in the Sky, The (1961) 279
shot down (1942) 5, 8, 47–8, 50,
    83–90
time in the cooler 71–2, 114–17,
    194, 201, 231–4, 280
training of 55
Under the Wire (2005) 278–9
Ash, Francis 275
Ash, Juliet 275, 279
Ash (née Porterfield), Margaret
    73
Ash Snr, William 73
Asselin, Eddie 78, 93, 96, 109, 155,
    228, 277
    background of 118
    escape efforts of 122–5, 132,
        139–40, 151–2, 154–5, 157,
        160–2, 165, 172–3
    capture during 179–80
Austria 186
    Innsbruck 165
Auxiliary Air Force 93
Avro Lancaster 266

Bader, Douglas 25, 27–9
    background of 28–9
    imprisonment at Colditz Castle
        31–2
Barber, Tony
    background of 153
    Chancellor of the Exchequer
        276
    escape efforts of 167, 176–7
    capture during 186
Barry, Flight Lieutenant L.B. 112

Barthropp, Elton Peter Maxwell
    D'Arley 56
Barthropp, Patrick ('Paddy') 9, 21,
    28–31, 57–8, 61, 64, 90, 96–7,
    199–200, 229, 233, 236, 262–3
    background of 10, 55–6
    escape efforts of 57–8, 63–9, 122,
        164–5, 169, 174, 231
    capture during 180–1
    family of 276
Belgium 47, 85, 171, 183, 254
Berliner Illustrirte Zeitung 140
Best, Flight Lieutenant Jack 34–5,
    39, 65
    background of 33
Binder, Major 56
Blakeslee, Don 78
Blatchford, Wing Commander
    Derek 'Cowboy' 82
Blond Beast 114–15
von Bodecker, Oberstleutnant 98
Boulanger, Julien 48
Boulanger, Marthe 48, 277
Brickhill, Paul 26–7
Bristol Beaufort 83
Bristol Blenheim 27
    pilots of 22
British Broadcasting Corporation
    (BBC) 112, 141–2, 244, 279
    External Services 275
British Communist Party 276
British Empire 238
Bryks, Josef 135, 146
    capture of 187
Buckley, Lieutenant Commander
    Jimmy 28, 32, 62–3, 188
    background of 62

disappearance of 188, 196
escape efforts of 151–2, 188
transfer to Oflag XXIB (1942)
109
Bulgaria
German entry into (1941) 140
Sofia 140–1
Burgess, Anthony 279
Bushell, Squadron Leader Roger
233, 238
escape efforts of 230–1, 237

Calnan, Tommy 17, 94, 97, 105, 110,
117, 121–2, 150–1, 193, 232
as Tomasso Calabresi 154
capture of 93
crash off Normandy coast (1941)
107–8
escape efforts of 105–7, 120,
122–3, 126, 132, 153–4, 157–60,
163–4, 166–7, 174–5, 182–3
capture during 183–4
Cambridge University
Trinity College 93
Canada 75, 84
Kingston 77
Montreal 118
Ontario
Windsor 76–7
Quebec 277
Toronto 77, 84
capitalism 195–6, 198, 231–2
free-market 75
Catholicism 10, 56
Catley, Jack 210
Černý, Flight Lieutenant Otakar
escape efforts of 187

Chamberlain, Neville 81
Chetniks 153, 165
Churchill, Winston 94, 181, 227
Codner, Lieutenant Michael 229
escape efforts of 230
Colditz Castle 31–2, 39, 236
Coles, Harry 48
Commonwealth 75–6, 149, 229
communism 115, 192
Conservative Party 81
Craig, Squadron Leader Dudley
146
escape efforts of 152
capture during 186
Crawley, Aidan 12, 21, 71, 96–9,
109, 131, 144, 203–4, 213–14,
244, 247, 249, 251–6, 275–6
background of 17, 93, 141, 240
capture of 94
escape efforts of 122, 127, 133,
137, 140–1, 165, 177–9, 184–6,
203–5, 239–40
capture during 186
intelligence gathering activities
of 141–2
later life of 276–7
writings of 44
Cross, Ian 235
escape efforts of 106–7, 122

Day, Wing Commander Harry
27–8, 32, 62, 127–8, 131, 144–5,
196, 236
background of 27
escape efforts of 118, 120–1, 137,
164
capture during 186, 236

transfer to Oflag XXIB (1942)
109
Deans, Warrant Officer James
'Dixie' 211–12
background of 202
Denmark 153, 186
Bornholm 168
Copenhagen 188
DH.98 Mosquito 205
Dodge, John Bigelow 94
escape efforts of 151–2
capture during 236
Dostoevsky, Fyodor 51–2
Dulag Luft 9, 18, 28, 46, 55
key personnel of 57–8, 62

Edge, Dickie 190
escape efforts of 136, 170
Edwards, Flight Lieutenant Robert
114, 212
Elbe, River 267
Elizabeth, Queen 81
Elliot, Walter
background of 81
escape committees 17, 32,
34, 62, 65, 93, 109, 121, 130,
136, 151, 196, 206–7, 215–16,
219

Fair, Flight Lieutenant Donald
278–9
death of 279
escape efforts of 199–200
Fairey Battles 77
Fanshawe, Lieutenant Commander
Peter 122
fascism 75, 196

First World War (1914–18) 19, 75,
94, 113, 163
Armistice (1918) 27
Gallipoli Campaign (1915–16) 94
imprisonment of British aviators
during 11
Treaty of Versailles (1919) 98,
143, 198
Western Front 94
Flockhart, Sergeant Cyril
escape efforts of 237
Flynn, Paddy 210
Focke-Wulf Fw 190 87–9
France 2–4, 25, 54, 84–6, 97, 112,
153–4, 165, 254
Boulogne 84
Calais 84, 100
Cap Gris Nez 84
Dunkirk 61–2, 85, 94
Normandy 107
Paris 8, 18, 49, 226–7, 277–8
Pas-de-Calais 10, 47, 226, 277
Neuville 47
Vielle-Église 8, 50, 54, 124, 277
Saint-Omer 2, 18, 25, 84

Galland, Adolf 26
de Gaulle, General Charles 277
Geneva Convention (1929) 184, 226,
236
provisions of 19–20, 30–1, 43, 45,
59, 100, 112
breaches of 31, 45, 72, 149
George VI, King 81–2, 127
Germany 11, 35–6, 54, 99, 140, 143,
172, 181, 193–4, 198, 226, 252,
266

Aachen 183
Barth 12
Berlin 12, 45, 165, 177, 182, 186,
    226–7, 246, 251
Bremen 202, 260, 262, 265, 267–8
Cologne 165, 182–3, 185
Essen 109, 181
Frankfurt 8
Hamburg 144, 267–8
Hanover 182
Heydekurg 42, 201–3, 205–6,
    208, 225, 228, 231, 237
Kirchtimke 270
Lübeck 269
Memel 205–6
Munich 184–5
Muskau 257–8
North-Rhine Westphalia 267
Nuremburg 181, 260
Sagan 11 12, 25, 32–4, 100, 108,
    114, 194, 201, 206, 229, 236,
    243–4, 250–1, 279
Spremberg 261
Steinau 243
Stendal 182
Tamstedt 262
Tilsit 206
Warburg 26, 100, 108
Wuppertal 184
Gibraltar 48
Gillet, Giselle 49–50, 278
Gillet, Joseph 49–50, 278
Glemnitz, Oberfeldwebel
    Hermann 16, 93–4, 252
Goebbels, Josef 181
Goldfinch, Flight Lieutenant Bill
    33, 36–7, 39, 65

background of 33–4
Göring, Hermann 19, 236
Great Depression 9, 74
Great Escape 235–6
    capture and killing of key
        members of 238–9
Greece 33
    Kalamata 33
Grimson, George 237
Guerisse, Albert (Pat O'Leary)
    founder of Pat Line 48

Harris, Sir Arthur 'Bomber' 227
    Chief of Bomber Command 32
Heinz 214
Hess, Myra 81
Himmler, Heinrich 226, 267
Hitler, Adolf 67–8, 76, 172, 176,
    181, 193, 198, 226, 236, 243–4
Horocks, Lieutenant General Brian
    266

India
    Independence of (1947) 275
Intelligence School 9 (IS9) 49, 149
    coded letters from 149–50
    personnel of 47, 54, 228
    relief parcels from 168
International Committee of the
    Red Cross 20, 45–6, 65, 145,
        148, 197, 232
    parcels 14, 42–3, 45, 59–60, 104,
        110, 117, 128, 133, 146, 148–9,
        191, 207–8, 243–4, 248–9, 254,
        259, 261, 276
    Canadian 134
Italy 271

Judaism 76, 115
Junkers Ju 88 82

Kayall, Joe
  escape efforts of 239
Kee, Robert 154, 246, 250, 252–3,
    276–7
  escape efforts of 106–7, 122,
    128–30, 157–9, 162–4, 166, 174–5,
    182–3
  capture during 183–4
  writings of 128–30
Keitel, Wilhelm 236
Kenya 33
Ketty, Rina
  'J'Attendrai' 48
King, William MacKenzie 80
Kirby-Green, Tom 235
  background of 238
Kowalski, Alexis 167
Krupp
  employees of 153–4

Labour Party 238, 240, 277
Lamond, Wing Commander Henry
    12, 33–6, 38–9, 65
  background of 33
Latvia 228
Liepaja (Libau) 228
Le Cam, Pauline 47, 54, 277
Leaman, Sergeant Ned
  capture of 237–8
Libya
  Tobruk 140
  von Lindeiner-Wildau, Colonel
    Friedrich-Wilhelm 19, 20, 30–1,
    111, 201

background of 19
following of Geneva Convention
    protocols 19–20
Lithuania 199, 222, 226
  Kaunas (Kovno) 228
London Weekend Television 277
Lovegrove, Flying officer Peter
  shot down (1942) 144
  suicide of 144
Loyola College 118
Lubbock, David 148
  background of 64–5
  capture of (1941) 65
  Feeding the People in Wartime 64

Marlag und Milag Nord 262,
    265–6, 268, 271
  personnel of 268
  SS quarters 271
Marshall, Charles 155
  background of 118
  capture of 109
  escape efforts of 154
  capture during 187
Marxist-Leninism 276
Massey, Group Captain Herbert 32
McNair, Robert 'Buck' 78–9
Merchant Navy 265, 268
Messerschmitt 109s 82, 87–8
Mesopotamia 113
Mihailović, General Draža 153,
    165
Miles Magister 79
Mogg, Ron 212
Montgomery, Bernard 112
Morris, Squadron B.G.
  escape efforts of 169, 187

Mountbatten, Lady Edwina 276
Murray, R.M. 79
Mussolini, Benito 75

nationalism 75
Nehru, Jawaharlal 275–6
Netherlands
    Holland 82, 202, 254
New Zealand 33
Norway
    Kirkenes 65
Nouveau, Louis 278

Oder, River 243
Oflag VIB 26
Oflag XXIB 95–8, 109, 133–4, 144–5,
    190, 209
    Abort 117–19, 122–3, 125–6, 132,
        155–6
    Appell 98, 129, 136, 154 5, 164,
        169
    Escape Clothing Department 145
    Hut 6 96
    cooler, the 104, 194
    movement of prisoners to 90, 93
    personnel of 98, 100, 103, 108,
        114–15, 127, 130–1, 144
    White House 130, 144
de la Olla, Jean 48, 51, 278
Orr, Sir John Boyd
    Feeding the People in Wartime 64
Oxford University 93
    Balliol College 275

Paget, Flight Lieutenant J.W.G. 145
Pakistan
    Independence of (1947) 275

Palmer, Bill 104–5, 109, 118
    escape efforts of 154
        capture during 187
Passmore, Richard 22, 24, 113
Pat Line 48, 278
Peschel, Major 16, 207, 219
Philipot, Flight Lieutenant Oliver
    escape efforts of 230
Pieber, Hauptmann 26
Pilz, Corporal Karl 17
Pitcher, Paul 78–80
Poland 12, 90, 108, 112, 226, 254
    Białogard (Belgard) 186
    Bromberg 99, 142, 165, 167–8, 177
    Danzig 101, 121, 143–4, 187, 237
    Graudenz 101
    Iłowa (Halbau) 251
    Inocwrocław (Hohensalza) 174,
        179–82
    Kolberg 168
    Kraków 179
    Kostrzyn nad Odrą (Küstrin) 182
    Lipna (Lieppa) 251–2
    Nakło nad Notecią (Nakel) 177
    Piła (Schneidemühl) 166–8, 175,
        177–8, 182, 184
    Poznán (Posen) 174, 184, 187
    Schubin 93–5, 100, 103, 108–10,
        112, 133, 140, 142, 148, 150,
        152, 169, 174–5, 180, 182, 184,
        186–7, 189, 194, 196–7, 204,
        209–10, 212, 229, 232
    Stettin 38, 204–5
    Warsaw 93, 143, 152–3, 166, 171,
        173–4, 187, 251
    Złocieniec (Falkenburg) 187
Pyrenees, The 165

Rambaut, Patricia 82
Ravensbruck 277–8
Republic of Ireland
  Dublin 55
Rhine, River 183, 267
Ricks, Joe 135–6
  escape efforts of 136, 187
Rimbaud, Patricia 275, 279
Rocourt, Emile 48
Rocourt, Gaston 48
Rommel, Erwin 257
  Afrika Korps 112
Roosevelt, Franklin D. 75, 193
Roth, Lieutenant General 269
Royal Air Force (RAF) 9, 11, 13, 18,
    23, 25–6, 32, 41, 53, 56, 84, 97,
    100–1, 111, 118, 145, 147–8, 153,
    168, 178, 185, 187–8, 196, 203,
    232, 269
  103 Squadron 106
  57 Squadron 27
  73 Squadron 140
  bombing campaigns of 181, 227
  Bomber Command 11, 32, 92–3,
    181, 183, 203, 205, 227
  escape efforts of personnel 44
Royal Canadian Air Force (RCAF)
    76, 84, 196, 275
  1 Squadron 78
  411 Squadron 79–80
Royal Marines 27
Royal Navy 262, 265, 268
  Fleet Air Arm 64–5, 122
  HMS Glorious 62
Russian Empire
  Moscow 253
Ryder, Lady Frances 81

Ryder, Norman
  background of 25

Sachsenhausen concentration camp
    236
Second World War (1939–45) 3, 5,
    75, 243, 273–4
  Battle of Berlin (Air) (1943–4)
    227
  Battle of Britain (1940) 10, 25, 56,
    78, 84, 276
  Battle of France (1940) 49, 84,
    97
  Battle of the Ruhr (1943) 181
  Battle of Stalingrad (1942–3)
    192
  Casablanca Conference (1943)
    192–3
  concentration camps in 18–19,
    54
  Dunkirk Evacuation (1940) 25,
    61–2, 94
  Eastern Front (1941–5) 16, 97, 207,
    243–5
  Holocaust 194
  Normandy Landings/D-Day
    (1944) 239–40, 266
  Operation Barbarossa (1941) 193,
    232
  Operation Market Garden (1944)
    267
  Pearl Harbor Attack (1941) 76
  US entry into (1941) 10, 76
  Western Desert Campaign
    (1940–3) 257
  Second Battle of El Alamein (1942)
    112–13

Secret Intelligence Service (MI6) 149
  Balkan section of 140
Shakespeare, William 43, 191–2
Short S.25 Sunderland
  pilots of 33
Sidhanta, Ranjana 279
Simms 98, 169, 189
South Africa 168
Soviet Union (USSR) 65, 193, 198, 214, 254
  Red Army 243, 252
  Stalingrad 192
Spain 48, 154
  Civil War (1936–9) 75, 196
  International Brigades 75
Special Operations Executive 149
Spree, River 261
Stapleton, Bill 61–2
Stalag Luft I 28, 33–4
Stalag Luft III 7, 11–16, 21, 24, 26, 39, 41, 72, 91, 95, 97, 99–100, 102, 106, 113, 131, 142, 148, 150, 190, 196, 198–9, 225, 238–9, 247, 253–4, 260, 276–7
  'A' Compound 209, 219
  administration area 8
  Appell 29, 36–7, 58, 66, 212, 235–6
  Barrack 64 58
  Barrack 69 63
  Block 64 9
  Central Compound 13, 191, 196, 199, 202
  'E' Compound 213
  East Compound 13–14, 31, 41, 66, 196, 199, 230–1, 233, 239–40, 245–9, 257–60

  evacuation of prisoners from (1944) 249–63, 265–6, 268
  expansion of 12–13, 228–9
  North Compound 229–31, 235, 248, 259–60, 279
  personnel of 15–16, 111, 136, 192, 198, 220, 244–5
  rations in 59–60
  South Compound 229, 247, 250
  Vorlager 14, 31, 63, 66, 93
  cooler, the 30–1, 71–2, 201, 231
Stalag Luft VI 42, 199, 205
Stevens, Flying Officer
  background of 153
Sturges, John
  Great Escape, The (1963) 114–15, 279–80
Supermarine Spitfire 1, 8, 25, 56, 85–6, 88
  pilots of 1, 9, 61, 93, 100, 107, 198
Sweden 12, 101–2, 188, 230, 237
  Halmstad 102
  Stockholm 143
Switzerland 12, 60, 65, 154, 165, 171, 184, 224–5
  Geneva 45, 197, 232, 248

Tally-Ho Club 206
Thalbitzer, Jørgen (John Thompson)
  background of 168
  death of 188
  escape efforts of 168, 188
Third Reich (1933–45) 3, 8, 18–19, 48–9, 75, 77–8, 104, 167–8, 176, 179, 193, 195, 211, 227, 243, 251, 260, 269

Abwehr 207, 237
bureaucratic systems of 146
Gestapo 8, 50, 52–3, 152, 173,
    179–82, 184, 186, 188–9, 201,
    203–4, 213, 219, 225–7, 236,
    238–9, 241, 277, 280
Hitler Youth 171, 181, 186
Luftwaffe 8, 15, 17–19, 25–6,
    53–4, 136, 201, 204, 235–6,
    238–9
Schutzstaffel (SS) 99, 170, 186, 194,
    239, 245, 251, 257, 261, 267–9,
    271
Selbstschutz 99, 115
territory occupied by 140, 143–4
Wehrmacht 95, 97, 99, 111–12,
    136, 184, 248
Tolstoy, Leo
    War and Peace 253
Tuck, Bob Stanford
    background of 25
Turkey 141
Turner, Squadron Leader Stan
    84–6

Ukraine 255
United Kingdom (UK) 16, 75, 77–8,
    82, 168, 241
    Coventry 56
    Dover 84
    Essex
        Hornchurch 80, 83
        Southend 83
    Lincolnshire 80
        Digby 78–9
        Kirton-in-Lindsay 80
        Lincoln 80

London 48, 52, 56, 65, 78, 80–1,
    117–18, 149, 155, 170, 190, 197,
    203, 246, 263, 279, 281
    National Gallery 81
    RAF Hendon 56
    military of 270–1
    XXX Corps 266–7, 270
    No. 57 OUT Hawarden 78
    War Office 149
    West Sussex
        Tangmere 25
United States of America (USA) 2,
    16, 76, 191, 195–6
    Air Force (USAF) 229, 280
    Chicago, IL 74
    Dallas, TX 4, 73
    Detroit, MI 74, 76–7
    Fort Worth, TX 73
    Kansas City, KS 75
University of Texas 74

Vistula, River 101, 171, 173, 187

Wareing, Sergeant Philip
    escape attempt made by 100–1
Webster, Flight Lieutenant
    capture of 187
Weimar Republic 19
Weser, River 267
Williams, Flight Lieutenant Eric
    229
    escape efforts of 230
Wise, Wilf 153
    escape efforts of 169, 174
    capture during 180–1
Wood, Flight Lieutenant J.W.
    capture of 187

Wood, Mike 104–5
Wooden Horse escape (1943) 230–1,
    239

Young, Digby 258
Young Men's Christian Association
    (YMCA) 148, 248
Yugoslavia 140, 153